Politics
and the Oval Office:
Towards Presidential
Governance

POLITICS

AND THE OVAL OFFICE:

TOWARDS PRESIDENTIAL

GOVERNANCE

Arnold J. Meltsner, *Editor*
Richard K. Betts
Jack Citrin
Eric L. Davis
Robert M. Entman
Robert E. Hall
Hugh Heclo
Everett Carll Ladd, Jr.
Charles Peters
Robert S. Pindyck
Francis E. Rourke
Martin M. Shapiro
Peter L. Szanton

Institute for Contemporary Studies
San Francisco, California

Inquiries, book orders, and catalog requests should be addressed to the Institute for Contemporary Studies, Suite 811, 260 California Street, San Francisco, California 94111—415—398—3010.

Library of Congress Catalog Number 80—69617
Cloth available through Transaction Books, Rutgers —The State University, New Brunswick, NJ 08903.

Library of Congress Cataloging in Publication Data
Main entry under title:

Politics and the Oval office.

Bibliography: p.
Includes index.
1. Presidents—United States—Addresses, essays, lectures. 2. United States—Politics and govern-
ment—1981—   —Addresses, essays, lectures.
I. Meltsner, Arnold J. II. Betts, Richard K.,
1974—
JK516.P59   353.03'1   80—69617
ISBN 0—87855—428—9 (Transaction Books)   AACR2
ISBN 0—917616—40—5 (pbk.)

CONTENTS

III
The Office

IV
The Current Policy Agenda

V
Coda

CONTRIBUTORS

RICHARD K. BETTS
Research Associate, Foreign Policy Studies,
The Brookings Institution

JACK CITRIN
Associate Professor of Political Science,
University of California—Berkeley

ERIC L. DAVIS
Assistant Professor of Political Science,
Middlebury College

ROBERT M. ENTMAN
Assistant Professor of Public Policy Studies,
Duke University

ROBERT E. HALL
Professor of Economics, Stanford University;
Director, Economic Fluctuations Program and
Project on Inflation, National Bureau of
Economic Research

HUGH HECLO
Professor of Government, Harvard University

EVERETT CARLL LADD, JR.
Executive Director, Roper Center for Public
Opinion Research; Director, Institute for Social
Inquiry, University of Connecticut

ARNOLD J. MELTSNER
*Professor of Public Policy, Graduate School of Public
Policy, University of California—Berkeley*

CHARLES PETERS
Editor-in-Chief, The Washington Monthly

ROBERT S. PINDYCK
*Professor of Applied Economics, Sloan School of
Management, Massachusetts Institute of Technology*

FRANCIS E. ROURKE
*Professor of Political Science,
Johns Hopkins University*

MARTIN M. SHAPIRO
*Professor of Law,
University of California—Berkeley*

PETER L. SZANTON
*Vice President, Hamilton, Rabinovitz
& Szanton, Inc.*

PREFACE

From 1932 to 1960 there were only three American presidents and all served for at least two full terms. Since 1960 there have been five, and none has served two full terms. The "imperial presidency" has come and gone, leaving President Reagan an inheritance of inflated expectations and widespread public disillusionment.

In light of recent experience, some commentators have argued that a president can no longer govern. They cite variously the huge complexity of the decisions a president faces, the decline of party support, the fragmentation of Congress, the hostility of the media, the intransigence of the federal bureaucracy, or the willfulness of foreign governments.

We at the institute do not share their pessimism. Last summer we published major studies in the two policy areas which featured most centrally in the presidential election campaign—national security and the economy. Each was written by a series of experts from diverse backgrounds, and focused on analyzing recent trends and suggesting feasible proposals for reform. They showed that improvements are possible.

Politics and the Oval Office is the institute's first book to address directly the institutional and political contexts for implementing substantive policies. Although the essential task is different here, this study shares the approach and the optimism of the earlier ones.

Our main objective has been to analyze recent trends in
the presidency from various perspectives, accepting the
negative developments while challenging the myth that
presidential leadership is no longer possible. The choice of
Arnold J. Meltsner as editor of the book was appropriate
because he combined a detailed knowledge of the subject
with considerable experience in the study of public policy and
its implementation. The twelve authors are acknowledged
authorities in their respective fields. We had no preconcep-
tions about the end product; but we are gratified by the fact
that all our authors share our view that, considerable though
the constraints may be, the president's job can be done, and
done well.

How can we justify adding yet another thick volume to the
already swollen literature on the presidency? We value this
book especially highly not only because, as I have said, it
highlights the implementation aspects of the presidency, but
because it is unique in bringing together so many diverse
perspectives in such a timely way and in such practical
terms. President Reagan's election resulted—at least in
part—from frustration with the failures of the previous administration; but if he is to fare better, he must understand
and come to terms with the major institutional and political
changes which our authors have outlined, and must turn
them to his advantage as he lays down his own style of
leadership. The book has in mind the particular problems of
the contemporary presidency and deals directly with how to
tackle them.

Politics and the Oval Office is in three parts. The first dis-
cusses recent institutional and attitude trends in public opinion, in party allegiance, and in the president's relations
with the media, Congress, the bureaucracy, and the courts.
The second suggests how President Reagan might organize
his office. The third—and again, we believe this is
unique—attempts to set the preceding analysis into a policy
context in the three critical areas of defense, energy, and the
economy.

The loud and clear message is that a president can govern, but that to do so effectively means steering a steady course towards a consistent and clearly articulated conception of the future. More immediately, it means establishing and sustaining good working relationships with the influential political leaders upon whose support his success depends.

We believe the time is ripe for the presidency to become once again a podium from which an imaginative and enlightened president can enunciate a coherent public philosophy. If today's opportunities are missed, they may never return. The new president has our best wishes for the complex and difficult but challenging days ahead.

H. Monroe Browne
President,
Institute for Contemporary Studies

February 1981
San Francisco, California

I

A Memorandum

1

ARNOLD J. MELTSNER

Memorandum

To: **President Reagan**
From: **Arnold J. Meltsner**
Subject: **Advice on Politics
             and Governance**

Some say the president can't govern because there is:

- A lack of public consensus and trust
- A nation that confuses its powers with your more limited power
- A decline in political parties
- A rise in single-interest groups
- A fragmented Congress with aggressive members
- A personality- and pathology-oriented media
- A policymaking judiciary

- A permanent and often independent bureaucracy
- A chronic and unanticipated policy agenda

But you can govern. Here's how:

1. *Start with yourself.*
   You cannot completely control the other political participants or their agendas, but you can control what you do. So:

   - Have a *short list*—three or four major objectives you want to accomplish in four years. *Be selective*
   - Have a conception of the future, where you want to go. Convert this conception into a theme for your administration
   - Set the policy agenda and frame the issues for other players
   - Guard your own time and political resources
   - Enjoy the job, but don't expect to be popular

2. *The short list.*
   Your policy agenda will soon become crowded with unanticipated problems, but in setting your objectives it will be essential that:

   - You consider that foreign, economic, and domestic policy issues are interrelated, because your advisors will tend to see them as compartmentalized
   - You recall that the electorate shares your views on the importance of the inflation problem, on the need to control taxes and spending, and on the need for strengthening our national security
   - In the economic area, you lower inflation and stimulate the growth of the U.S. economy

- In the national security area, you improve the readiness of our forces and regain parity with the USSR

- In the energy area, you work towards getting rid of oil and gas controls on prices; you also protect the poor, keep the government out of commercialization, and fill the strategic oil reserve

3. *Direct your office.*
Your Executive Office and White House are not solely your own; a large part of this presidential bureaucracy is there to meet legal requirements and to maintain linkages with various public and private interests. Nevertheless, you can do much to shape your office so it can meet your needs. Therefore:

- Set up a structure that fits *your* personality, operating style, and informational needs

- Select knowledgeable aides and staff members who reflect *your* views and whom you trust, but also have informal outsiders who will tell you what you don't want to hear

- Don't make symbolic cuts in the level of staffing—you will need all the help you can get. Focus the staff on the objectives of your *short list*

- Use your cabinet as you see fit—as a collective decision-maker, as a sounding board, as an implementor of your policies, but don't rely entirely on its members for any of these things

- Don't become a prisoner of your own and others' organizational arrangements; feel free to reach out and make end runs for information and advice, and encourage the expression of dissent within your office family

- Don't become completely dependent on others. Sure, you must delegate and use other people to do the job, but don't let them use you

4. *Implement your short list.*
The short list is the key to the success of your administration. Don't let it get confused or sidetracked with other people's objectives. You must keep personal control of policymaking for *your* objectives by:

- Formulating the policies in the White House

- Consulting extensively with congressional leaders, interest group representatives, and bureaucratic experts, but always reserving decisions for yourself

- Building political support into the process of policy design and not expecting that good or right policies automatically carry support

- Remembering that, for each major policy initiative, a new coalition will have to be built

- Using the media to help provide information to you, but also to inform the public about the issues

- Continuing to build your party, but working through others such as the Republican national chairman as you will not have much time

5. *Avoid mistakes.*
Every president makes mistakes; you will, too. But you can avoid the serious ones by:

- Being particularly reflective and cautious in your first six months in office

- Having an in-house devil's advocate who leans on every policy proposal after a decision has been reached but before you are identified with it

- Developing, at a distance from you, policies and programs which are not on the short list. Commissions, task forces, and teams from both inside and outside government are useful for formulating these proposals

- Paying attention to congressional timing and scheduling. Do not overload Congress

- Accepting the independence of the judiciary and the fact that there is not much you can do to influence the Supreme Court, but avoiding legislation which creates rights and encourages judicial intervention

- Using the expertise of the permanent bureaucracy and insisting that it provide you with "early warning" information

- Shooting for long-range policies while incurring short-run political costs

6. *Make things work.*
You will make many decisions, but don't stop there. If government is to be efficient and to perform, you must also be concerned about implementation. To be effective, you should:

- Select low visibility, low political cost means — informal over formal, administrative rulings and executive orders over legislation

- Avoid costly reorganization battles. Shuffling boxes will not save money

- Use your cabinet secretaries and their assistants to do necessary coordination between departments and to follow through within an agency. You can't control the bureaucracy from the White House

- Praise the civil service in public; many bureaucrats will support you if given the chance

- Concentrate on appointments for independent agencies
- Recognize that some interest groups will support you and that you need not always be a victim of "iron triangles"—where agencies will be tied to congressional committees and interest groups

7. *Restore the public's confidence.*
Right now the public is distrustful and negative about government and about whether anything can work. It is essential that you bolster the public trust in our public and private institutions. You can do so by:

- Promoting the performance, efficiency, and responsiveness of government at all levels: federal, state, and local
- Being *consistent* in your public actions
- Shaping public expectations and defining national goals persuasively
- Educating the public about what government can do and can't do—particularly during the honeymoon
- Adopting highly visible austerity measures—cut the budget so the people know you are dealing with waste
- Not scapegoating *your* government. If you need a scapegoat, blame national or international *conditions*, never agencies, courts, or specific people
- Keeping some distance from the media for yourself and for those close to you
- Not overusing "media events," because they can backfire and create public cynicism
- Trying to keep conflicts within your administration and with Congress as quiet as possible. Negotiate in private, and don't respond publicly to every charge and attack

In the following chapters you will find a detailed discussion of many of the points I have sketched in this memo. While we do not always agree on some of these points, the authors of this book do share an optimistic view of the presidency: despite the many difficulties and problems, you *can* govern.

II

The Political
Environment

2

CHARLES PETERS

What Has Happened to the American Public?

The challenge of tedium. Handling reform. Washington's survival networks. Lobbyists, bureaucrats, and the cabinet. The movement toward self-protection. Rivalry in the White House. Information and Congress. The danger of insulation.

During the almost twenty-eight years between the inauguration of Franklin Roosevelt and the inauguration of John Kennedy we had but three presidents. In the twenty years since Kennedy took the oath of office we have had six — twice as many presidents in eight fewer years.

This says a lot about what has happened to the American public—or, to be more precise, to the two publics that deter-

mine the fate of the presidency. One is the American people;
the other is Washington. Both have been hard on recent occupants of the Oval Office.

With the people as a whole, I think television has been a
major factor in their apparent fickleness. During the 1950s
the nation became saturated with television sets. By 1958
television had acquired enough power to turn what had been
a minor sport called professional football into something that
dominated the Sunday afternoons of American men for the
next two decades. In 1960, with its presentation of the
Kennedy-Nixon debates, television became a major factor in
presidential politics.

But with television came a phenomenon that might be
called Almost Instant Boredom. Attention spans were
trained to one hour, thirty minutes, even thirty seconds.
Quick fame was often followed by equally rapid obscurity.
And so it was in politics.

Switch the channel, change the show—enough of Jimmy
and Rosalynn and Miss Lillian and Billy. They seemed
engaging enough four years ago, but now they belong with
Tricia and Lynda Byrd and Betty Ford. It's time for Ron and
Nancy. And Ron and Nancy had better watch out if they
don't want to suffer the same fate.

Is it possible for Reagan to avoid what happened to his recent predecessors? I think the answer is yes. And I will try to
explain why.

FACING THE PUBLIC CHALLENGE

Beneath the public's boredom, beneath the urge to change
channels, there lies a hunger for purpose, a hunger for
leadership, for a life beyond media titillation. Reagan recognized at least some of that hunger when he sought to stir
memories of Franklin Roosevelt. Roosevelt appealed to his

countrymen's idealism. And that is the great secret of leadership in this nation. When Woodrow Wilson was criticized for being an idealist, he said, "That's how I know I'm an American."

Reagan may prove to be content with just the appearance of being another Roosevelt, with being an attractive, ceremonial leader, with making an occasional eloquent speech, with reigning instead of governing. But assuming that he does want to govern, that he does want to lead, what does Reagan have to do?

He must conduct himself so that the people can be proud of their president. John Kennedy, Dwight Eisenhower, and Franklin Roosevelt should be his models from recent history. Humor, grace, dignity without pomposity, should be what he attempts to convey. Pettiness, never. Just after Jimmy Carter was elected in 1976, I wrote about what had troubled me in his campaign (Peters 1976) — "the occasional evidence that Carter can be petty, vindictive, even nasty."

One case that most people can remember was when Hubert Humphrey withdrew from the race and Carter graciously commented that his only regret was being deprived of the chance to beat the senator in the New Jersey primary. Another was after Carter criticized Clarence Kelly for accepting the free valances from the FBI carpentry shop and reporters reminded him that Kelly's wife had been dying at the time. Carter replied, "Well I see he's remarrying now."

These examples of pettiness may be of trivial importance in a Carter presidency, but nothing did more to deflate my enthusiasm for Carter than the mean spirit displayed by the Humphrey and Kelly remarks. And I can't help thinking that a president can't get away with too many remarks of a similarly ungenerous nature without losing the affection and respect of his people.

The president must be a great teacher, educating first himself and then the people on the central issues facing the country. Recent presidents have tended to avoid facing the problems that lie ahead, both because they are complex and

because their possible solutions are often a threat to powerful individuals and groups.

Take, for example, the problem of income maintenance.
Social security payments and the pensions of former federal
employees are increased each year. According to the National Taxpayers' Union, the unfunded pension liability of
the federal government now exceeds $5 trillion. Yet no politi-
cians want to face the problem. And with good reason—they
remember that Barry Goldwater mentioned the possibility of
changing the social security system during the 1964 campaign and proceeded to be buried under one of the great electoral landslides of American history. The problem is that the
recipients of the various income maintenance programs tend
to panic whenever the prospect of reform is mentioned
because they fear it will result in the loss of the particular
benefit they receive.

Reagan's first test on this issue came when the federal
employees' unions asked him if he would support continua-
tion of the twice-a-year cost-of-living increase in federal pensions. Reagan, in the heat of the election campaign, said yes.
One hopes that he does not feel trapped by that endorsement, that he will be willing to step back, examine the issues
himself, and help the people examine them as long-range
problems that must be faced.

It is essential that this examination be conducted in a way
that threatens no one with immediate loss. Take social
security. If you tell my poor Aunt Minnie that you're going to
take away her social security check or reduce it, she's going
to be panicked and outraged. And so are the members of her
family who might have to pitch in and make up the
difference. If, however, you say that you are going to com-
mence an examination of the social security program that
might in a few years result in changes—not in benefits to
the present beneficiaries, but to people now in their forties,
thirties, and twenties who would be told they could not expect to receive social security in their sixties if they didn't

need it—this is one of the changes we're going to have to make. We can no longer afford social security or any of the other income maintenance programs—like unemployment compensation or veterans' pensions—for people who don't need them. Too many such payments now finance trips to Europe or Florida for people like my rich Aunt Alice, for whom the social security or the unemployment compensation or the pension is gravy, something they don't really need.

If Reagan is serious about controlling the federal budget, the income maintenance programs are where he should strike first. He should eliminate all such payments except those based on need alone.

FDR would have explained the problem in just this way, so you could almost see Aunt Minnie and Aunt Alice as he talked. That's why the people loved his fireside chats. Carter tried to use the fireside chat, but failed because he is a terrible speaker. Reagan, on the other hand, can hold an audience's attention and should be able to use the fireside chat to arouse the support he needs. And he's going to need a lot of support because of that other public he has to deal with: Washington.

Washington and its survival networks

Washington is the world of the insider, the world of the permanent government, the world that watches presidents come and go but always seems to take care of itself. It's a world of survivors, and that's the main thing for Ronald Reagan to understand about it. People care more about surviving, about staying in Washington, than they do about solving the country's problems. It hasn't always been this way. From 1933 through 1945 the city was focused on action—on defeating the Depression or on winning the war. But after the war the tendency toward self-protection—one that had always been present in public officials—became increasingly dominant. The McCarthyism of the 1950s only exacerbated their concern about survival and made them more cautious, less likely to sponsor or risk identification with possibly controversial programs of action.

Washington, in other words, became a city where the lowest value is put on action and the highest on survival. The city is, in fact, composed of *survival networks*, and each person the president brings into his administration either will already be connected to a local survival network or will quickly be invited to join. When a new cabinet secretary goes to his first Washington dinner party, he'll find himself meeting one person after another who can help him in his career and they, in turn, will see the secretary as someone who can help them. Because they and he will perceive this mutual advantage, they will tend to like one another and to form friendships, alliances in which the unspoken assumption is that each will help take care of the other. These networks soon become strong forces in their members' lives. And it won't be long before President Reagan will realize that at least some of his cabinet members are acting more out of the interest of their networks than out of the interest of the Reagan administration. This is why the skilled lobbyist devotes much of his time to building survival networks for those officials he wants to influence. Here's how he does it.

Suppose the cabinet member is the secretary of labor and the lobbyist is entertaining him at dinner. The other guests might include the chairman of an appropriations subcommittee that decides on the budget for the Department of Labor, high officials from several unions, a prominent reporter or two, with possibly a celebrity thrown in. (The celebrity may be from the worlds of society, sports, or the arts—it depends on what will impress the secretary.) All of them the new secretary will recognize as people whom he needs, whom he wants to know. And all of them—except, perhaps, the celebrity, whom the lobbyist will take care of in some other way—want to know him. And the better the lobbyist, the more likely he is to have invited to that dinner someone who represents power in the direction the secretary wants to travel in the event his political career languishes. Suppose the secretary's fall-back ambition is to be a university president. Then another guest might well be the chairman of the board of trustees of a leading university. This is seduction Washington-style. And it is a seduction Ronald Reagan must fear.

Not for himself. Most lobbyists do not concentrate on the White House. At least not in the sense of seeking favors directly from the president or the senior members of his staff. The wise lobbyist knows that it is enough to be known as a friend, either of the president or of one of his top assistants. He will then never have to ask for the favor because the friendship itself will be enough to signal the lower ranks of the administration that the lobbyist is to be treated with respect and his concerns are to be given sympathetic attention.

When the lobbyist actually asks for the favor, he seeks it where the interest groups he represents can have the strongest effect—from the departments where those groups are most likely to be looked upon as key constituencies. And because lobbyists are working on those departments that are affecting them, the bureaucrats in those departments give the most sympathetic attention to the lobbyists because the lobbyists are the ones who are paying most attention to them.

Each bureaucrat is, after all, worried about his own survival. And it's important to understand what threatens his own survival. The only real threat is a cut in his agency's budget. Since it's virtually impossible for the civil servant to be fired, the only way he can lose is through a budget cut that abolishes his job. So his deepest instinct is to protect the budget of his agency and to encourage its growth so that it can provide for his two salary increases each year. The last person he wants to offend is the lobbyist with a constituency powerful enough to cause congressmen to take a critical look at his department's budget.

Cabinet and federal personnel

So what the president is likely to hear from his cabinet departments is the combination of the selfish interest of the lobbyists working on that department and the selfish interest of the bureaucrats working within it. Reagan, like our last four presidents, has talked about having cabinet government. But, as each of his predecessors has found out, cabinet government does not work. And the precise reason that cabinet government does not work is that the interests of the cabinet departments are different from the interests of the country as a whole. The president has to ask what is in the best interest of the country, not of the Department of Labor or the labor unions.

Take minimum wage reform, for example—it's practically certain that Reagan's secretary of labor will soon find himself favoring maintenance of the minimum wage at its present level or increasing it; certainly not reducing it for teenagers, a move that might make sense in solving the current teenage unemployment program. But the unions oppose such a reduction, and any secretary of labor who intends to maintain access to his constituency is going to be hard pressed to support it. His interest is labor, while the president's is the country, and the president should never forget that difference.

Because of the bureaucracy's tendency to protect and advance its own interest, the president must be particularly skeptical of information he receives from bureaucrats. When they tell him, as the Central Intelligence Agency told John Kennedy, that a Bay of Pigs invasion will work—or, as the Department of Defense told Carter, that an Iranian hostage rescue mission will work—the president had better take a good look on his own. If he finds he has been lied to—as Kennedy found he had been lied to by Allen Dulles—he should fire the man who lied, fire the people who misled him, and signal to his subordinates that, whatever their bureaucratic interests seem to be, their own self-interest is clearly to avoid being fired. That's what Kennedy did and that is why he was later successful in handling the Cuban missile crisis—he did get accurate information from his subordinates then. Carter, on the other hand, didn't fire anyone after the failure in the desert.

The assistant-secretary level is where the government is actually run. Cabinet secretaries are usually too busy with speeches, ceremonial duties, congressional testimony, and relations with the White House to attend to the day-to-day running of their departments. This is why it is so important that the president fill these jobs with people he can trust to both administer his programs and tell him what is going on. Carter let his cabinet secretaries make these appointments, so he never really got control of the government.

But even these appointments are not enough to run the government effectively. Implementing policy is just as important as making it. The president needs the power to hire and fire officials much more easily. Carter's civil service reforms were incremental, in the millimeter range. Firing is now slightly—but very slightly—easier than it was before, which means it is still virtually impossible. The Office of Personnel Management boasts that firing has increased by 10 to 15 percent since the civil service reform passed, and the media have generally accepted this claim as a genuine accomplishment. But the truth is that the 10 or 15 percent is 10 or 15 percent of the *one-seventh of one percent* of all career employees who have been fired in an average year preceding the "reform." If Ronald Reagan wants to control the government and if he is serious about cutting its costs, he must get the right to fire many more—I would suggest that only half of all government jobs should be tenured, which means there has to be a lot more civil service reform.

As for hiring, the president can select only one-tenth of one percent of all federal employees. The other Carter civil service reform—the Senior Executive Service—does permit the president to move around an additional one-fifth of one percent, but not to dismiss them. Even these modest reforms are threatened by court decisions holding that federal employees have property rights in their jobs and therefore not only may not be fireable—but perhaps may not even be transferable—without a hearing.

In other words, that postwar movement toward self-protection has been spectacularly successful. The permanent government is entrenched and very close to immovable.

So the new president is faced with one public, the people as a whole, who want him to solve the country's problems, and with another public, Washington, which doesn't care about solving those problems—which, in fact, sees itself threatened by such solutions.

If, for example, you work for the Department of Energy, somewhere in the back of your mind is the knowledge that a solution to the energy problem would mean there would be no further need for a Department of Energy or for your services. Your zeal to take effective action to solve the energy problem is therefore not excessive. Better to merely *pretend* to solve the problem. That's why I have written that the fundamental Washington equation is make-believe = survival. Bureaucrats confer, the president proclaims, and the Congress legislates, but the impact on reality is negligible, if evident at all.

Take legislation. When a bill has passed Congress, reporters standing on the Capitol steps tell us about it on the evening news and everyone acts as if something had really happened. But nothing actually happens until the bill is implemented. Only then will it work or not work. But seldom will a congressman or a reporter be around to find out.

The president must remember that the Congress, the press, and the bureaucracy are all joined in the game of make-believe. They want to survive, to stay in Washington.

They don't want to go out to inspect the coal mine in West Virginia and find out whether that mine safety legislation is working. And so they don't go. Only the president is likely to suffer from such inaction, because the people out there in the country ultimately expect some real action.

The White House staff

The one part of the Washington public that will share the president's concern for action is the White House staff. They see their interest as his and, because of the way Washington has changed since 1945, presidents have steadily increased their number because they provide that increasingly rare quality—loyalty.

President Reagan's immediate predecessor made a serious mistake in dealing with his staff—an error from which, one hopes, Reagan will learn: Carter relied almost exclusively on the presentation of information by memorandum. He did not encourage oral argument from his staff. He tended to accept or reject proposals on the basis of written information. FDR should remain a model to President Reagan in this respect. FDR, it will be remembered, would call up someone who had a deep and abiding distrust for the person who made the proposal. If Harold Ickes made it, Roosevelt would ask Ickes's number-one enemy, Harry Hopkins, "What do you think of that, Harry?" And when Hopkins made a proposal, Roosevelt would call up Ickes and say, "What do you think of that, Harold?" Roosevelt would also do end runs down the chain of command, calling assistant secretaries and their deputies to see if there was any dissent within the department levels beneath the secretary who had presented the proposal to him.

Rivalry on the White House staff is inevitable, and the president should not suppress it as Carter did but should use

it to find out everything he can about the deficiencies of one
person's ideas against those of another. The main danger of
these rivalries is that the staff members will try to outper-
form one another in doing obeisance to the president, in saying "Yes, sir, you're absolutely right." There's a remarkable
story told by Chester Cooper (1970), who was a member of
the National Security Council under Johnson, in his book
The Lost Crusade. He describes a White House meeting:

The president in due course would announce his decision and then
poll everyone in the room—council members, their assistants and
members of the White House and NSC staff. "Mr. Secretary, do you
agree with the decision?" "Yes, Mr. President." "Mr. X, do you
agree?" "I agree, Mr. President." During the process I would frequently fall into Walter-Mitty-like fantasy: When my turn came, I
would rise to my feet, slowly look around the room and then
directly at the president, and say very quietly and emphatically,
"Mr. President, gentlemen, I most definitely do not agree." But I
was removed from my trance when I heard the president's voice
say, "Mr. Cooper, do you agree?" And out would come, "Yes, Mr.
President, I agree."

Capitol Hill

At the opposite extreme from the White House staff stands
the president's most important Washington public, the Congress. Congress has not only failed to click its heels for recent
presidents; it has been downright hostile to the executive
through much of our history. Indeed, in the last fifty years
only two brief periods of three years each, 1934–1936 and
1964–1966, stand out as periods of congressional cooperation with the president. The reason may lie in their different
approaches to getting reelected.

Congressmen are like the president in that they want to be
reelected. But for them, getting reelected means something
different. The president must seem to be solving national
problems; the congressman must seem to be solving the

problems of his individual constituents. The president needs to bring groups together in broad coalitions to support his program; a congressman simply seeks to avoid offending these groups so they won't vote against him. That may be why congressmen are especially susceptible to the persuasions of a lobbyist, no matter how small a group he represents, because every congressman lives in mortal fear of losing the election by one vote.

So how can the president deal with a Congress that is not concerned with the broad national issues? LBJ twisted arms, but that does not seem to fit Reagan's style. FDR appealed through his fireside chats to the people, and the people let their congressmen know they wanted them to support Roosevelt's programs, which is what I hope Reagan will do. I also hope he will try cooperating with congressmen. They have the information and the votes (for his bills) that he needs. He has the information and the signatures (for their bills) that they need.

The information they have that the president needs comes to the congressmen as the result of their role as ombudsmen. The average member of Congress spends 80 percent of his time on constituent service, dealing with problems his voters have with the federal government. Taken together and carefully analyzed, the complaints congressmen get could tell the president a lot about what his government is doing wrong. The Carter administration (in the person of a White House staff member named Richard Pettigrew) was the first to even try to get this information from the Hill, and while its success was modest, future presidents should continue and intensify the effort.

One reason that congressmen might not have been as forthcoming with their information is that the Carter administration, like all its recent predecessors, was not good about giving executive branch information to the Congress. The case of A. E. Fitzgerald is useful in understanding the executive branch's attitude. Fitzgerald, a civilian accountant for

the air force, testified before the Congress in 1968 about the
C–5A. His testimony was truthful but embarrassing. The
Johnson administration berated him for not being a "team
player." Then the Nixon administration, instead of hailing
him as a hero, fired him. By going to court Fitzgerald won his
job back, but the air force continues—more than a decade
after the event—to treat him as a leper.

There is, as this story illustrates, a lack of candor in executive branch testimony on Capitol Hill, particularly where the
testimony reveals faults in the executive branch program.
The president could take a mighty step toward changing this
situation simply by reminding all the administration's
employees that they and the Congress work for the same
employer, the people of the United States, and that there is
absolutely no excuse for any kind of dishonesty or misleading
testimony.

The problem of leaks

One reason presidents may not have taken this simple step
in the past is their fear of the leak. This fear often has a
reasonable basis. Certainly you don't want to give the sailing
schedule for Polaris submarines—or even our fall-back
negotiating position on SALT III—to the Russians. But from
such reasonable concerns the fear often turns into panic
about any information embarrassing to the administration
leaking out to the public. This state of mind can even result
in the president himself not becoming aware of embarrassing information because his subordinates have grown so
secretive. Since, as I've tried to point out, the natural tendency of the chain of command is to suppress unhappy information, the president—in order to make sure he gets such information himself—must not display fear of any leaks except those that truly compromise national security.

A great example of what the fear of the leak can do is the
Bay of Pigs. It was clear somewhere midway in the planning

of that event that John Kennedy had begun to have grave doubts about it. How did Allen Dulles persuade the president to continue in the face of those doubts? Dulles and his deputy, Richard Bissell, said that should Kennedy cancel the operation, the fact that he had done so would ultimately leak out and Kennedy would look like a coward. So Kennedy, afraid of the criticism the leak would inspire, let the operation go ahead.

And fear of the leak may have contributed more than anything else to the downfall of Richard Nixon. Remember, it was this fear that led to the founding of the plumbers and the hiring of E. Howard Hunt.

At the root of the fear of the leak is a president's fear of the press, one of the most influential of the Washington publics with which he must deal.

Most recent presidents have feared and disliked the press. They have tried to distract—perhaps even to bribe—reporters by arranging trips to glamorous places like Paris and Venice and by arranging for discount vacations for reporters' families at Key Biscayne, Sea Island, San Clemente, Vail, and Palm Springs. The most fabulously successful of these distractions was the 1972 trip to Peking, which probably got Nixon the most benign coverage of his presidency.

Generally, however, presidential attempts to curry favor with the press have proved to be fruitless. Indeed, perhaps because it felt lied to by the Johnson and Nixon administrations, the press has become increasingly hostile to the occupants of the Oval Office.

Still, if Reagan will follow the examples of FDR and JFK, he may have some success with reporters. Both Kennedy and Roosevelt enjoyed their press conferences and used them to get their views across to the nation.

There is another way that I would urge Reagan to make use of the press. In the first year or so of his administration he does not have any reason to be defensive about most of what the government does or does not do, because fair-minded people will realize that he has not had enough time to change things. So why not invite the press, just as I have suggested he invite the Congress, to help him find out what is wrong with the government and its programs? Challenge the press to do constructive reporting, to use its wit and guile not only to find out what is wrong but also to figure out why it's wrong and to determine what needs to be done.

ADVICE TO REAGAN

If I were Reagan, I would have less fear of the press and the Congress and the other publics he must deal with in Washington than I would of the city itself, of its insulation from the rest of the country. Northwest Washington and suburban Montgomery and Fairfax counties, where Reagan and his people will all live, make up one elegant country club. It's Rodeo Drive all over again, with elegant shops and scores of expensive restaurants and hundreds of new homes selling for $300,000 to $500,000. You can drive to work without encountering a single shack, much less a slum.

Reagan's critics charge that he is a prisoner of Rodeo Drive —it, by the way, is a super-chic, super-protected part of Beverly Hills. My guess is different. I think he is a prisoner of the Norman Rockwell view of the United States. It's a view that has a nice side. Those old *Saturday Evening Post* covers represent a world of simple but good values—family, community, church, and country, united by warm affection, gentle humor, and an engaging absence of pretension of any kind. There was, and still is, some truth in this picture of America. But it leaves a lot out—like the race problem, the mud and blood of war, and the stairwells reeking with the urine smell of poverty.

So whether Reagan's prison is Rodeo Drive, Norman Rockwell, or northwest Washington, he must find a way to break out, to connect with his people; to remember—as he seemed, for example, to forget at one point during the campaign—that blacks and others of his fellow citizens do have real problems that he alone, because he alone is president, can tackle. No one else represents the country as a whole; no one else is so clearly charged with responsibility for the nation's tomorrow; no one else can summon his countrymen to sacrifice, to give up their own insulation—and he can do that only if he is willing to give up his own.

Perhaps even more important to avoid than being a prisoner of Washington is to avoid being a prisoner of events. This is the way most recent American presidents have failed the people. From Johnson with Vietnam to Carter with the hostages in Iran, they have become victims of the agendas of others, of the events presented by the newsticker, of the bills to sign and the proclamations to issue that the Congress and the bureaucracy always have ready. The only way to avoid this fate is for a president to have an agenda of his own—to have things that he wants to accomplish, that he wants to do for his country. If the president says no, I'm not going to be governed by the things that come up—I'll do my best with them, but I've got these other things that I think are equally or more important for this country, and these are going to be the most important things for me to do each day—he will be giving the kind of leadership that the American people respect. And that might even move Washington.

3

JACK CITRIN

The Changing American Electorate

Political disaffection in 1980. Partisanship, electoral apathy, and the presidency. Attitudes toward government regulation and waste. The effect of voter cynicism on politicians. Television and the press. Recommendations to restore public confidence. Points on style.

The news about the state of the nation for the past fifteen years has been mostly bad, and the public has held the government responsible. The apparent decline in American power and prestige, a widespread economic discontent, and continuous revelations of official corruption and cronyism caused a pervasive loss of confidence in national leaders and institutions. Frustration over these failures and a desire for a fresh start, rather than a major shift toward conservatism, were the basis of President Reagan's victory. An obvious recommendation for restoring public trust in government would be better performance. But the complexity of issues, particularly those involving conflicting objectives and goals, makes undiluted success improbable. While it is beyond the scope of this chapter to recommend substantive policies, the new president's style of communication may prove critically important as he attempts to rebuild public confidence by shaping public expectations and persuasively defining national goals.

Developing a new style of presidential leadership will require focusing on big issues, promising less and delivering more, being decisive and consistent in policy commitments, seeking respect before affection, resisting the ascendancy of the mass media, expanding participation as part of the policymaking process, and pressing for early successes during the initial six-month "honeymoon."

THE CRISIS OF CONFIDENCE

President Reagan, when he took office on 20 January 1981, had a great opportunity to reverse a fifteen-year trend towards political cynicism. Yet as he mounted the "bully pulpit"* to expound national policy and act as the country's

---

*This, of course, is Theodore Roosevelt's description of the presidency, which Mr. Reagan employed during his televised debate with Mr. Carter.

moral spokesman, the president faced a skeptical and dis-
gruntled flock. Mr. Reagan's victory had been satisfyingly
decisive, but during the long campaign neither his own
reaffirmation of the traditional verities, John Anderson's
call to self-denial and sacrifice, nor Jimmy Carter's promise
that four years of patient suffering were about to be
rewarded had inspired the multitudes. Indeed, pollsters and
journalists had littered their reports with the public's complaints about the inadequacies of all the candidates. Leading
pundits had echoed these popular misgivings, and as election
day approached some took to quoting Samuel Johnson. To
vote at all, like marrying for the second time, represented
"the triumph of hope over experience." To debate which candidate constituted the lesser evil was as pointless as "settling
the precedency between a louse and a flea." The "crisis of
competence" joined the "crisis of confidence" as a recurring
title of political commentary, and the episodic romance of
American scholars with parliamentary institutions and disciplined parties flourished anew.

The current mood of public disenchantment predates the
1980 election. For several years opinion polls have warned of
increased cynicism about public officials at all levels, of the
decay of party loyalty, the crumbling of attachments to traditional institutions such as family, school, and church, and of
a growing readiness to go beyond the formal channels for
seeking redress.

Mr. Carter himself sounded the alarm in a televised address to the nation late in 1979. He voiced the concern of
many scholars that the loss of trust in political institutions
reduces citizens' willingness to cooperate with official
policies (see, for example, Easton 1965; Crozier et al. 1975).
This, it is argued, damages the effectiveness of a government
already beset by a troubled economy and overburdened by
rising public expectations; the failure to meet these expectations further attenuates public confidence, which makes it
even harder for the government to act effectively.

The purpose of this chapter is to assess in detail current public opinion. What is the prevailing constellation of political habits, expectations, and attitudes among Americans, how does this constrain presidential leadership, and what can the president do to free himself?

TRENDS IN APATHY AND INVOLVEMENT

Although the designation of leaders at competitive elections is the principal mechanism for achieving popular sovereignty in a democracy, participation in American national elections has been declining. In 1960, 62.8 percent of the population old enough to vote went to the polls, the highest rate of turnout in the twentieth century.[1] Figure 1(a) shows that in 1976 only 54.3 percent of those eligible cast ballots. Preliminary estimates are that 52.5 percent of the electorate voted in November 1980.

Lacking the drama of a widely publicized personal contest for the ultimate prize in American politics, the off-year congressional elections have always had a more limited drawing power. But here, too, the trend is toward reduced turnout. In 1966, 45.4 percent of the electorate voted in the elections for a U.S. representative; eight years later only 36.2 percent went to the polls. Figure 1(b) shows that there was an additional small decline in participation in 1978, confirming that more is involved than a temporary revulsion from politics induced by Watergate.

In an interesting analysis of trends in political participation, Richard Brody (1978) calls the recent drop in turnout "puzzling" because it has occurred during a period in which numerous restrictions on voter registration were eliminated or eased and the electorate became steadily better educated, at least in formal terms. Between 1969 and 1975 a series of reforms enfranchised many black residents in the South,

Figure 1
Participation in National Elections:
1960–1978*

{a}
Vote for president

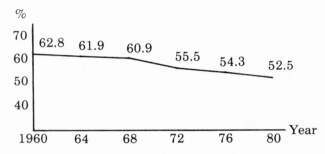

{b}
Off-year vote for U.S. representative

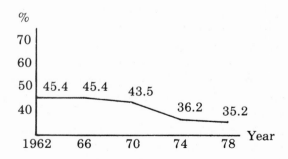

Source: U.S. Statistical Abstract 1979, Table 835, compiled by U.S. Bureau of the Census. 1980 estimate from *Los Angeles Times,* 5 November 1980, p. 1.

*Figures refer to percent of those eligible *by age* to vote.

where turnout increased by 6 percent. Without this, as Brody (1978, Fig. 2) points out, the decline in voting nationwide would have been much steeper.

In 1976 more than one in four Americans over eighteen had received some postsecondary education, a threefold increase in twenty-five years. Other things being equal, this change in the social structure should have resulted in more voting. Education increases exposure to politics, along with interest in them and greater comprehension; Wolfinger and Rosenstone's definitive study (1980, p. 102) concludes that it is the "transcendent" influence on electoral participation.

Another reason for surprise at the slide in turnout for national elections is that almost all Americans still express the belief that one ought to vote, come what may. In 1968, 92 percent of the electorate *rejected* the position that "it isn't important to vote when you know your party doesn't have a chance"; over 90 percent in 1976 felt as dutiful.

The increased abstention from voting in national elections is more accurately viewed as the product of growing doubts about the efficacy of those elections in directing the course of government than as a rise in the active repudiation of political involvement. More people are indifferent to the outcome of contests for national office. As Table 1 shows, 67.5 percent in 1964 believed that elections helped make the government pay "a good deal of attention" to the public's desires; by 1976 only 51.6 percent believed this was so.

In addition, the fraction of the electorate that evaluated the presidential candidates equally—whether they felt equally positive, negative, or neutral—grew from 8 percent in 1968 to 14 percent in 1976.[2] Those who vote occasionally or not at all are distinguished from regular voters by their detachment from and ignorance about the issues of the day but may be attracted to the polls by the candidacy of a charismatic personality. Newly enfranchised and independent voters seem to be especially responsive to the stimulus of an appealing candidate, so it is plausible that the spread of

Table 1

Trend in Attitudes toward the Electoral Process

	1964	1968	1972	1976
Percent caring about the outcome of the presidential election	65.1	62.5	58.1	56.1
Percent agreeing that "those we elect to Congress lose touch with people pretty quickly"	—	44.6	32.1	27.9
Percent who say elections make government pay a "good deal of attention"	67.5	59.5	55.1	51.6

Source: Codebooks of U.S. National Election Studies, Institute of Social Research, University of Michigan.

indifference to the available choices in recent presidential elections is a cause of lower turnout.

It is important to note, however, that increased apathy on election day is not a sign that the public is passive. Indeed, forms of political participation requiring more skill and effort than the simple act of voting have become more widespread. The so-called "tax revolt" is largely a story of citizen activity aimed at placing proposals to limit taxes and government spending on state ballots. Within six months of its passage in June 1978, California's Proposition 13 had spawned fifteen similar measures in other states. And in contrast to the growing cynicism about elections of public officials, there is widespread approval of initiatives and referenda. A California poll conducted in December 1979, for example, showed that 72 percent of the electorate believed ballot propositions were a more effective way of influencing the government than "voting for candidates."

Although we lack hard evidence of this, it appears probable that membership in politically relevant interest groups, particularly single-issue groups, has grown. With the advent of computerized direct mailing and the proliferation of radio talk shows and telethons, exposure to political messages and requests for contributions has increased. There is evidence that more people are contacting public officials. Figure 2 shows that disapproval of such political tactics as protest marches, disruptive sit-ins, and refusing to obey "unjust" laws has declined. Tolerance of such protests prepares the ground for actual participation in them, so it is significant that the change in attitude appeared in every demographic and ideological subgroup in society (see Citrin 1977). Once the wives of medical doctors occupy a governor's office to complain about the cost of malpractice insurance and the dwindling yeomanry parade in tractors across the Washington Mall, it is clear that tactics once viewed as extreme have acquired legitimacy as a means of stirring an unresponsive government to action. The president thus must deal with an electorate of which a large proportion did not seize the chance to vote, yet which is poised to protest when aggrieved about matters of immediate personal concern.

TRENDS IN PARTISANSHIP

The Democrats—the majority in American politics since the New Deal—have now lost five of the nine presidential elections since 1946. In 1980 they lost control of the Senate for the first time in twenty-six years, which may prove as essential as the loss of the White House in altering the course of public policy. Longstanding fissures in the party were evidently only temporarily closed in 1976, and a debate is now under way as to whether the latest wave of defections from its ranks signifies a lasting change in the balance of partisan forces, the growing rejection of both political parties as objects of loyalty, or merely a short-run movement toward the "out" party due to frustration with the "ins."

Future elections will settle this debate; my purpose here is to consider trends in partisan sentiment and their implica-

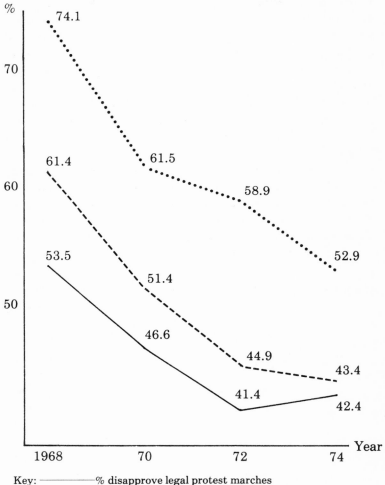

Figure 2
Trends in Approval of Protest Tactics:
1968–1974

%

74.1

70

61.4   61.5

58.9

60

53.5

52.9

51.4

50

46.6

44.9

43.4

41.4

42.4

Year

1968   70   72   74

Key: ―――――% disapprove legal protest marches
― ― ― ―% disapprove disruptive sit-ins
· · · · · · · % disapprove disobedience of "unjust" law

Source: Codebooks of U.S. National Election Studies, Institute of Social
Research, University of Michigan.

tions for presidential leadership. In the vocabulary of U.S. politics, the political party historically has been a symbol of divisiveness and selfish ambition; as such, it has not been widely admired. But negative judgments of the parties are growing. Data provided by the University of Michigan's biennial election studies show that the proportion of the electorate who felt that parties do "a good deal" to make government responsive to the people fell from 43.5 percent in 1964 to 21.9 percent in 1978.

Those who predict the imminent demise of the parties cite the growth in the number of voters who prefer to identify themselves as Independents rather than as Democrats or Republicans and the increase in split-ticket voting in the late 1960s and 1970s (De Vries and Torrance 1972). According to the Michigan election studies, 37 percent of the electorate called themselves Independents in 1978 compared to 23 percent in 1960. Both parties lost adherents during this period; the proportion of Democrats dropped from 46 percent to 39 percent, while the Republicans' share of the electorate's attachments shrank from 27 percent to 21 percent. These figures taken by themselves, however, greatly overstate the erosion of party loyalties (see Clubb et al. 1976). When asked, most Independents expressed a preference for one of the major parties over the other. In 1978 only 14 percent of the Independents were indifferent as between the Democrats and Republicans, and turnout among this group was much lower than anywhere else along the spectrum of party identification. Table 2 indicates that those who "lean" toward a party tend to participate and to vote for the presidential nominee of that party as often as people who "weakly" identify with it.[3] In short, as the collapse of the Anderson candidacy starkly demonstrated, many voters *talk* Independent but *act* partisan.

A recent study that tracked the attitudes of the same people between 1972 and 1976 concluded that while the strength of party affiliation may change, the direction of party iden-

Table 2

Party Identification and Presidential Voting
1952–1976

	Mean percent	
	Turnout	Vote for Democrat presidential candidate
Democrats		
Strong	82	84
Weak	73	64
Independent	74	70
Pure Independents	66	35
Republicans		
Independent	80	12
Weak	81	15
Strong	90	3

Source: These data were provided by Professor Raymond Wolfinger and were compiled from the Michigan National Election Studies for his forthcoming book on Independents.

tification is enduring; it is more stable, in fact, than most other political attitudes (Converse and Markus 1979). The trend in partisanship is thus best viewed as a decline in the intensity of partisan feeling. In view of the reluctance of a better-educated electorate to defer to party leaders and the tendency of current nomination procedures, campaign finance laws, and techniques of electioneering to fragment the parties and encourage campaigns centered on "the man," this trend is likely to continue.

The fluidity of partisan sentiment represents both a danger and an opportunity for President Reagan. The danger is that he will misread the electoral support of many Democrats as a sign of an ongoing commitment to all aspects of his party's dominant outlook. Voters cross party lines more readily than they stay across. The opportunity is that the president's proposals are less likely to encounter reflexive

opposition based on partisan hostility. The president should
benefit from the similarity of views among Democrats and
Republicans—in the electorate if not in Congress—on the
main themes of his candidacy: the primacy of inflation
among the nation's problems, the need to control taxes and
public spending, and the desirability of strengthening
America's military capabilities.

TRENDS IN POLITICAL OUTLOOK

The 1980 elections reflected a rightward swing in American
opinion that began several years ago. Public opinion polls
conducted during this period show an increasing number of
respondents identifying themselves as conservative rather
than liberal in politics. The liberal commitment to government as the agent of social and economic progress seemed to
be waning. In 1964, 44.5 percent of respondents with an interest in the issue felt the federal government had become
too powerful for the good of the country; fully 71 percent in
1976 believed this. In several states voters defied warnings
about the disruption of social services and passed measures
that cut taxes or limited public spending. Attitudes about
defense spending, an issue that divides liberal and conservative politicians, also changed: between 1971 and 1979 the
proportion of the electorate adopting the conservative pro-
spending posture rose from 11 percent to 60 percent. Finally,
Lipset and Ladd (1980, pp. 55–59) have compiled evidence
indicating increased support for restricting the rights of accused criminals and imposing severe punishments on those
convicted.[4]
    On the issues cited above, then, President Reagan's stated
views seem to be shared by a majority of the public. The same
set of polls, however, raises important questions about how
fundamental and complete is the movement toward conser-

vatism. In several areas of policy, liberal opinions predominate or are growing. In others, people frequently adopt a conservative posture when issues are posed in abstract symbolic terms but express contradictory opinions when concrete measures aimed at realizing their general values are proposed. These inconsistencies in the public's outlook constrain the president's ability to be an ideological purist without risking the public's retribution, although the power of his own actions and events to reshape mass attitudes must be acknowledged.

To illustrate, there is an increasing tendency to adopt a liberal outlook on "life-style" issues. Racial, religious, and political tolerance has increased in the past decades.[5] Americans are also more supportive of equal rights for women. And increasing numbers are tolerant about drugs, pornography, homosexuality, and abortions, even if they express a continued personal commitment to traditional norms. For example, 31 percent of the public in 1979 approved of the legalization of marijuana and 40 percent favored allowing a woman to have an abortion simply because she wanted no more children; in 1969 the comparable proportions were 13 and 15 percent, respectively.[6] These liberal views clash directly with the opinions of the highly mobilized "Moral Majority," who supported the president, yet they are concentrated among the college-educated and affluent voters who frequently share his conservative views on economic policy.

Public attitudes toward the proper scope for state intervention in economic and social policy provide important examples of the uneasy amalgam of conservative and liberal views. Hostility toward government regulation of business disappears or is transformed into support when certain industries or dangerous products are mentioned. In 1979 those who felt the amount of government regulation was too great outnumbered those who believed there was insufficient regulation by a small margin of 33 to 29 percent.[7] And a 1978 Harris Survey found that 44 percent of the public believed that businessmen's complaints about excessive regulations were justified, compared to 32 percent who disagreed and 24 percent who were undecided. Other polls conducted in 1979 revealed widespread approval of deregulation of the transportation industry and a reduced government role in the steel and auto industries.

Yet by margins ranging from 40 to 23 percent the extra costs of government rules to ensure product safety, provide security for workers, guarantee equal opportunities for employment, and protect the environment were deemed worthwhile.[8] And Figure 3 shows that the public would like to see more government control of pricing and manufacturing procedures in a variety of industries. In short, Americans accept both the conservative's condemnation of government intrusions as a cause of inefficiency and inflation and the liberal's fears about the willingness of business to safeguard the consumer's interests unless coerced. Policies that reduce the cost of regulation without protecting the benefits people value will surely elicit sharp protests.

Similarly, while the predominant rhetoric inveighs against the size of government in general, people continue to insist on a full range of expensive public services. Indeed, public opinion regarding the way government should carry out its responsibilities can be summarized as "Taxes, no! Spending, no! Services, yes!"

Antagonism toward taxes is hardly recent, but resentment about the size of the burden has grown. In 1957, according to Gallup, 61 percent of the American public felt the amount they paid in taxes was too high. This proportion actually fell below 50 percent in the 1960s, those halcyon days before "stagflation," but then rose steadily to 72 percent in 1976. In 1978, 66 percent of a national sample felt they had reached the "breaking point," up by 12 percent since 1969, and 42 percent agreed that "taxes are now so high that people should refuse to pay them until taxes and spending are cut."[9]

While support for a tax cut declines when respondents are

Figure 3
Opinions on the Need for Regulation:
1980

Question: Now I'm going to name some things, and for each one would you tell me whether you think there is too much government regulation of it now, or not enough government regulation now, or about the right amount of government regulation now? First, automobile safety.

Government regulation of...

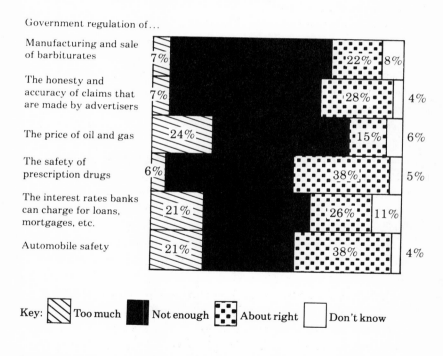

Manufacturing and sale of barbiturates — 7%, 22%, 8%

The honesty and accuracy of claims that are made by advertisers — 7%, 28%, 4%

The price of oil and gas — 24%, 15%, 6%

The safety of prescription drugs — 6%, 38%, 5%

The interest rates banks can charge for loans, mortgages, etc. — 21%, 26%, 11%

Automobile safety — 21%, 38%, 4%

Key: ▨ Too much   ■ Not enough   ▦ About right   ☐ Don't know

Source: Survey by the Roper Organization February 1980, reported in *Public Opinion* 3,3 (June/July 1980):38.

warned that it would mean the loss of services they value, the polls show that in the abstract people prefer that both taxes and spending be lowered. For example, an NBC News Poll conducted in late 1978 found that people favored a one-third cut in federal taxes by 55 percent to 34 percent and in state and local taxes by 52 percent to 39 percent, "even if it meant the things you like about government would have to be cut substantially." More recent surveys indicate that the public is even more anxious to limit spending than to reduce taxes; since 1978 several CBS News/*New York Times* polls have found a better than three-to-one margin in favor of cutting expenditures first.

More significant, however, is the evidence of a widespread desire to maintain specific government services, particularly in health and education. A 1980 National Opinion Research Center (NORC) survey found that while citizens saw the government as spending more than they—in the aggregate—desired, by a margin of 43 to 31 percent they preferred to maintain existing services even if this meant no reduction in expenditures.[10]

Table 3 reports on the trends in replies to questions about whether the government should increase, decrease, or maintain spending in a variety of areas. It is striking that the majority continue to desire more spending on health, education, crime prevention, and environmental protection. Other data indicate widespread public support for a national health insurance, the existing social security program, and a guaranteed job.[11]

Quite predictably, programs whose benefits are available to everyone, at least in principle, are more widely favored than those with a specialized clientele. Universal access to such programs makes them expensive, of course, so we are left with the irony that the public simultaneously demands reduced taxes (and spending) along with costly insurance against the financial risks of illness, old age, and unemployment.

Table 3
Trends in Spending Preferences 1973–1980

Percent believing government is spending *too little* on:	1973	1980
Halting rising crime rate	69	72
Health	63	57
Defense	12	60
Education	51	55
Environment	65	51
Problems of big cities	55	46
Conditions of blacks	35	25
Welfare	21	14
Foreign aid	4	5
Space exploration	8	20

Source: National Opinion Research Center, reported in *Public Opinion* 3, (October/November 1980):22.

How is the circle squared? The psychic resolution of this inconsistency, apparently, is to insist that huge savings lie in the elimination of bureaucratic "waste," a worthy if politically formidable objective. That the public believes that the government is wildly profligate there can be no doubt. Between 1968 and 1978 the proportion of Americans believing that the national government wastes "a lot" of the taxpayers' money leaped from 47 to 79 percent. And a 1978 Gallup poll found that the median estimate for the amount of each tax dollar wasted by the federal government was 48 cents.

THE CONTOURS OF POLITICAL DISAFFECTION

The statistics of declining confidence in government are by now widely disseminated.[12] The change in the public's out-

look has encompassed a loss of faith in the integrity and
effectiveness of a wide range of institutions and has cut
across all traditional class, racial, regional, and ideological
boundaries.

The rise in disenchantment can be clearly seen in the
responses to five questions appraising "the government in
Washington, regardless of which party is in power" that have
been included in the University of Michigan's national surveys since 1964. For every aspect of national government,
the proportion of unfavorable opinions (the government can
be trusted *only some* of the time, is run for the benefit of *a few
big interests*, wastes *a lot* of money, and is staffed by *many* officials who *don't know* what they are doing and *quite a few*
crooked administrators) rose substantially over the past fifteen years. Indeed, the *average* proportion of such answers
doubled—from 30 percent in 1964 to 60 percent in 1978.

Figure 4 tracks the movement in the proportions of "politically cynical" citizens, those who give at least four negative
answers out of the five possible, and those classified as
"trusting" by virtue of giving no more than one such
response. The erosion of confidence in government was
spawned after 1964 by civil strife and the war in Vietnam,
and it continued steadily until 1970. From 1970 to 1972 there
was little overall change, but Watergate and economic recession renewed the downward slide. And while the level of
cynicism stabilized between 1974 and 1978, it seems certain
that the results of more recent polls will show another rise.
In any event, 50 percent of the sample in the 1978 National
Election Study were "cynics" and 15 percent "trusting."

Since 1966 the Harris Survey has asked people how much
confidence they had in "the people running" primary American institutions, both governmental and private. As Table 4
confirms, the central institutions of national government
consistently have a low comparative standing. But public
confidence tended to shift in a concerted fashion. Between
1966 and 1979 dissatisfaction with all institutions increased

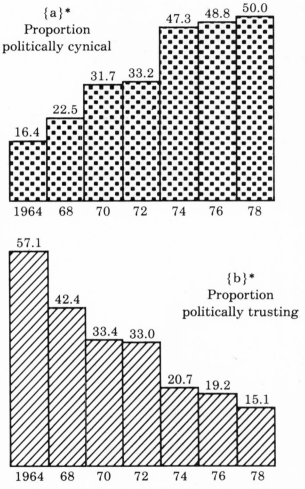

Figure 4

Trends in Political Cynicism: 1964–1978

{a}*
Proportion
politically cynical

16.4 22.5 31.7 33.2 47.3 48.8 50.0

1964 68 70 72 74 76 78

57.1 42.4 33.4 33.0 20.7 19.2 15.1

{b}*
Proportion
politically trusting

1964 68 70 72 74 76 78

Source: U.S. National Election Studies, Center for Political Studies, University of Michigan.

*Figures (a) and (b) add up to less than 100% because the middle category or respondents is excluded.

sharply. These data suggest that a diffuse sense of pessimism about the state of the nation has developed. Between July 1977 and April 1979 the proportion of the public which felt the country was "in deep and serious trouble" rose from 41 to 67 percent. And only a small minority thought the government would be able to solve the country's main social and economic problems (see Caddell 1979, p. 7).

Table 4
Confidence in Institutions 1966–1979

Percentages expressing a "great deal of confidence" in:	1966	1972	1974	1976	Nov. 1977	Feb. 1979
Federal executive branch	41	23	28	11	23	17
Congress	42	19	18	9	15	18
Nongovernmental institutions*	47	36	31	24	31	23

Source: The Harris Survey.
*Average of medicine, higher education, organized labor, major companies, the press.

Table 5 compares the level of trust in government expressed by various sectors of society in 1978. The balance of attitudes in a group is obtained by subtracting the proportion of cynical respondents (classified according to answers to the five Michigan questions about "the government in Washington") from the proportion within it which is trusting.[13] These Percentage Difference Index values thus vary from +100 in a totally trusting group to −100 in one that is totally cynical.

Clearly, political cynicism is shared by all demographic and partisan groups, although the precise timing and the extent of the shift varied among them (see Citrin 1977 for more details). And a change in the political coloration of the presidency makes some groups more trusting while others become

Table 5

Political Cynicism in Selected Groups 1978

	Percentage Difference Index*
Race	
Blacks	−36
Whites	−32
Education	
Grade school	−38
Some high school	−39
High school graduate	−38
Some college	−35
College graduate	−26
Income	
Under $10,000	−36
$10−15,000	−32
$15−20,000	−32
$20−25,000	−34
$25,000 plus	−25
Age	
Under 30	−26
31−40	−31
41−50	−36
51−60	−37
61 plus	−47
Party identification	
Democrat: strong	−25
weak	−31
independent	−34
Pure Independent	−39
Republican: independent	−39
weak	−36
strong	−34

*PDI values: % trusting less % cynical.

more cynical. After Mr. Carter's election in 1976 blacks and
self-identified Democrats in the aggregate became more con-

fident in government, whereas whites and Republicans voiced increasing levels of mistrust; the opposite movements took place when the Republicans won power in 1968. These are nuances of shading, however, in a picture dominated by an across-the-board rise in disaffection.

Before commenting on its origins and implications, several fragments of evidence are worth noting which point the other way. First, when given the choice of several unfavorable answers, most respondents eschewed the most negative. People today are more likely than they were in the mid-1960s to express "some" rather than "a good deal" of confidence in our institutions, but they are not much more likely to say that they have "hardly any." Government now tends to be regarded as "fair" but not "poor," rather than "good." Given the adverse events Americans have endured in the past decade, this changed outlook might be more appropriately described as realistic skepticism, not unreconstructed cynicism.

Second, faith in the underlying form of government remains pervasive. In 1976, for example, 66 percent of the National Election Study sample stated that the government in Washington was run for the benefit of just a few big interests. But 80 percent of the same sample and fully 71 percent of the politically cynical respondents expressed pride in the American form of government. Forty-seven percent felt that no real change in the system was needed, and the 25 percent who felt a big change was necessary tended to mention relatively minor alterations in the electoral process when asked to propose reforms.

Third, several studies show widespread satisfaction with personal contacts with government officials and agencies (Kahn et al. 1975b). More generally, specific institutions such as the presidency usually receive more favorable ratings in the polls than do vague entities such as "the government as a whole" or "the people in charge of" an institution. Indeed, despite the considerable grumbling about recent presidential nominees, the individuals concerned tend to be viewed in at least mildly positive terms. Similarly, a nationwide poll conducted by CBS News in 1978 showed that, whereas only 30 percent of the public approved of the performance of Congress as a whole, 60 percent felt their own elected representative was going a good job.

CAUSES AND CONSEQUENCES OF POLITICAL MISTRUST

The main cause of the prevailing cynicism is the past decade's succession of failures to meet expectations in crucial areas of national policy. The government is expected to provide peace, prosperity, order, and integrity in the management of public affairs. Instead, despite changing national administrations twice—in 1968 and 1976—Americans have experienced a costly and indecisive war, massive civil disorders, corruption in the highest offices, a sustained period of high inflation, and finally the humiliating Iranian hostage crisis.

Arguably, it is the relative mildness of the public's response, not the fact of increased dissatisfaction, which is surprising. Possibly the tendency to compartmentalize one's personal well-being from events in the political arena has limited the impact of the government's shortcomings on more fundamental political loyalties. Personal grievances only become politicized when they concern problems which the government is expected to solve yet has not done so. Inflation, of course, is such a problem; moreover, its economic and psychological effects are pervasive.[14] When the goals of government policy are universally shared, public confidence falls if they are not reached. But when opinion about what is right and desirable is polarized, as with the abortion issue, a consensual outcome is unlikely and the tendency of govern-

ment to steer a centrist course simply alienates both sides to
the conflict (see Miller 1974).

To a certain extent, the current skepticism about political
leaders and institutions reflects a more general decline of
deference to authority that is seemingly inherent in the economic and social transformations of modern life. As Nisbet
(1975) has pointed out, geographic mobility, the bureau-
cratization and nationalization of economic life, and the
spread of secular, liberal education have loosened the ties of
affection and obedience to authority figures in the home,
the school, and the local community. Political leaders cannot
expect to be immune to this trend—which is likely to continue, however well particular administrations perform.

It should also be repeated that many of the negative comments we now hear are merely casual verbalizations of a
widely accepted stereotype. Sneering at politicians has a
venerable history in the United States and, once open disdain for public officials begins to spread, many people join in
to conform to the current fashion. These rhetorical sallies
against the political process are unlikely to disappear, but
whether they lead to action is another matter.

The role of television and the press in creating feelings of
political malaise is controversial (see Miller et al. 1979). The
mass media are clearly the main source of learning about
current affairs; television, in particular, disseminates the
grisly details of remote events in Washington and abroad.
But while one may quibble about the balance of good and bad
news that is transmitted, the media can hardly be blamed for
the failures and misfortunes that caused the public to lose
confidence in government.

It is easier to be critical of the manner in which recent
presidential campaigns have been reported. Recent studies
by Robinson (Robinson et al. 1980) and Patterson (1980) conclude that news coverage is inclined to be objective but
shallow. Public confidence cannot be helped by the tendency
to present the campaign as a contest, a horse race in which

interest can only be maintained by raising doubt about the front-runners and glamorizing new entrants—who are then cast aside with faint ridicule when they falter. The undignified spectacle of potential presidents scrambling for the attention of reporters also makes it harder for them to inspire respect. Again, however, one should not be too hard on the media for spreading cynicism when presidents campaign by attacking the bureaucracy they head and congressmen run against Congress.

Turning now to the consequences of political mistrust, conventional wisdom holds that disaffected citizens are normally apathetic, withdrawing from political participation; that most politicians are corrupt and insincere; and that government institutions are unresponsive to popular desires. When the alienated act, the argument continues, it is only to protest against the status quo.

Table 6 reproduces and adds to the results of an earlier study which refuted the idea that the politically cynical develop a distinctive style of participation (Citrin 1978). For example, the rates of turnout among trusting and cynical respondents in the 1976 and 1978 elections were virtually identical.

It does appear, though, that politically cynical voters consistently favor the candidate of the "out" party for president; they were more likely than were trusting citizens to prefer Carter in 1976, McGovern in 1972, Wallace in 1968, and Goldwater in 1964. If this pattern held, the main electoral consequence of mistrust of government in 1980 was, understandably, to boost support for Mr. Reagan. In earlier elections, however, this pattern of negative voting did not extend to congressional elections; incumbent candidates for Congress were not more likely than other candidates to be rejected by people cynical about government as a whole.

As to the influence of disenchantment with government on people's willingness to cooperate with official policy, there are few empirical studies. One that is relevant is the analysis

Table 6

Cynicism and Political Participation*

Percentage	Cynical	Trust-ing
Not much interest in politics	22	16
Wrote letter to editor	30	28
Voted in 1976 election	71	75
Talked to someone else about election	42	43
Worked for candidate	3	3
Voted for Carter	56	39
Voted against incumbent congressman, 1978	31	28
Voted in 1978 congressional election	55	52

Source: Inter-University Consortium for Political and Social Research, 1976 and 1978 National Election Studies.

*Figures are proportions of cynical and trusting respondents who engaged in a particular activity.

by Sears, Citrin, Tyler, and Kinder (1978) of reactions to the energy shortage in 1974 in Los Angeles. In that situation, politically disaffected and trusting citizens were equally likely to conserve electricity and curtail their driving; when it came to behavior, the demands of self-interest prevailed. Attitudes toward the political system did influence beliefs about the energy crisis, however; disaffected citizens were more likely than the trusting to deny official claims about the gravity of the crisis and to blame the U.S. government for the shortage of oil.

A negative climate of opinion about government affects policy largely through the reactions of political leaders. One possible response, of course, is for officials to simply avoid taking necessary decisions for fear the public will refuse to go along. Alternatively, those in power may redirect their attention to the grievances underlying the public's cynicism. For example, official perceptions that citizens were concerned about morality in government led to the reform of campaign finance laws and the creation of ethics committees in Congress.

For their part, opposition leaders and organizations out-side government may be emboldened by prevailing attitudes to resist and obstruct the president's programs, hopeful that he will suffer the blame fur delay or inaction. The most serious consequence of the spread of political mistrust may be to discourage the cooperation of significant elites in a political system in which cohesive policymaking is already hampered by institutional fragmentation and weak political parties.

LEADERSHIP IN AN AGE OF CYNICISM

At one level, the obvious recommendation for restoring the public's trust in government is better performance, particularly on the economic front. This advice is sound, but it is insufficient. The diversity and complexity of the government's problems—for example, how to cope with both inflation *and* unemployment in an economy that is vulnerable to uncontrollable actions by unsympathetic outsiders—make it unlikely that any president will enjoy a steady stream of successes. The prevailing lack of deference toward political leaders, moreover, has roots in American culture and is reinforced by trends in social structure. Like religious faith, political trust is more easily lost than regained, so the president must be prepared to govern a cynical constituency.

There is ample evidence in the polls, however, that the public yearns for strong leadership, that people are tired of "normal" politics—with its cycle of overpromising followed by self-justification—and would prefer an unadorned analysis of problems which they already know are serious. Overcoming the present sense of drift is the first step toward rebuilding citizens' faith in government; one aspect of effective leadership is the ability to shape public expectations and define national goals persuasively. It is beyond the scope of this chapter to recommend substantive policies to the president. Instead, I shall make some modest suggestions about leadership style which may begin to solve the intertwined crises of confidence and competence.

Concentrate on the big issues. The president is the focal point of American government and the ultimate authority for decisions of all degrees of importance. His time and attention are finite, and the public is likely to be reassured if he is perceived as concentrating on appropriate issues where his goals are universally shared. The president should stand aloof from divisive conflicts on symbolic issues; whatever he decides, he is bound to antagonize some group. When he is called to account for the misdeeds of officials as remote from him as they are from the people, he should be in a position to take the responsibility but not the blame.

Promise less but deliver more. There is no convincing evidence that people actually expect a continuous rise in their standard of living (Sniderman and Brody 1977). Indeed, the increased pessimism about the nation's future that appears in the polls can be viewed as a realistic scaling-down of expectations of future growth. What people do demand is the essence of the welfare state: a guaranteed minimum standard of income, health, and education. Reassurance on this point is important, but what should be promised is a floor of services and assistance, not a permanent escalator in a room with no ceiling.

Sacrifice begins at home. Given the widespread perceptions of massive waste in government, highly publicized gestures toward austerity—such as the reduction of staff, introduction of cost management procedures, or complete elimination of an executive department—can positively influence public opinion. In the longer term, it is probably more important to convince people that the public sector will not be spared the vagaries of the business cycle and given special protection from inflation. Employees of the federal government are well paid relative to the private sector, and allowing this differential to decline would testify to official frugality without causing a mass exodus of talent from government.

Have a scapegoat when bad news comes. Attacking "government" from within is unlikely to foster cooperation between elected officials and administrators, nor can the head of government convincingly describe himself as an outsider for very long. In the short run, the blame for bad times can be placed on the errors of one's predecessors; later on, international conditions[15] or unpopular domestic interest groups may be more convenient scapegoats.

Be decisive; be consistent. Although one aspect of lowering public expectations is to frankly admit that there are problems which government lacks the knowledge and resources to solve, a retreat into inaction as a general strategy would further damage public confidence. The president is expected to lead, to be decisive. Once action is taken, consistency and perseverance are critical. If his decisions fail to produce immediate results, they may result in negative judgments in the public opinion polls; but vacillation reduces credibility and portrays an image of weakness to constituents and other leaders alike.

Seek respect before affection. Much is expected of an American president. As Head of State he must be dignified; as Chief Executive he must be capable; as Man of the People he must be lovable. In other less-populist cultures, confidence in government remains intact despite the predominance of cynicism about politics (Okamura 1979). In Japan, for example, attitudes toward the political parties and elected officials are largely negative, but the government has an undeniable capacity for mobilizing the public to cooperate with its decisions. One reason for this is the high degree of respect, though certainly not affection, for the bureaucracy. The appointment to high positions of people whose technical expertise and objectivity are acknowledged can boost the president's credibility.

Resist the ascendancy of the mass media.   No one questions the public's right to know or the central role of the mass media in making the exercise of that right possible. Yet one cannot help feeling that the current role of television and the press in shaping both the political agenda and the public's image of political life is too large. An increased distance between the president and reporters might add an aura of dignity to the office. More important, the president should make use of television as a medium of public education; doing so will further his own interests and his vision of the public interest rather than the interests of the media.

Consult the public; expand participation.   A frequent complaint about government is that it is remote and unresponsive. One avenue toward restoring trust is to allow the public a greater sense of involvement in policymaking. Decentralization of authority to the local governments which currently inspire more confidence, the expanded use of presidential commissions, and town meetings, are possible devices to explore.

Extend the honeymoon; break in front.   Presidents are at the peak of their popularity when they take the oath of office. At this juncture they have known only victory; the seemingly inevitable failures are yet to come. Out of caution or goodwill, Congress traditionally allows for a "honeymoon" period of about six months. This is a time in which institutional and partisan rivalries are muted and the president is given a chance to initiate a legislative program. Success in this period of harmony would not only please the public, but might also help sustain a spirit of cooperation between the branches of government.

IN SUM: PRESENT A UNITED FRONT

The structure of American government encourages conflict and deadlock. This tendency is enhanced when different parties control Congress and the presidency, and is overcome only in rare moments of national crisis (Sundquist 1980). The bickering, confusion, and delay promoted by the fragmentation of power create obstacles to effective leadership and intensify the public's disaffection from the political process.

It is natural and desirable that the new president refashion policy to follow the direction of his ideological following and to consolidate his party's gains. Nevertheless, a style of governing that recognizes the concerns of the country's main centers of economic and political power, including the Washington community, and commitment to a process of consultation and conciliation in the management of the nation's problems could contribute significantly to improved performance and increased confidence in government. Bipartisanship in foreign policy and unity among institutional elites have symbolic value. Consideration of diverse viewpoints during the formulation of policy makes it more likely that decisions, once reached, will be generally accepted, and that key groups will concur and will mobilize support among their constituencies.

The public's loss of confidence is the effect—not the cause—of failures in government; current attitudes are not serious constraints on effective leadership. Firm leadership and the development of cohesion among elites, a measure of restraint in their competitive struggles, and a concerted effort to convey a genuine sense of national unity and purpose should begin to overcome the current malaise.

4

EVERETT CARLL LADD, JR.

Political Parties and Governance in the 1980s

Representative and direct democracy. Political parties as linkage. The Progressives. Independence and the decline of partisanship. Recent party reforms. The Winograd Commission. Congress and the "iron triangle." Interest-group liberalism. The need for party competition. National committees, the national chairman, and the cabinet. Discipline, funding, integration. The president as party leader.

The new administration, as it begins its work and surveys the diverse problems that confront the nation, should give special attention to the deterioration of political parties, which are the primary institutions of American representative democracy. While substantive matters involving the economy and national security may seem to be more immediate and pressing, the present incapacities of political parties stand as serious barriers to attaining a coherent and successful public policy. Fortunately, without clashing with current American political values and expectations and without requiring change in the Constitution, the president and Congress may take a number of actions that would revitalize the political parties and would permit them again to assist in development of successful public policies.

THE CLASH OF ALTERNATE
CONCEPTS OF DEMOCRACY

Political leaders in the United States, from one perspective, should be the last group to need reminding that political parties are critically important to successful governance in the broadest sense. After all, the country has benefited from some remarkably well-designed governmental machinery for 190 years. But in fact this experience—living under generally successful political institutions—seems to have contributed to a remarkably casual attitude toward the institutional requirements of successful governance.

Although the United States is the world's oldest *representative democracy*, its politicians and political commentators frequently fail to distinguish that basic approach to governance from *direct democracy*. What is worse, they often append direct-democracy changes to America's representative institutions while announcing that in so doing they are making the system "more democratic." For the last two decades American presidents have been regularly chewed up and enfeebled; not one has been able to complete a second term. Yet there has been little real urgency to pursue institutional

changes that might help presidents in the immensely
difficult tasks of governing. Many members of Congress de-
cry its present condition and express doubts that the institution, as now arranged, can enact the responsible policy the
nation needs; but no serious attempt has been undertaken to
reform congressional organization and operation. Although
the American people have made clear their frustration with
government—including the extent to which policy is in-
fluenced by special interests—no sustained effort has appeared to educate the public on how to retune the engine of
government and make it run more effectively.

THE PROBLEM WITH THE
POLITICAL PARTIES

Political parties have an extensive role and place in representative democracy. They are the essential "linkage" institution—linking the general public to government and
those in government to one another. In Congress and the
state legislatures, for instance, parties are instruments for
organizing and directing legislative affairs, and the recent
decline of parties—especially over the last fifteen years—
has had profound implications for legislative operations.

Some factors weakening political parties in the United
States have had recent origins; others are of long standing.
American political culture itself has been foremost among
the latter. Though Americans gave the world its first party
system, they have always been highly ambivalent toward
parties, largely because of their distinctive cultural individualism. Americans resist collective structures like parties that in any way deny the individual's claim to more
direct participation. Thus our strong attraction to various of
the assumptions and practices of direct democracy, which
tends toward direct participation by individual citizens in

public affairs. During the Progressive Era this cultural inclination to direct democracy encouraged actions designed to
weaken parties, which accomplished that precise end. The
Progressives advocated, with great success, that voters in
primaries rather than party organizations control nominations for state and local office. This emphasis on making the
parties internally democratic is unequaled in any other democratic system; the direct primary remains almost exclusively an American institution.

Despite these general cultural inclinations, political parties remained reasonably strong. After World War II,
however, various changes seriously eroded many supports
holding up the parties. One development is the extraordinary
increase in formal education, especially in higher education.
Since World War II the American population has become
more educated, has many more sources of political information, and clearly feels less dependent upon parties. People
thus are irreversibly more inclined to be independent—twice
more, in fact, than they were three decades ago. In 1952, 22
percent of voting-age Americans described themselves as independents.[1] By September 1980 that figure had reached 40
percent, compared to 37 percent Democrats and 24 percent
Republicans.[2] These trends in self-description are paralleled
by a dramatic increase in independent political behavior—
crossing party lines and ticket-splitting in elections.

Extending governmental responsibilities through the New
Deal and post–New Deal "service state" further weakened
party organizations by taking functions away from them.
Parties once provided a number of concrete social services,
including aid to the needy. Nonpartisan public bureaucracies
now administer such services, of course, at a vastly higher
level than the parties ever did. While party leaders still serve
as fixers or "ombudsmen" for citizens with needs or grievances regarding governmental action, in some areas in the
United States the ombudsman role has increasingly been
taken over by public bureaucracies.

The rise of the national mass media has also weakened parties, increasingly assuming communications roles once performed by party organizations. David Broder observed in a perceptive essay that newsmen now serve as the principal source of information on what candidates are saying and doing. They act as talent scouts, conveying the judgment that some contenders show promise while dismissing others as lacking talent. They also operate as race-callers or handicappers, telling the public how the election is going. At times they function as public defenders, bent on exposing what they consider a candidate's frailties, duplicities, and sundry inadequacies. They sometimes even serve as assistant campaign managers, informally advising a candidate and publicly, if discreetly, promoting his cause (Broder 1970, pp. 3–22).

Most Americans once got their political information from the political parties, including a party press. Today parties have lost the communications function to a professionalized and bureaucratized press and have thus lost an important role.

Responding to these developments that weaken the parties, the American public's regard for political parties and confidence in them has declined. In May 1980, for example, only 28 percent of the public gave the Democratic party a "highly favorable" rating—down from the 42 percent in 1967.[3] The Republicans' support also fell, from 34 percent highly favorable in 1967 to just 17 percent in 1980. Growing proportions of the population doubt that there are major differences between the parties—in the sense of what government actually does when one party or the other is in office. "Do you think there are any important differences in what the Democratic and Republican parties stand for?" the CBS News/*New York Times* poll of 10–14 September 1980 asked respondents nationally. Just 43 percent of the respondents said yes—and, what is most striking, only 52 percent of registered Democrats and 49 percent of registered Republicans saw important differences.

These trends were dramatically confirmed in a 1980 Connecticut poll which asked state residents, "Which party, the Republicans or the Democrats, does the better job [handling a specified problem] or don't you think there is much difference?" As Table 1 shows, between 70 and 80 percent of the respondents indicated that they saw little partisan difference. Some questions produced a pro-Democratic edge, others a pro-Republican margin, but this was beside the point: large majorities simply didn't think one party was better than the other. Another poll taken eight months later found that the presidential campaign had rekindled some partisan fire, but not much.[4] On the question of which party does better in handling inflation, for instance, 70 percent saw no difference in September compared to 75 percent at the beginning of the year.

PARTY REFORM SINCE 1968

Many of the developments that have weakened American parties lie largely beyond our control. The United States has always been an intensely individualistic society and parties as intermediary institutions will always confront profound cultural biases. Given the current structure of American society, the communications and service functions simply cannot be returned to the parties to any substantial degree. Voters today necessarily are less dependent on party leaders than those of the 1890s or 1920s. In those areas susceptible to control, one might have hoped for some modest doses of "countercyclical policy" to bolster a deteriorating but important institution. Just the opposite has occurred, however, in the name of "reform." Since 1968 we have gratuitously weakened an already feeble institution.

The reforms made thus far are actually not as sweeping as sometimes suggested. The changes since 1968 are not com-

Table 1

"Which party, the Republicans or the Democrats, does the better job on the specific problem or don't you think there is much difference?"

	Republicans	Democrats	Not much difference	Don't know
Controlling inflation	20%	5%	69% (75%)	6%
Energy	10	10	64 (80%)	16
Foreign affairs	19	11	60 (70%)	10
"For people like you"	8	14	73 (78%)	5
Running Connecticut	9	17	66 (74%)	8

Source: Connecticut Poll No. 4, conducted between 31 January and 6 February 1980.

parable to those of the Progressive Era; nothing nearly as intrinsically consequential as the general introduction of direct primaries has happened in the recent period. The reform initiatives of the last decade have been significant—and their impact unfortunate—because they came at a time when political parties were already critically weak. Without this background of weakness, the reforms since 1968—initiated by the Democratic party's Commission on Party Structure and Delegate Selection (McGovern-Fraser Commission)—would not be nearly as important as they are.

Proliferation of presidential primaries was the major formal response to the many new rules affecting the operations of the national parties. After McGovern-Fraser, the Winograd Commission (1978, p. 24) acknowledged in its re-

port the relation between the proliferation of primaries
following 1968 and the McGovern-Fraser reforms. The commission wrote:

Delegate selection processes in 1968 were criticized as closed to
rank-and-file participation. The reformers emphasized the value of
participation in the delegate selection process. While the
McGovern-Fraser Commission was neutral on the question of primaries, many state parties felt that a primary offered the most protection against a challenge of the next convention.

There were seventeen Democratic presidential primaries in
1968; the number rose to twenty-three in 1972 and to thirty
in 1976. Whereas less than half of all delegates to the 1968
presidential convention were chosen by primaries, nearly
three-fourths of the 1976 Democratic delegates (and two-
thirds of the Republican delegates) were thus selected. The
proportions were even higher in 1980.

Reviewing the developments whereby presidential primaries became the dominant instrument for choosing convention delegates, the Winograd Commission quietly and
cautiously concluded that state parties have taken "more of
an administrative role than a decision-making role in recent
Presidential nominations."

The Democrats initiated the party reforms of the late
1960s and early 1970s, and they are clearly responsible for
these actions—which have further weakened rather than
revitalized the parties. Still, the Republican party moved
haltingly in the direction pioneered by the Democrats, and
the GOP did little to challenge the Democratic initiatives.
The low-profile Delegates and Organizations (DO) Committee was the Republican counterpart to the McGovern-Fraser
Commission, and after the 1972 convention the Rule 29 Committee continued the Republicans' reform efforts, adopting
new procedures for delegate selection that reflect the Democrats' concern with internal democracy. Even if the Republicans had done nothing, however, they still would have felt
the effects of reform since many of the Democrats'

changes—particularly the increased use of primaries—
have since been mandated by state law.

PARTY DECLINE IN CONGRESS

In the name of reform, the political parties have been substantially removed from selection of presidential nominees.
As the parties have withered, candidates for Congress and
other elective offices have been left to operate as independent entrepreneurs. "Because these new candidates did not
rise through disciplined organizations," James Sundquist
(1980, p. 198) noted, "they are individualists from the beginning of their political careers. As candidates they were self-
selected, self-reliant."

Congress responded to this new individualism in the early
1970s by scrapping its old organization, the seniority system.
It also allowed its members large staffs which came to function as personal electoral "machines," and it proliferated the
number of largely autonomous subcommittees so that virtually every member of the majority could have his own
show.

The effects of this general absence of mechanisms for integration and leadership were immediately apparent. In this
setting, interest groups—whose governmental presence had
grown as governmental interventions became more
numerous and widespread in the 1960s—found they could
take their case, without any party mediation, directly to individual congressmen and establish close working ties with
the subcommittee or subcommittees in their areas of interest. They also further developed strong links to the
federal bureaucracy. The end product is the notorious "iron
triangle," whose three angles are the interest groups, congressional subcommittees, and their relevant federal
agencies.

One typical triangle joins tobacco growers and dealers with the House Subcommittee on Tobacco and with an obscure corner of the Department of Agriculture imposingly titled the Agriculture Stabilization and Conservation Service, Price Support and Loan Division, Peanuts and Tobacco Section. The policy worlds thus defined are remarkably impervious to outside influence and are closed off from general public scrutiny. "Molecular government" is what Joseph Califano (1978, p. 6) called it when he was secretary of Health, Education, and Welfare and thus unusually well placed to observe the problem. "Washington has become a city of political molecules," he observed, "with fragmentation of power, and often authority and responsibility, among increasingly narrow, what's-in-it-for-me interest groups and their responsive counterparts in the executive and legislative branches." National policy is now made not for the nation at large but for narrow, autonomous sectors defined by the special interests. The sum total of programs determined in each sector makes up national policy—but a national policy that the nation does not want.

One of the first to describe this malady precisely was Theodore J. Lowi (1969), who dubbed it "interest-group liberalism." Almost every group had come to look to government for help—that's where the "liberalism" came in—but Big Government had been carved up into a host of independent satrapies. Interest-group liberalism is harmful in two different ways. It encourages government to act on individual measures without attention to their cumulative consequences; and it erodes popular confidence in the process of government by permitting decisions to be made in closed arenas effectively removed from popular control.

Politically active interest groups are a necessary and proper part of a free society. Given the far-flung activities of modern government, a vast proliferation of organized special interests was unavoidable. What is very avoidable is the current political environment—with its gravely weakened polit-

ical parties and hyper-individualistic, fractured Congress —
which allows interest groups to dominate the policy process.

THE ROLE OF PARTIES AS REPRESENTATIVE INSTITUTIONS

The decline of political parties in the United States is serious
because parties have such a central role in representative democracy. They are necessary for achieving popular control
over government and for assuring that public institutions
respond to popular wishes. There are so many different elective offices in a country this size that citizens cannot consider their votes meaningful instruments for controlling
policy unless the myriad separate contests are linked in some
understandable fashion — unless, for instance, balloting for
the 435 seats of the national legislature can be seen as competition of one party against another rather than as the
unrelated, detached competition of individuals. Woodrow
Wilson (1885, pp. 331–32) stated the problem well nearly a
century ago:

The average citizen may be excused for esteeming government at
best but a haphazard affair [he lamented] upon which his vote and
all of his influence can have but little effect. How is his choice of a
representative in Congress to affect the policy of the country as
regards the questions in which he is most interested?

Only parties can organize the issues so that mass publics
can speak effectively on them. If they make elected officials
in some sense collectively — rather than individually — responsible to the electorate, parties enormously expand the
level of meaningful public control over government.

Americans today in record numbers feel that governmental institutions are unresponsive and out of control. This feeling lies at the heart of the loss of confidence in public decision-making.[5] Although the problem is complex, the weak-

ness and ineffectuality of political parties as intermediary
organizations have greatly aggravated the decline of confidence in government.

REBUILDING THE PARTIES

The now widespread perception that things are not working
has spurred interest in sweeping changes in our governmental institutions, including the call for an end to the separation of powers and for the introduction of some version of
parliamentary government (Cutler 1980). In this view, the
constitutional separation of the executive and the legislature
is the main culprit in the now excessive fractionizing of
governmental power. In the fall of 1980 Lloyd Cutler, then
counsel to President Carter, was one of those arguing the
case for some form of parliamentary government. This case
has never been convincing. Ending the separation of powers
would require nothing less than a wholesale rewriting of the
Constitution. Americans rightly believe that they have been
well served by their constitutional arrangements. Broadly
successful political institutions, all too rare on this planet,
should not be scrapped. Apart from this, the political
prospects of getting so momentous a change are zero.

Fortunately, no massive transformation of the American
constitutional system is necessary to achieve more coherent
representative government. Some modest actions, well within the powers of the parties themselves and of Congress,
could produce the desired results. The task is straightforward—to find means of rebuilding the parties so that they
can better perform their integrative and representative
functions in ways compatible with American traditions and
expectations.

The almost universal acceptance of primaries suggests
they are here to stay as the central institutions for nominee

selection. Parties can also have a vital role in the nomination process. At the presidential level, the party roles could be strengthened by requiring that a substantial portion of national convention delegates—perhaps one-third—be chosen wholly outside the primaries in their capacities as party officials and officeholders. All of the following might be made voting delegates *ex officio*: each U.S. senator of the party, each member of the House of Representatives, each governor, the party's national chairman and cochairman, each member of the national committee, and the chairman and vice chairman of each state party. The total number of *ex officio* delegates to the two national conventions would thus be on the order of 1,100 to 1,200. With such specific acknowledgement of the formal role of their leaders, the political parties would acquire new vigor. Conscious and reflective planning by the party would again be possible in the selection process. This constructive change in presidential nominee selection can be made, it should be noted, by the Republican and Democratic national parties themselves, without any legislative action whatsoever.

Party leaders will not be taken seriously until they once again have resources. As long as funds go directly to individual candidates, party discipline will be weak. Party leaders must have the means to achieve a significant measure of party discipline, and that can best be accomplished by increasing the flow of political funds to leaders. The most direct way to accomplish this would be by providing government funding for congressional campaigns, routing funds through the party leadership, while imposing strict limitations on interest-group contributions to candidates.

Giving party leaders in Congress this "power of the purse" should help them to get support for other actions they know are needed but which they are now too weak to propose. Both the number and the autonomy of congressional committees and subcommittees should be greatly reduced. In general, far greater powers to coordinate and direct the legislative process need to be delegated to the elected party leadership. The president has a large stake in any effort to rebuild congressional leadership, since the achievement of coherent new public policy depends upon it. He should work with the Republican members of the House and Senate to promote a substantial measure of party government.

Financial resources can be used to strengthen not only congressional leadership, but also the leadership of the national committees. Congress should consider providing major financing for each of the two national committees, on the approximate order of $15 million per year for activities chosen by the committees themselves pursuant to their general mandates. Such activities might include buying television time to present party programs, voter-registration efforts, and candidate recruitment and development. The two committees would be permitted to raise additional funds privately, consistent with other provisions of the federal campaign legislation. They would be required to account precisely for all of their expenditures, and full publicity would be the primary regulating mechanism.

Although the idea of *substantial* public support for the Republican and Democratic national committees has not yet been tried, federal funds ($4.4 million in 1980) already go to each committee to pay the cost of its national convention. Nine states also now provide public funds to state party bodies. The total of $30 million here suggested is small indeed in the context of an annual federal budget of more than $600 billion. But this support could be decisively important in rebuilding the parties.

SPECIAL ROLE OF THE PRESIDENT

Another Republican president, just after the turn of this century, recognized the special educative possibilities of his office when he called it a "bully pulpit." Certainly the successful rebuilding of American political parties today requires a broad educational effort built around presidential leadership. Measures to revitalize the parties can be implemented—but they will not be unless Americans are shown that the objective is the strengthening of the machinery for effective democracy, not a return to the day of the "bosses" and the "smoke-filled rooms."

Present defects in what government does, the president should point out, result from defects in the way in which it does its work. Congress cannot function properly without the integrative mechanisms of party. Without the capacity for integration that parties can so well provide, the president and Congress cannot cope successfully with the dispersal of power which distinguishes the U.S. government. The public at large can exercise proper control over political leadership only through more disciplined parties—when governmental decision-making is made less individualistic, more coherent, and more unified. What Woodrow Wilson wrote in 1885 rings true today—that for the public "there are so many cooks mixing their ingredients in the national broth that it seems hopeless, this thing of changing one cook at a time."

The president has a responsibility to help strengthen the party system generally as part of the machinery of representative democracy, but he has a special responsibility and unique resources as leader of the Republican party. In exercising his party leadership for the long-term objective of party revitalization, the president should enhance the position of Republican national chairman and make the chairman his principal officer for activities in this area.

The position of national chairman has been underutilized by presidents of both parties over the past quarter-century. To make effective use of what is potentially an important administration position, the president should have the chairman attend and participate in cabinet meetings. He should as well designate the chairman as the administration's principal liaison officer with the Republican congressional leadership. With his credibility thus enhanced, the national chairman could articulate convincingly the administration's interest in party rebuilding, while the resources gained from giving the Republican party more coherence could be employed almost immediately to advance passage of the administration's programs.

The practical importance of a president of the United States legitimizing the strengthening of the party role in the governing process can scarcely be overstated. The United States badly needs an unequivocal presidential endorsement of a carefully developed and continuously pursued program to reinvigorate its representative institutions. The stakes are particularly great for President Reagan, faced with the need to control the federal budget—which has gone out of control in the grips of the special interests groups that have filled the vacuum left by the decline of parties. Rebuilding the party, therefore, will be an indispensable step in fulfilling his policy objectives.

5

ROBERT M. ENTMAN

The Imperial Media

Journalists and their need for friction. Public office and private leadership. Press treatment before and after election. Warring expectations of the president. The double binds. The press, Congress, and guilt by association. Reshaping news coverage. The value of confidentiality. Managing media relations—how to handle the press.

President Reagan was elected after a lengthy campaign which dominated the domestic news and stimulated widespread expectations that his presence in the White House would really mark a fresh start for the nation. The media will be quick to focus on how well his performance matches his promises. In recent years—particularly since the Vietnam war—presidents and the media have seemed to be adversaries. For presidents, the question has not been *whether* the media would obstruct their leadership, but *when* and *how*. And journalists have suspected presidents of manipulating them and even of lying in order to further political objectives. At best, relations have been cool; at worst, hostile.

The media clearly have a responsibility to report what they find and to criticize effectively the institutions of government. It is right for reporters to be alive to the hazards of manipulation. On the other hand, from the president's point of view, they should not be allowed to reduce his capacity for firm leadership.

This chapter will outline some of the ways in which the media can and do obstruct the president.* They include confusing the president's responsiveness to their demands with sensitivity to the public interest; inhibiting private negotiation between the president and other national leaders, particularly those in Congress; complicating executive management by magnifying conflict within the cabinet; and imposing conflicting standards of behavior which mean that, whatever he does, he cannot escape unfavorable judgment.

But the president is far from helpless. If he understands the limitations of his office, he can circumvent some of these problems and turn others into opportunities. He can use his "honeymoon"—the first few months in office—to reduce the unrealistic expectations which soon lead to frustration. He can negotiate with Congress in private. He can staff and manage his press office with discretion and care. And he and his staff can use the media selectively and with precision.

*James David Barber and Francie Seymour offered helpful comments on an earlier draft of this paper. I am grateful to them.

PRESIDENTS CAN MANIPULATE BUT NOT DICTATE THE NEWS

The president's resources for managing media relations are well known (see Paletz and Entman 1981, pp. 57–59; Crouse 1973, pp. 227–56; Grossman and Rourke 1976, pp. 455–70). They include monopolizing and selectively releasing information; controlling the forum and timing of contact with the press; secrecy (Grossman and Rourke 1976, p. 459); co-optation of reporters and editors through personal friendship; televised news conferences orchestrated to convey favorable impressions (Paletz and Entman 1981, pp. 60–61); and applying licit and illicit pressure through government agencies such as the Federal Communications Commission. In general, these resources give the president an unmatched capacity to get the news he wants into the press. But keeping news out is another matter. Politicians and others with power—as well as journalists themselves—contribute significantly to the composite depiction of a chief executive.

Media practices thrust the president into the news

Presidential management of the media is often compatible with journalists' needs. In choosing and defining political news stories, journalists look for a powerful cast of characters, for conflict or controversy between its members, and for potential personal impact on audiences. The prevailing definition of news allows a president to make news virtually whenever he wants to do so. Over the past two decades attention to the president has increased; 25 percent of all domestic national news now concerns presidents or presidential candidates.[1]

Among the processes that journalists use to construct political news stories are: *personalization*, the neglect of histori-

cal or structural explanations by concentrating on individuals whose deliberate choices cause events; *source stan-
dardization*, the use of the same group of informants on the
beat; *dramatization*, the depiction of interactions of news
personalities so as to generate audience interest, pity, fear,
catharsis, where possible; and *surrogate representation*, the
enforcement of government responsiveness to the public by
pressing politicians to explain candidly their actions, motivations, and plans. Because these practices are almost universal, different media (and even the same ones) tend to repeat
similar stories, themes, questions, and answers. These practices often help presidents. Personalization, for example, permits them to claim credit for just about anything the government does well; the duplication of content enables them to
reach the entire electorate with the same basic message (cf.
Paletz and Entman 1981, pp. 16–22; Kumar and Grossman
1980, pp. 5–7, 10–11).

The tone of the news—set by journalist incentives and elite opinions

Hindered by the president's control over much newsworthy
information and constrained by conventional definitions of
news, reporters and their editors nonetheless have considerable autonomy, especially in seeking out news that can
be narrated as drama unfolding. In stories like these, their
interests and his often diverge. Drama lies in stories of presidential involvement in domestic conflict and in history-
making ventures, usually overseas. Drama is magnified
when the outcomes are either highly uncertain or likely to
mark a major change from previous patterns, or both. Reporters and editors face personal incentives—having little to
do with ideological bias—to emphasize any drama they can
find. Good for journalists' prestige but often bad for that of
the president, dramatic stories which center on domestic

conflict tend to convey the impression that the chief executive is incompetent, rigid, or cynical.

Aside from the president and his administration, the normal sources of national political news are Washington elites. When these congressmen, bureaucrats, and other powerful individuals generally agree with the president, journalists have few sources for concocting dramatic narratives. Such reports emerge mainly when some elites decide to publicize their criticisms of the president.

Clashes among Washington newsmakers over presidential policy and purpose stimulate news. The more conflict, the more the media will fill with criticisms of the president. These undermine the president's preferred image as a competent consensus-builder. They publicize alternative views of policy problems and suggest solutions the president opposes. The conflict feeds on itself: the more discord, the more dramatic the story possibilities. Coverage which is damaging to the president further emboldens his opponents, as shown by the presidencies of Lyndon Johnson, Richard Nixon, and Jimmy Carter (Paletz and Entman 1981, pp. 65–78, on Nixon and Carter).

The contest between press and president is normally played out somewhere between the basking of the early John Kennedy and the thrashing of Richard Nixon. Within these bounds a president's skill at media relations can make news a little brighter. Maladroit media management does the reverse. But more important for the tone of the coverage may be the level of elite support the president enjoys and the treatment that news organizations and employees, acting out of their own habits and interests, afford presidential activities.

FOUR MEDIA IMPACTS ON PRESIDENTIAL LEADERSHIP

Journalists have taken a more aggressively critical stance

toward the presidency since the perceived betrayals of Vietnam and Watergate. One facet of the practice of surrogate representation, the critical perspective assumes purely political motives behind presidential ideas and actions and then tries to confirm that theory by doggedly pursuing presidents and their aides until they admit its accuracy. Confined largely to the major national media, the technique seeks to enforce a moral and responsive *process* of presidential leadership. It casts a president less as a leader with special legitimacy than as a politician—one with a special calling and high responsibility, but a politician nonetheless.

The country has benefited from this approach, to a point. But the advantage of process-oriented reporting recedes if it prevents presidents from reaching their policy objectives; democracy requires effective policy as well as pristine process. This section explores four potentially damaging consequences of the media's skeptical mood.

Confusing press interests with the public interest

The press tends to judge a president's responsiveness to the public on the basis of his cooperativeness with reporters. They demand that he reveal and fully explain all his major decisions. This expectation is as unrealistic as it is self-serving. Unrealistic, because all presidents will—and to some degree should—make decisions they neither disclose in detail nor justify to the press. Self-serving, because the emphasis on full disclosure seems to be rooted more in the media's production practices than in a well-grounded theory of journalism's proper political role.

Open White House news sources make for cheaper production—fewer reporters and less hard work are required to ferret out information. James Deakin of the *St. Louis Post-Dispatch* (quoted in Purvis 1976, p. 49) defines the mission of White House news hunters: "We are . . . making a consistent attempt underneath all the bombast and fury of the press conference and the briefing, to find out why the president did what he did in the past."

The other major goal of the White House news corps is to find out what the president plans to do in the future. Yet a politician cannot explain past actions or future plans without trying to fit news reports to his political needs, to the expectations of his elite audiences. So the president and his staff are among the less-helpful sources on the president's plans. Better answers could be found by digging about Washington, probing the innards of the bureaucracy, plowing through congressional hearings and reports. To ask a president or press secretary why the president did something offers the appearance of critical reporting without its reality.

Consider televised press conferences. In most of them we learn mainly how the president parries, rephrases, and ignores tough queries. A president who has significant information to release will rarely do so involuntarily in response to a reporter's question; he will choose his own time and place. The event becomes a ritual of predictable thrust and parry. Reporters give a show of undaunted inquisitiveness; presidents, of ersatz candor.

Why a president does something should be less newsworthy than *what* he does. The "why" we largely know in advance: partly to help the country, partly to advance his policy goals, partly to protect his political future; post-Watergate reporters highlight only the latter. Citizens and voters need also (perhaps mainly) to know the "what"—what effects presidential policies will have on inflation and economic growth, on their children's education and health, and on national security (cf. Barber 1979, p. 21). But again, providing such information would require a more diligent, tedious brand of reporting along with a diminution of the drive to unmask the selfish political goals behind every presidential action.

Present practices often compel the president and his staff

to reveal information they do not want to divulge. While on
occasion this is beneficial to the public, press officers sometimes answer prematurely, incorrectly, or unwisely. They are
upbraided if they backpedal, abandon, or repudiate the
earlier position and excoriated if they refuse to respond at
all. Yet this "news" may be hollow. Ron Nessen has described
an egregious example. As the Vietnam war drew to its sorry
finale in 1975, White House reporters continually hectored
him with questions about when the United States would
evacuate Saigon (Purvis 1976, pp. 45–46). But the Ford administration could hardly have revealed the answer—even if
it knew—without jeopardizing the safety of those still in
Saigon. More important, even if the answer had been forced
out of the White House, knowing it would not have
strengthened the citizen's voice in government in any
meaningful way.

Dissolving the distinction between
public office and private leadership

Leadership has both public and private dimensions. One of a
president's major tasks is to inspire the public. But publicity
alone does not propel policies through the bureaucracy and
Congress and into action. Leadership also entails private
communication—in person, over the telephone, by letter—
with power brokers and decision-makers. Presidents and
their staff deploy technical arguments, emotional appeals,
veiled threats, deft flattery, adroit bluffs, tantalizing hints—
the whole repertoire of persuasive tools—*in private*.
Publicity vitiates these tools. Media coverage of the tactics,
their rationales, and different actors' reactions adds an extra
dimension of strategic complexity into a president's already
Byzantine political calculus.

   A president once could manipulate tacit knowledge or nag-
ging suspicions to his advantage. A member of Congress
might say to himself, "I know he's flattering me but I like it"

or "He sounds as if he might really carry out his (wholly implicit) threat," and then conclude "I'd better go along." Now,
quite frequently, the president's underlying strategy is
publicized. The press tells those on the receiving end what
the president is trying to do to them, how, and why.

Consider Jimmy Carter's early run-ins with House
Speaker "Tip" O'Neill. Carter failed to appoint one of
O'Neill's cronies to a top administrative post. The personal
offense given and taken was detailed in the press, as was
Carter's calculated attempt to regain O'Neill's affection.
Similar developments occurred in Carter's relationship with
AFL—CIO president George Meany. Granted the Georgian's
apparent ineptitude in such matters, it is doubtful that wide
media coverage of his strained relationships and awkward
attempts at reconciliation efforts made things easier.

This phenomenon corrodes presidential leadership in a
number of ways. First, it increases the tactical intelligence of
those he is trying to persuade. Without publicity, a president's manipulative maneuvers might not be recognized as
such by his less-insightful adversaries and allies; when his
tricks are exposed and dissected in the news, even the most
obtuse lobbyist or senator can fend better. Second, once a
president's technique for handling a particular task of persuasion is publicized, other actors are forewarned and hence
forearmed. Third, the publicity changes the decision calculations of those the president attempts to lead. Public
knowledge that a president is trying to soothe or strong-arm
an individual may compel the latter to spurn the president's
offer; it ill-behooves most politicians to appear to respond to
presidential pressure or flattery. Fourth, such publicity may
embarrass a president, generating pressure to avoid perfectly legitimate tactics of political life and reducing his list
of options. It may also make his own responses to the political acts of others more problematic; he of all politicians must
avoid appearing too willing to compromise with interests
which are merely powerful or cunning. Finally, these per-

suasive tactics are quintessentially those of party maintenance: to the list of formidable centrifugal forces operating
on party organizations and politics must be added the journalistic foible of publicizing a president's private leadership
activities.

Complicating executive management

Beyond the direct focus of the chief executive himself, the
White House staff, cabinet officers, and departments sometimes tumble into the media net. They are all politicized,
loyal to the president, and thus part of his story. The media's
attraction to presidential subordinates can pose management problems because of three strong media impacts—on
the agendas of executive officials and agencies, on the relationships between those individuals and offices and the
president, and on the president's control over information.

First, public attention is drawn only sporadically to most
federal offices. When the Federal Aviation Administration,
the Environmental Protection Agency, or the White House
Counsel's office make major news, it is generally because reporters scent controversy over, say, a plane crash, a hazard-
ous waste spill, or an ethically questionable legal maneuver
on behalf of the president. These offices are hypersensitive
to such publicity because they make the papers relatively in-
frequently. One bad story comprises a substantial portion of
an entire year's coverage. Those involved tend to believe that
the stories harm the agency's public image and reduce its
clout with the president and Congress, so they scurry fran-
tically to redress publicized misfeasance, clearing their normal and long-range agendas to focus on the object of attention. Not surprisingly, the bureaux anticipate and fear negative media reactions. They may become overly cautious and
rigid in applying their rules to stave off future onslaughts.

Second, publicizing personality feuds and policy debates
within the administration complicates the president's task of

coordinating his top officials. Stories about whose influence is ascending, whose plummeting, who is at whose throat or in whose pocket, can only exacerbate jealousies and tensions. Recall Rogers and Kissinger, Vance and Brzezinski. Highly publicized internecine quarrels make the president look like a poor manager, even if they are not his fault. Such reportage discourages frank and open dialogue between a president's advisors as it poisons the relationships among them.

Third, news can turn reputation into reality: a press imputation of clout can actually bestow influence (see *Fortune* 1979, pp. 36–49). So, innocently enough, cabinet officers and White House staffers cultivate reporters. But then they may leak information that undermines a president's proposals or credibility. The media's craving for conflict within the administration provides a tempting opportunity. The threat of disobedience gives the president an incentive to limit access to the most important information to a very small group of trusted personal aides. This practice in turn overloads him with decisions and with public expectations.

Reinforcing double binds

Americans expect a great deal of their president. Above all, they want leadership; survey respondents indicating the country needs strong leadership increased from 49 percent in 1976 to 63 percent in 1979 (Wayne 1980, pp. 5, 9). But citizens are ambivalent; they have traditionally disapproved of many of the traits exhibited by strong leaders. Post-Watergate journalists have made this element of tradition into a creed. By subjecting presidents to a daily buffeting of charges and countercharges of failure to fulfill the contradictory high standards of presidential office, news reports reinforce a number of double binds that tie the hands of leadership. For news of presidential defaults is unavoidable and unremitting; by satisfying one standard, a president frequently violates another.

The Man on the White Horse verses the Man in the White House. A president usually begins his term after a long election campaign during which media practices have encouraged him to indulge in oversimplified attacks on opponents, to promise to solve policy problems while simultaneously remaining fuzzy and uncontroversial, and to avoid too many expressions of doubt, hesitation, and realism about the intractability of problems. Dominating the domestic news of election years, the very magnitude of campaign coverage implies that the selection of a new president can really make a difference. After the election, the press brims over with paeans to the overworked transition staff as it culls applications for posts in the new administration and selects only the brightest and the best. The composite picture is of a fresh beginning glistening with promise.

Then reality moves into the White House. Contradictory promises that slipped by in the hurly-burly of the campaign lose their luster. News reports call attention to the incompatibilities among proposals. Attacks on predecessors and opponents return to haunt the new incumbent as he realizes the complexity of the problems he faces or acknowledges them for the first time. Fuzziness is no longer an option, for a president's legislative proposals have to be specific: they force him to take a stand. Contumely and controversy inevitably follow, and with them, negative reporting. Supporters who relied upon the fulfillment of campaign slogans and symbols, or who read into them a message of future commitment, become disillusioned. Opponents see their charges confirmed.

If a president does propose a bold initiative to fulfill a campaign pledge, he often faces energetic opposition. The media are drawn to policy shoot-outs. Their eagerness to focus on his critics may implicitly impel him to avoid proposing innovative policies. The cautious president takes refuge in incrementalism—only to be assaulted all too often by accusa-

tions of failure to provide the courageous, visionary leadership the country's predicaments demand.

The media do not cause the cycle of boom and bust in
public expectations; but their campaign coverage encourages
the boom, their Washington coverage, the letdown. The new
president needs to recognize the change in the logic of media
relations that occurs when the campaign becomes incum-
bency. President Carter never did.

Machiavelli versus St. Francis. Journalists require the
president to observe the norms of two distinct levels of discourse. On the first, which might be called personal discourse, journalists demand the same kind of decency and
candor that people depend on for rational communication in
everyday life. On the second level, that of political discourse,
journalists recognize the significance of language for controlling the behavior of others, that is, for leadership. Yet reporters cry "Foul!" when a president responds to them as
they expect him to respond to all other political actors—with
strategic artifice and a calculated choice of data and words.

Consider another example from James Deakin. He has expressed deep resentment at the Nixon administration's
misleading statements during the India-Pakistan war of
1971, calling them "an affront to the intelligence of reasonable people" (Purvis 1976, p. 48). Judged by norms of personal
discourse, the administration's words *were* deceitful and
offensive. But on the political level it would have been an
affront to intelligence for the administration to subvert its
own delicate policy initiative by announcing its strategy
openly. And journalists would have pounced on any such
careless and unstrategic revelation, as they later did when a
different administration's United Nations ambassador
(Andrew Young) spoke too freely. This problem confronts
presidents in domestic policymaking as well.

A profile in courage versus a finger to the wind. One
journalistic standard calls for the president to do what is best

for the country, not what is popular. In this view, he should not pander to public opinion; he should point the populace in the right direction; where it is unmovable, he should plow ahead and damn the political consequences. Yet a president who takes this tack often gets into trouble. Attacks on his stewardship proliferate as his reported isolation from public opinion grows. It is alleged that a president who neglects the evidence of surveys and other public expressions misuses his great office, misreads his traditions and purposes.

John F. Kennedy's book, *Profiles in Courage*, revealed the continuing American ambivalence on this issue. But none of Kennedy's profiles were subject to the continual and contrary public jostling of these two incompatible standards which suffuses recent media reporting.

Again it should be emphasized that the press alone does not create these three warring expectations. It does, however, repeatedly thrust them into public consciousness — and thus into the calculations of the elites — by its intimate and insistent coverage of the presidency. In that way press reports frequently diminish a president's potential to transcend the double binds that tradition imposes.

LEADING CONGRESS BY SEEKING PUBLIC SUPPORT: ONWARD OR DOWNWARD?

Under the circumstances just depicted, presidential leadership has become increasingly problematic. More than ever, a president's ability to lead comes down to his capacity to persuade (Neustadt 1980; cf. Sperlich 1975, pp. 406–30). Supportive public opinion may be a significant component of a president's stock of persuasive resources. Yet the double binds reinforced by the media have magnified the difficulty of meeting the public's expectations and retaining its approval.

There is a growing body of research on presidential popularity based on the Gallup Poll question, "Do you approve or disapprove of the way [the incumbent] is handling his job as president?" But there is little understanding of its impact on presidential power or its roots in media coverage. What follows, then, is one observer's speculative version of the relationship between the press, public support, and presidential success in Congress.

Why the Congress decides

A president is only one of the forces acting on a Congress member. The most recent comprehensive studies have found that the president has little direct and distinct impact on most roll call votes.[2] This should not be surprising: Congress members cultivate independent local power bases which minimize their dependency on the president (cf. Mayhew 1974). As Congress has enhanced its ability to initiate and analyze proposals in recent years, even the president's power to dominate the congressional agenda has suffered.

The key to presidential success is probably in convincing legislative leaders, committee heads, and interest groups to support the president's policies. These three, along with members' constituents and their own personal beliefs, determine most decisions. If a president's position coincides with the dominant slant of these forces, legislators will go along. If not, under conditions of weak party organization, presidents have relatively little to offer individual members to induce them to buck the tide.

Enter public support. A president who has high public approval can argue that voting with him against the wishes of interest group moguls or legislative leaders will win accolades for the solons back home. Such claims may sway some members.[3] Public support might also enhance a president's ability to obtain the cooperation of committee, party, and interest group chieftains.

If there are any advantages to individual members in voting with a president against the push of other Washington power brokers, however, they must disintegrate when the president is perceived as unpopular. Then, going along with the president exposes members and leaders to guilt by association, as some Democrats discovered in the 1980 election.

Media impact: more harm than good?

Congressmen, along with the rest of the citizenry, receive a major part of their information about presidential popularity through the media. It comes not only from direct reporting of the Gallup Poll results but from the tone and content of editorials, columns, and news stories. Although research evidence is scant, it appears that lower Gallup ratings may stimulate less-positive portrayals of the president. When presidents seem to be in declining favor, the practice of surrogate representation may lead reporters to probe more sharply. Low approval rating and negative media coverage feed each other, heightening the perception that the president is floundering, deepening the drumbeat of decline—dissolving one of his few persuasive resources, the notion that public opinion is on his side.

Some scholars have unearthed a relationship between media content and approval rating. They find that when news of presidents' actions is good or better than what came before, presidential popularity tends to increase (Brody and Page 1975, pp. 136–47; Haight and Brody 1977, pp. 41–59). But other research indicates that economic conditions, national calamities, and partisan feelings have the major impacts on the approval rating. Growth in real income and employment is especially helpful; decline, harmful (Hibbs et al. 1980, p. 29; cf. Kernell 1978, pp. 506–72). Prosperity may contribute more to a president's support than can media notices, however glowing. If so, and if the above analysis of Congress is accurate, it may be that negative coverage can sap the president's leadership strength more decisively than positive news can fortify it.

The argument would go as follows. The economic situation, and the presence or absence of such disastrous domestic or foreign entanglements as Vietnam or Watergate, establish a baseline of approval. If events go well and the economy perks along, elite support will tend to be high and press coverage will tend to be favorable without a great deal of presidential machination. Approval ratings will rise—or not deteriorate unduly. If the economy remains volatile, if the international situation continues to be tense, the news will obtrude in two ways. The press will cover the economic dilemmas or the unresolved world tensions; because of popular expectations of the presidency, this news implicitly indicts the incumbent. And the press will report the elite controversy that generally envelops such problems. Lower approval ratings follow and help to produce more unfavorable coverage. A downward spiral ensues, compounding the president's difficulty in garnering elite support for the solutions the public expects.

WHAT IS TO BE DONE? REDUCE AND SHIFT MEDIA FOCUS

Although this paper focuses on the negative impacts on leadership, all is not lost. Particularly if he enjoys an ideologically sympathetic majority in Congress, the president still possesses the potential to fashion favorable media images, to garner public and elite support, and to get things done. And the positive contributions of good media relations should not be gainsaid. But neither should this potential obscure the obvious and veiled costs of the media's unyielding concentration on the White House. On balance, a chief executive would probably profit from engineering a reduction in the media's inordinate obsession with him. Then he should work to reshape the character of the coverage remaining.

Reduce reliance on media events

Do not make a fetish of getting on television. One of the noteworthy changes in reporting since Vietnam and Watergate is that journalists now depict politicians' overt attempts to create media events just so. With a president involved, the media do cover the events—the Rose Garden ceremony, Carter's putatively nonpolitical hegira through the hinterlands, the minor announcement cloaked as major pronouncement. But if, as they transmit the events, reporters convey the political strategy behind them, they vitiate both.

Presidents have helped erect barriers to their own leadership by overemphasizing media events, which frequently only reinforce the cynicism of journalists and citizens alike.

Use the honeymoon to dampen, not raise, expectations. All new presidents enjoy a glowing press. Washington waits, journalistic deference prevails, as the pomp of inauguration and drama of peaceful transfer of power unfold (Kumar and Grossman 1980, p. 12; cf. Morris 1975, pp. 49–52). Coming directly after the legitimizing hoopla of an election, this coverage tends to raise approval levels—and expectations—to their highest points, whence they can only tumble. Although media-induced exhilaration encourages otherwise, the honeymoon is precisely the best time for new administrations to inject caution and realism into public (and journalistic) consciousness. If offered only after the inevitable failures come, such caveats appear as apologia rather than as prudence.

Reduce publicized conflicts with Congress

Handle the media's tendency to amplify conflict with Congress by negotiating in private. A president should not automatically assume that taking to the airwaves to publicize his position against that of a recalcitrant Congress will help. There is no assurance that the public will be swayed by his speech (recall the failures of President Ford's WIN, Carter's energy talks; cf. Mueller 1973; Sigelman 1979, pp. 542−61) or that an independent Congress would necessarily respond even if the public were moved. Moreover, televised appearances can inject precisely the element of open discord that draws attention to a president's congressional adversaries, elevating them to page one (and Walter Cronkite) rather than page thirty-six (*sans* TV). When Congress attacks publicly, presidents should not automatically respond in kind. It is astonishing how quickly the media lose interest when there is only one voice clamoring instead of two—especially when that one is *not* the president's. Consider the nearly instant disappearance from page one of the Iranian hostages (post−rescue mission) and Billygate (post−press conference) when President Carter stopped his constant public commenting. The lack of publicity might allow other, more effective, means of persuasion to operate.

Encourage party revival. For too long presidents have neglected their party organizations to build up personal followings through the media. This may make sense in primary and even fall election campaigns, but once in office the party organization, especially in Congress, should be his most valuable friend. Indirectly pressuring congressional party leaders through the media's putatively favorable impact on public opinion is less likely to work than is patient cultivation of organizational bonds.

Attempt to change news practices

Reduce reporters' expectations. Tame White House–
beat reporting by decreasing reporters' expectations of full
access to officials, by directly asserting that the demands of
leadership require a modicum of confidentiality. Take advantage of the country's growing preference for strong leadership to legitimize this approach. And repeat frequently that
bargaining and mutual adjustment are the essence of democratic politics, not its antithesis.

**Shift reporters' attention from politics and plans to
facts and figures.** While discouraging discussions of the
president's political motivations and strategies, staffers
should be open and accommodating with the technical policy
analysis that undergirds decisions. This tactic should defuse
complaints about total inaccessibility. It could reduce the
total volume of reporting, since dry data are often defined as
unnewsworthy. To the extent data are covered, Americans
would obtain more of that elusive information about the
"what" of presidential policy. Such information, better than
the current skeptical but banal stress on the "why," would
enforce democratic accountability by telling citizens more
clearly just "what" government is doing to and for them.

**Discourage personal mingling between press officers,
other White House staff, and journalists.** While something surely is gained by social interaction, and it probably
cannot be reduced very much, the president should realize
that the advantages of personal friendships dissolve when
the news gets juicy—as Ron Zeigler, Ron Nessen, and Jody
Powell found. Co-optation works both ways. Reporters may
get more out of presidential staff (for instance, through "off-
the-record" backgrounders that can be used to frame on-the-
record questions, or through alcohol- or fatigue-induced
slips) than vice versa.

Beware the pitfalls of cabinet government. In the current environment of intense media attention, cabinet government could saddle the president with more responsibility for media relations without enhanced power to control them. The media might hold presidents accountable both for the decisions cabinet departments make and for the bad news they generate. Nixon, Ford, and Carter all promised a larger role for cabinets, yet their moves in that direction were stymied in part by media pressures. For the buck not only stops at the Oval Office; it inexorably *goes* there, no matter where it originated. The president will be asked to explain and justify the newsworthy controversies a cabinet member arouses, as suggested by the storms over Earl Butz's bad jokes and Joseph Califano's antismoking campaign. More autonomy for cabinet officers may make sense, but it might be wise to limit their authority to the less-newsworthy (which are not always less-important) matters.

Staff the press office and use the media with selectivity and precision

Employ a press staff that understands how the national media cover incumbent presidents. This means selecting journalists or others who know well the operations of the Washington press corps. Those whose experience is limited to running advertising campaigns or state and local press offices should generally be avoided.

Keep the press staff (except the secretary) in the dark about the politics of White House decision-making. If press officers are not privy to the president's political strategies and future plans but are well briefed on policy substance, they can honestly fend off reporters' gossipy "why" inquisitions and steer the focus to the "what."

For pushing policy proposals, the media are most helpful early or late in the decision cycle. In the beginning, before there are set views, presidential talks can weave a favorable aura around a proposal. Later, near decision time, undecided members of Congress can occasionally be swayed by the swell of media attention a president kindles. But note the boomerang threat: if voting with the president means voting against home-district sentiment, publicity and visibility may be the last thing potential allies need.

Use the different media for the purposes they can best accomplish. For example, television is best for ephemeral rousing of mass sentiment through symbolism. It is not the medium for rational persuasion. Jimmy Carter's energy and inflation speeches provide a paradigm to avoid. The *New York Times, Washington Post,* and *Wall Street Journal* are the papers of record for the powers that be. These are the best places for agenda setting and reasoning with elites. These papers also guide the news judgments of the networks. *Time* and *Newsweek* are read by the better-educated and politically interested public. News magazines can shape the issues their audience ponders and some of the standards their readers use to evaluate presidents and policy.

Pumping up approval ratings through the media is feasible mainly in connection with foreign policy initiatives and crises. The approval question probably taps a combination of what the public thinks the main job of the president is and how well he is doing it. When a chief executive is immersed in a major diplomatic quest (Begin and Sadat at Camp David, Nixon in China) or a threat to national sovereignty (the *Mayaguez,* Iranian hostage seizure), elites generally support him and drama suffuses the story. The president receives reams of positive coverage that focus overwhelming public attention on one aspect of his job: handling the foreign affair. Approval ratings usually spurt upward. But elite support, media favor, and public approval may fade as second guesses supplant the cheers. More important, the approval increase is linked to the initiative or threat. As these become old news, perceptions of the president's "job" revert to other (usually domestic) matters on which he is less likely to enjoy an elite consensus and beneficent press. But this story contains a useful lesson: to the extent that he can, a president should encourage circumscribed perceptions of what his proper "job" should be. That way, when asked if they approve of the way the president is handling it, more people are likely to respond affirmatively.

All the above tactics could fizzle or backfire. As Watergate showed, the media have considerable autonomy; if antagonized, they can strike back in many ways. The president must mix new techniques with traditional ones. Others will appear in time. Their success would measurably enhance his leadership.

6

ERIC L. DAVIS

The President and Congress

The redistribution of congressional power. Subcommittee government. The Budget Act and the War Powers Resolution. Restrictions on the president's foreign policy power. The legislative veto. Capitol Hill and the White House—the political value of respect, consultation, and liaison.

Many observers of the Washington scene have reported that Jimmy Carter had to deal with a more resistant Congress than any other recent president, even though his party had a clear majority in both the House and the Senate. Whatever the truth of this account, it is said that President Reagan will have an easier time on Capitol Hill; despite the Democratic majority in the House, the magnitude of Reagan's electoral

victory and the swing to the right in Congress should place
few obstacles in the way of his programs. Furthermore, Republican congressmen have, historically, complied more
readily than Democratic ones with the proposals of presidents of their own party.

Yet any analysis which explains relations between Congress and the president in terms of a particular partisan line-
up—or, like the argument that Carter's "Georgia Mafia"
were responsible for his failure to establish good legislative
liaison, in terms of personality and political skills—must
also acknowledge some fundamental developments during
the 1970s which would reduce any president's influence over
Congress, whatever the circumstances of the moment.

By "fundamental developments" I mean, first, the diffusion of power and shift in goals within Congress, which have
together made it substantially more difficult for the White
House or any other central leader to steer legislation through
Congress; and second, the increasing tendency for congressmen to view the president as an adversary whom they are
obliged to constrain. I will review these developments and
their implications before offering some advice to the new
president.

DEVELOPMENTS IN CONGRESS

The first major development was a series of changes in the
distribution of power within Congress. The second was a
series of laws through which Congress attempted to reclaim
some of the institutional authority many of its members
believed it had lost to the executive branch during the
Johnson and Nixon years.

The distribution of power in Congress

Two interesting trends were observed in congressional elections during the 1970s. The first was a sharp decline in the

number of marginal House seats—those which were not safe for the incumbent member. In 1976, 1978, and 1980 more than 90 percent of House members who sought reelection were successful and many faced little if any competition. The principal explanation for this phenomenon was that House members were changing their role. Instead of representing the collective preferences of their constituents on a variety of public policy issues, they increasingly saw themselves as representing and helping individual constituents who had specific problems with government agencies. Rather than campaigning on such issues as military spending, tax policy, or education policy, members advertised their ability to find lost Social Security checks and to speed the processing of pension claims (Fiorina 1977). It was easier for members to be reelected on this basis than on their stands on controversial issues.

The second trend in congressional—particularly House— election results ran in the opposite direction. Throughout the 1970s membership turnover in the House of Representatives ran at about 15 percent per election. Only in 1974, the first election year after Watergate, was this turnover accounted for by the electoral defeat of incumbents; otherwise it resulted from voluntary retirements. Thus, a majority of the Democratic members of the 95th House sworn in along with President Carter in January 1977 had never served in Congress while a Democrat occupied the White House; and a majority of the members of the 97th House, which assembled in January 1981, had six or fewer years of congressional experience.

Turnover in the Senate was also relatively high during the 1970s, with a majority of senators in the 97th Congress having served one term or less. However, the Senate turnover owed more to electoral defeat than was the case in the House. In 1976, 1978, and 1980, when more than 90 percent of House incumbents were reelected, fewer than two-thirds of Senate incumbents were. Perhaps senators, with their

greater visibility and larger constituencies, were not as successful as their House colleagues in presenting themselves to
their electorate as helpful intermediaries.

These changes in the membership of Congress contributed
to certain important changes in the way the legislature conducted its business. Members of Congress, and especially
House members, began to see a greater distinction between
their Washington role as policy-oriented legislators and their
new constituency role. In a way, their emphasis on constituent service gave them more leeway in Washington since, by
enabling them to establish trust and goodwill with their
voters, it made it easier for them to justify their actions in
Washington (Fenno 1978). Paradoxically, members became
better able to focus attention on policy issues as they gave
more time to constituency service.

In the early 1970s many of the newly elected members
became dissatisfied with the way Congress was organized,
especially the House. Power was concentrated in the hands
of the chairmen of the standing committees—fewer than
twenty—selected through the seniority system. The new
members tried to change this system, but until 1974 they
were too few. After the 1974 elections, however, seventy-five
new members joined the House Democratic caucus, and the
latter swiftly enacted some far-reaching organizational
changes which have had important consequences for the distribution of power within Congress.

The most important change substantially reduced the
autonomy of the standing committee chairmen by eliminating seniority as the criterion for their selection. Since 1975
House full-committee chairmen have been nominated by the
Democratic Steering Committee—controlled by the party
leadership—and all House Democrats have voted on the
nominations. The caucus's rejection of three nominees for
committee chairs in 1975 demonstrated that committee
leaders can no longer behave autocratically. Rank-and-file
members who do not sit on a particular committee are in-

creasingly willing to take on that committee and its chairman on the House floor, with an increasing probability of
success. In the Senate, too, both parties have turned away
from seniority as a criterion for the selection of committee
chairmen and ranking minority members.

During the 1970s both the House and Senate substantially
increased the number of their subcommittees, and today
there are more than 100 subcommittees in each chamber.
Their responsibility for drafting legislation has steadily increased. Most of them are assured of institutional autonomy,
since they have the authority to appoint their own staff and
have fixed jurisdictions and rules of procedure which protect
them from manipulation by the chairmen of their principal
committees.

Two important results should be noted. The first is that
power is dispersed much more widely in today's Congress
than was the case as recently as ten years ago. Instead of
being concentrated in the hands of fewer than twenty full-
committee chairmen, power is now dispersed among nearly
150 full-committee and subcommittee chairmen in the House
and among all Republican senators, each of whom chairs at
least one full committee or subcommittee. However, while
there are more positions of formal power in today's Congress,
none of them confers much real influence. The dispersal of
power has made it increasingly difficult for any central
decision-maker to move the Congress in one direction. The
Speaker, the House and Senate majority leaders, and other
party leaders have almost no way of controlling a
recalcitrant member.

A second consequence of the rise of subcommittee government is equally important. The proliferation of subcommittees has led to an increasingly narrow and specialized focus
among congressmen. Fewer members attempt to look at the
trade-offs on various issue areas or to set priorities among
desired goals. The difficulty the Budget Committee faced in
achieving "reconciliation" for the 1981 fiscal year is only one

example of the power of specialists to block generalists within Congress. Furthermore, this specialization is leading more and more members of Congress into "issue networks" (Heclo 1978), the alliances among members of Congress, interest groups, and political executives in the bureaucracy, which have proved so successful in protecting their own programs against the encroachments of "outsiders" such as budget committees, cabinet secretaries and, yes, presidents.

This dispersal of power in Congress imposes many constraints on the president. Before discussing them, though, I want to mention a second fundamental development which has made Congress less susceptible to presidential influence: the legislative initiatives with which Congress reacted to what it saw as presidential encroachments on its institutional authority, particularly during the Johnson and Nixon years.

Reasserting the authority of Congress

Watergate led many congressmen of both parties to believe that something had to be done to restore the proper constitutional balance between the legislative and executive branches. They felt that the presidency had usurped powers which they had abdicated, and that Congress had failed in its constitutional role as a check on the presidency. During the mid-1970s this sentiment was reflected in a number of legislative initiatives designed to restore the Congress to its proper place as "the first branch of government." (For an extended discussion of these initiatives, see Fisher 1978.)

The Congressional Budget and Impoundment Control Act 1974

The 1974 Budget Act was passed by a rather unusual congressional coalition. On one side were the "conservatives" who wanted to restore fiscal discipline. On the other side were the "liberals" who wanted the legislature to consider more explicitly the trade-offs among national priorities, and especially between military and social spending, and who also wanted to restrain Nixon from using his power to impound funds to resist the implementation of social programs which Congress had authorized.

The 1974 act led to some fundamental changes in the budgetary relationship between Congress and the presidency. To begin with, Congress no longer depends exclusively on the president's Office of Management and Budget for information on federal spending programs. The Congressional Budget Office, and to some extent the staffs of the House and Senate budget committees, now serve as countervailing sources of information.

The act also restricted the president's ability to impound funds. If the president wishes to terminate a program which Congress has funded, he must obtain the separate consent of both chambers. The president may, on his own initiative, delay the spending of appropriated funds, but such delays may be overturned by the vote of just one chamber.

In its first six years the Budget Act has not worked out as well as its supporters intended. The budget process itself has become the subject of intense partisan conflict, as exemplified by the Democratic leadership's refusal to bring the fiscal 1981 second budget resolution up for a floor vote before the 1980 election in order to prevent the Republicans from amending it to include budget-balancing or tax-cut provisions. Furthermore, the two budget committees have had great difficulty in persuading the authorizing and appropriating committees to bring their spending programs into line with the congressional budget resolutions. Finally, the impoundment control provisions have generated a great deal of paperwork, but have not enabled Congress to impose its spending priorities on the president.

The War Powers Resolution 1973

In an attempt to prevent future Vietnams, in 1973 Congress passed the so-called War Powers Resolution over President Nixon's veto. This provides that the president can commit American armed forces to military action only in three circumstances:

(1) after Congress has approved a declaration of war;

(2) pursuant to specific statutory authorization previously given by the Congress; or

(3) in a national emergency resulting from an attack on the United States or on American forces or citizens overseas.

In the last of these circumstances, the president is required to justify the commitment of forces to the Congress at once and to terminate it after sixty days unless Congress has by then declared war. If the president declares that "unavoidable military necessity" requires the continued use of forces after sixty days, he may be allowed another thirty days to withdraw the forces, after which time Congress may order them to be disengaged by means of a concurrent resolution not subject to presidential veto. Another section of the War Powers Resolution requires the president to consult the Congress "in every possible instance" before sending American forces into action (Cronin 1980, p. 197).

Twice since its passage congressmen argued that presidents have violated the spirit of the War Powers Resolution. In April 1975 President Ford ordered a military operation to rescue the crew of the S.S. *Mayaguez*, an American merchant ship which had been captured by Cambodian forces. Ford did not consult with the Congress until after the military operation had ended, but the release of the ship's crew made much of the congressional criticism on this point rather moot. In April 1980 President Carter did not consult with the Congress prior to ordering the unsuccessful attempt to rescue the American hostages in Iran. The president claimed he was not required to do so, since the mission was a "humanitarian" and not a military one; many observers wondered, however, how the secrecy essential to the rescue operation could have been preserved had members of Congress been notified of it in advance.

Other restrictions on a president's foreign policy powers

The Case Act (named after Senator Clifford P. Case of New Jersey) requires the executive branch to submit to the Senate, within sixty days of signing, the text of any executive agreement with another government. Many senators are concerned that their treaty powers have been diminished by the increasing use of the executive agreement as a means of making pacts with other countries, but it seems unlikely that the mere reporting requirements of the Case Act will redress the balance.

In 1974 Congress restricted the president's ability to sell defense equipment to other nations. Any sale worth more than $7 million may be vetoed if both chambers vote against it within thirty days. Congress has attempted to block the sale of fighter aircraft to Egypt and Saudi Arabia, but no major arms sale has yet been rejected.

Finally, legislation appropriating funds for foreign aid programs has often prevented either the U.S. government or international agencies such as the World Bank from helping certain named countries. In recent years they have included Brazil, Argentina, Uruguay, Ethiopia, Uganda, Vietnam, Angola, Cambodia, and Cuba. (For a complete list of statutory provisions restricting a president in international affairs, see Cronin 1980, pp. 206–9.)

The legislative veto

A fourth example of the recent assertiveness of Congress is its increasing tendency to attach so-called legislative veto language to many pieces of authorizing and appropriating legislation. Although legislative vetoes come in many forms—committee vetoes, one-house vetoes, and concurrent resolutions requiring the consent of both houses—their object is the same: greater oversight of the executive administration of programs. Congressmen who support the legislative veto claim that it is one of the few devices Congress has to ensure that the federal bureaucracy will remain responsive to congressional and public opinion.

The legislative veto has been the subject of intense political and constitutional controversy in recent years (Dry 1980, pp. 1, 20–22; Seidman 1980, pp. 1, 22–23). Presidents Ford and Carter considered that legislative vetoes, especially the committee and one-house versions, were unconstitutional infringements on their executive powers. The Department of Justice has argued consistently since the mid-1970s that the legislative veto violates the principle of the separation of powers. The Supreme Court has yet to issue a definitive opinion.

Legislative vetoes have also been opposed on political grounds. Critics often contend that Congress is simply unable to adequately review every one of the thousands of regulations issued by the bureaucracy every year, and will veto only those regulations opposed by vocal interest groups. They also point out that the veto enables Congress to avoid difficult substantive choices when it enacts legislation but to retain the opportunity to claim political credit by overturning agency regulations in response to pressure from interest groups.

IMPLICATIONS FOR THE PRESIDENT

Both the changes in the distribution of power within Congress and the reassertions of congressional authority can be seen as representing fundamental changes in congressmen's basic goals. These probably result more from the extensive membership turnover of the 1970s than from senior members altering their previous goals. Richard Fenno (1973) has noted that members of Congress can emphasize different combinations of three goals: reelection through helping constituents, acquiring power in Congress, and helping to make good public policy.

It is obvious that members of Congress increasingly value the goal of seeking reelection through constituent services. This increased emphasis, unfortunately, has adverse implications for a president's promotion of his legislative program on Capitol Hill. As noted earlier, if a member of Congress can be reelected primarily for the particular benefits he provides his constituents, that gives him much more freedom to vote as he wants in Washington. This greater leeway makes members less responsive to the argument from the White House that voting for the president's program would be in the members' own electoral interests back home. With more and more members now adopting representational stances not based on policy issues, such arguments from the president and his legislative staff have become less persuasive. If the member believes that he will be reelected on the basis of his constituency service regardless how he votes on issues (with the exception of intensely controversial issues such as abortion), he will not be especially responsive to White House arguments that it will be good constituency policy to support the White House. The president cannot coerce congressmen into voting for his programs, since he has few sanctions to use against them. As appeals to the member's constituency interests have become increasingly less effective, presidents have had to attempt to convince congressmen on the merits of issues. This, of course, is often much more difficult than an appeal to self-interest.

Alternatively, the president can offer congressmen inducements in the form of benefits which might increase their support among their constituents. Certain of these inducements, however, such as patronage jobs, are today in shorter supply than they were a few years ago, while others, such as federal public works projects, are no longer seen as "cost-free" activities.

Fenno's second goal is that of acquiring power in Congress. As Fenno describes it, internal power was, until the recent organizational reforms, a particular attraction of membership in such prestigious House committees as Ways and Means or Appropriations. Influence was seen as unevenly distributed, with only a few positions offering much. One interpretation of recent House reforms is that the new members have decided not to wait many years before attaining positions of great influence; they can now obtain moderate power after a relatively short wait. These reforms have made the House more like the Senate, where power has always been relatively widely distributed. From the president's point of view, however, this leveling of the congressional influence structure is undesirable. Because there are now relatively few members in both chambers who can influence many of their colleagues, the president must contact many more members when lobbying for his legislative programs.

Fenno's third member goal is helping to make good public policy. Here again some undesirable changes, from the president's point of view, have come about in recent years. Before the reforms, "making good public policy" usually meant helping the executive branch to make good policy; Congress viewed its role as one of ratifying and legitimating the policy proposals of the executive branch. For today's Congress, however, "making good public policy" seems in many respects to involve strengthening Congress relative to the executive branch so that it cannot be manipulated by presidents. Personal and committee staffs have been expanded, and specialized staff units such as the Congressional Budget Office have been established to provide Congress with sources of advice alternative to the executive branch. Congress seems to be placing less emphasis on developing new policy ideas and more emphasis on subjecting executive branch policies to closer scrutiny. In part, this is because the congressional reforms have made it almost impossible for central leaders such as the Speaker or key committee chairmen to coordinate a legislature grown increasingly fragmented and disjointed. Even if congressmen cannot agree on how to put their own policy house in order, they can often agree on the need to "gang up" on the president. Thus, through more extensive legislative oversight, legislative vetoes of the executive branch regulations, and provisions restricting the president's freedom of action in international affairs, Congress can impose greater restrictions on the executive's freedom to act without legislative consent.

At the same time, however, it is not required to exercise the self-discipline of restraining its own independent-minded members, which it must do if it is to develop positive policies of its own. It is certainly appropriate and desirable for Congress to strengthen its policymaking role; Congress should do more than merely legitimate the president's policies. But if legislators view Congress and the presidency, not as partners working together but as antagonists each seeking to deny the other "victory," then presidents have a substantial hurdle of suspicion and mistrust to overcome before their ideas can receive a fair hearing on Capitol Hill. Perhaps because of the lingering effects of Vietnam and Watergate, in recent years members of Congress have too often seemed more determined to protect the legislature's institutional role than to work with the president to improve the public condition.

WHAT CAN A PRESIDENT DO?

As we have seen, the contemporary congressional environment is not hospitable to presidents. Still, there are things which a new president can do to make life easier for himself on Capitol Hill. Following are some suggestions on how he might create a more favorable legislative environment for his programs.

Develop personal rapport

Congress should not be viewed in purely instrumental terms. The president should not limit his contacts with Congress to occasions when he needs votes to get a bill passed. If members view the president as coming to them only when he needs them, they will be less likely to respond positively than if they see that he is concerned with their general personal and political welfare.

From the first day of his term in office, a president should work diligently to develop a favorable relationship with Congress. If this can be achieved in the early weeks of an administration, it will give the president a resource he can draw on throughout his term. It is especially important that the president be seen as making a personal effort to establish close relationships; while the White House legislative liaison staff is important, this is a task which he cannot leave exclusively to his staff. In this respect, President Reagan's proposal to maintain an office on Capitol Hill is of considerable symbolic and practical significance.

A comparison between Lyndon Johnson and Jimmy Carter might be instructive at this point. Johnson went to great lengths to cultivate members of Congress. Not only would he invite them to the White House on a regular basis, but he would also provide them with small tokens of his esteem for them such as rides on *Air Force One*, autographed pictures, and pens used in bill-signing ceremonies. Carter, on the

other hand, seemed to go out of his way to slight congressmen. The Carter White House billed the House and Senate
leaders for meals they ate at the regular leadership break-
fasts. Telephone calls from Capitol Hill were frequently not
returned. And at one Carter fund-raiser the Speaker of the
House was seated at the table farthest away from the president—a privilege for which he had paid $300!

A series of social gatherings may be particularly useful at
the White House early in the president's term. All congressmen of both parties should be invited to these functions,
which would give the president an opportunity to get to know
them on a personal basis and would give them a sense that
they could express their views directly to him.

He should consult widely on Capitol Hill when making
staffing decisions. A few senior positions, such as cabinet
secretaryships, should be filled by members of the Congress.
President Reagan's nomination of Congressman David
Stockman as director of the Office of Management and
Budget is a step in the right direction. Such appointments
will give him ambassadors on Capitol Hill, even on issues outside their own agency's particular areas of concern. Other
positions, particularly those requiring frequent contact with
Congress, should be offered to people respected on Capitol
Hill who understand the norms and folkways of Congress.

Consultation during the formulation of new policies

A president's legislative programs are likely to receive more
favorable consideration on Capitol Hill if Congress has been
consulted during their development. The president should
make it clear to his domestic policy staff, as well as to appropriate agency officials, that regular consultation with
Congress is an important part of their job. In most instances,
these consultations should be undertaken with the senior
members of the committees and subcommittees responsible

for writing legislation in particular policy areas. In addition, though, it is important that congressional leaders be made a part of these consultations since they will be responsible for shepherding the president's programs through the congressional maze. Again, these consultations should not be limited to members of the president's party. While congressmen of the other party may not be sympathetic, such discussions might convert opponents into neutrals.

The people responsible for policy formulation, both in the White House and in the departments, should combine technical expertise and political skill. Relying solely on technical experts will not lead to positive results for the president. Technical experts may come up with substantively sound proposals, but it is not certain that their proposals will have a realistic change of congressional approval. Politically skilled people will also be able to advise the president on strategies to avoid in developing new policies. For example, they could tell him which congressmen not to consult, so that damaging leaks will not appear in the press. They could also discuss with the president the costs and benefits of going over the heads of the Congress to the public in situations in which there is congressional resistance to a presidential program. Jimmy Carter could have used some of this advice, for his frequent attacks on the Congress during its consideration of his energy programs did not make the passage of either that program or any other of his legislative initiatives any easier.

The president himself should never forget that Congress has an important role to play in the development of public policy. He should not hesitate to incorporate ideas initiated in Congress into his legislative programs, both to increase their chances of passage and to improve their quality. The president should continually recognize that congressmen are elected, and that it will on occasion be necessary for a member generally sympathetic to the administration to vote against the White House to avoid weakening his own electoral base.

Effective legislative liaison

Given the recent tension between the two ends of Pennsylvania Avenue, the president must have an effective legislative liaison staff which can act as a buckle between two institutions which have been increasingly moving apart.

To begin with, staff members must have an extensive knowledge of Congress, particularly if the president himself does not have much Washington experience. As noted earlier, Congress is becoming an increasingly complex and differentiated institution. Only people with prior experience can give the president sound advice on how to maneuver his legislative programs through its procedures. Furthermore, experienced individuals are likely to have their own associates on Capitol Hill—contacts who might help push presidential programs.

White House liaison staff will be more effective on Capitol Hill if they are perceived as having played a role in developing the legislative program and not as mere messengers. The president should see to it that both his domestic departments and agency heads consult with them regularly.

The legislative liaison staff must be seen as having the president's confidence and as being able to speak in his name. This means being able to respond to an amendment which comes up unexpectedly on the House or Senate floor without having to check back with the White House. It is also important that the liaison staff see the president regularly, since members of Congress should feel assured that their messages are passed on to him. Otherwise it is unlikely that they will use the liaison staff as a channel of communications.

Effective legislative liaison consists not only of the White House congressional relations staff, but also of agency liaison staffs. The president should pay particular attention to finding substantively expert and politically skilled people to fill assistant secretaryships for legislation in the various departments and should meet them regularly, allowing agencies to exchange information on pending legislation and to seek each other's support in difficult legislative battles. These meetings would allow the president to tell the agency staff members that they were indeed part of an administrationwide team and were *his* firm allies on Capitol Hill.

Both departmental and White House legislative liaison staff can and should develop effective relationships with interest group lobbyists who support elements of the administration's program. These interest groups should be consulted during the process of policy formulation or, if they can be included in a coalition supporting parts of the president's programs, they may well be able to help it through Congress. Effective legislative liaison agents will seek to divide the workload between government and interest group lobbyists. This will avoid duplication of effort and will often produce a more complete and accurate count of congressional preferences on legislation.

Again, however, politically skilled liaison staffers will be able to advise the president when *not* to ally himself with interest groups. While such alliances are usually beneficial to the White House, there are some situations in which using interest groups to fortify the administration's position today leads to being too closely tied to the programs of those groups tomorrow.

Finally, all legislative liaison staff should remember that congressional politics is coalition—not party—politics. By no means should the White House and the departments confine their efforts to the president's party. When the president's party is the minority in the Congress, it is obviously necessary to reach out to the majority; but even when the same party controls both ends of Pennsylvania Avenue, the president should seek the support of the minority party. Partly because of the increasing separation between presidential and congressional elections discussed earlier, presidents can no longer rely on common party loyalties to obtain legislative support.

There is another sense in which congressional politics is coalition politics. It is imperative that presidents recognize that patterns of power differ considerably from one decision point to another in Congress because of the internal division of labor, and that different sorts of coalition often have to be put together at different stages of the legislative process. For example, the coalition which will get legislation reported out of the House Ways and Means Committee is not necessarily the same as the coalition which will get support from the Senate Finance Committee, and it may be that neither of these will ensure success on the floor.

CONCLUSION

No one serving as president during the 1980s is likely to find legislative relations easy. Congress will not be supine as it was during the 1950s and 1960s. While some moves to re-centralize power in offices such as the House speakership might be successful, Congress is likely to retain its indepen-dence and to continue to respond to constituencies other than the White House.

But there is a great deal that a president can do to improve his chances of success on Capitol Hill. By treating Congress with respect, by consulting with it during the policy formula-tion process, and by selecting liaison staff of the highest quality, a president can create a climate in which Congress will in turn look toward the White House with respect and with an inclination to give him a fair hearing. If a president does not follow these suggestions, the trend towards a mere adversarial relationship evident during the 1970s is likely to continue into the 1980s.

The election has given President Reagan the opportunity to lead the nation in an era of legislative/executive cooperation unknown since Lyndon Johnson's Great Society. His sweeping victory, coupled with the substantial Republican gains in the House and Senate, will make the Congress potentially more receptive to White House legislative proposals than has been the case in recent years. However, this cooperation is only potential. The House of Representatives will continue to have an opposition majority at least through 1982; Reagan himself has not had extensive personal experience on Capitol Hill, and his budgetary policies will not permit him to award very many congressmen pet projects and constituency benefits. Thus, if President Reagan is to translate this opportunity into concrete legislative accomplishments, he must give great care and attention to Congress from the very beginning.

7

FRANCIS E. ROURKE

Grappling with the Bureaucracy

The implementation gap. Executive and agency policies—continuity or change? Time and autonomy in regulatory commissions and administrative agencies. "The president needs help." White House aides and political appointees. Controlling the bureaucracy. The White House information system. Current trends affecting White House control.

To presidential candidates, making promises is easy. And a new administration, thrust forward on a wave of post-election euphoria, is generally good at designing broad programs for honoring them—perhaps after a great deal of negotiation and compromise within the president's inner circle. But recently both presidents and policy analysts have shown increasing concern about the "implementation gap"—the difference between the promise embodied in program design and its tangible outcome in the real world. And it has become almost a tradition for presidents and their supporters to blame bureaucratic resistance for at least part of the problem. Although there is some justification for this, the experience of several recent presidents suggests that effective leadership can overcome bureaucratic intransigence. Moreover, current trends should make the job of controlling the bureaucracy easier.

BUREAUCRATIC RESISTANCE

Presidential leadership turns not only on the chief executive's ability to bridge the constitutional gap between the White House and Congress, but also on his capacity to induce the executive branch to work toward his objectives. Historically, the cleavage between the White House and the executive bureaucracy has held presidents back from their policy goals as much as has poor relations with the coequal branch of government on Capitol Hill.

Indeed, there have been times when presidents have had greater leverage over congressional committees than they have had over some of the more autonomous agencies in the executive branch. The U.S. Corps of Engineers and the Federal Bureau of Investigation have provided notorious examples of bureaucratic independence. Presidents commonly encounter agencies tightly allied to congressional committees and constituency groups, "iron triangles" that strongly resist efforts by the White House or any other outsider to influence "their" area of policy.[1]

Recent presidents have certainly been aware of the importance of establishing good relationships with the major executive departments and agencies. Even presidents elected after campaigning against the waste and incompetence of bureaucracy, like Richard Nixon and Jimmy Carter, have felt compelled to make early visits to executive offices to assure as many civil servants as possible that the White House needed their support to achieve its goals and that it had no intention of doing anything that might jeopardize their agencies or their programs.

But such visits cannot alter a fundamental fact of life new presidents must face. The bureaux, departments, and independent agencies that make up the executive branch have their own agendas set by laws that long predate the president's arrival in office. Thus, while the president may view his election as a "mandate for change," there is a massive undertow throughout the bureaucracy that pulls, not in the direction of change, but toward continuity.

White House officials commonly see this bureaucratic resistance as a major obstacle. This is a major theme running through the chronicles published in recent years by former White House aides. Were it not for foot-dragging on the part of the rest of the executive establishment, they commonly argue, they would have written a much more impressive record of achievement while in office; things only really went well when they were able to wrest control of a policy area from the tenacious grip of the bureaucrats in whose keeping the law had placed it.[2]

Sometimes the White House complains not so much about the actual resistance of bureaucrats to change as about the slowness with which agencies respond when they are complying with presidential directives. The time frame in which the White House operates is far different from that of ordinary agencies. When he is first elected, the president has less than four years in which to make a record of accomplishment. The agencies on which he must lean feel no sense of urgency. They have usually been administering their programs for a long time when the president arrives, and they expect to be doing so long after he has departed.

Agencies that enjoy legal protection from White House interference, like the independent regulatory commissions, are particularly hard to control. They have jurisdiction over a vast range of social and economic activities and have been established by statutes that guarantee against any presidential interference in their everyday decisions. This legal autonomy is designed to prevent sudden shifts in policy — when a new president takes office —that might disrupt large segments of the economy. Indeed, officials in independent regulatory commissions commonly argue that their agencies are not part of the executive branch at all. It is one of the anomalies of the American political system that the public expects the president to manage the nation's economy while he is limited in his ability to influence regulatory agencies which have the legal power to make or break large sectors of that economy. This is not the least of the gaps between responsibility and power that a president faces.

Whether or not they enjoy legal independence, virtually all administrative agencies have close ties with external groups, ties that give them a strong political base from which to resist White House direction. The ties may be to organizations representing the population groups the agency serves, to professional groups to which many of the agency's employees belong, or to congressional committees that sponsor and monitor the agency's activities.

Beyond the independence that statutes may confer on agencies or that they may wrest for themselves out of an uncertain political environment, every agency has certain bureaucratic characteristics that make it difficult for any president to control. Administrative agencies are repositories of specialized skills. They generate information that they have first—and sometimes sole—access to, and they have long ago mastered routines through which to frustrate efforts to establish outside control. To say that every executive agency is a bureaucracy is to say that it directs itself to a large degree, driven by the ethos of the profession that shapes its programs and always concerned with its own welfare as an organization.[3]

WHAT CAN THE PRESIDENT DO?

The task of getting the bureaucracy to follow his leadership is a formidable assignment for any president. But some things a president can do himself. He can convey to rank-and-file government employees his appreciation of the work they do. Of course, this may not be easy when "putting down the bureaucracy" has become a favorite pastime of presidential candidates. While bureaucracy in general may have unfavorable connotations for many voters, the people it serves may value it highly. "Americans Love Their Bureaucrats" was the title of a recent study of citizen attitudes toward government agencies which showed that people dealing with agencies like the Social Security Administration had highly positive feelings about their personal experiences (see Kahn et al. 1975a, pp. 66–71).[4]

So presidents can help themselves by speaking out in public on behalf of civil servants and the work they do. But there is little more that a president can do personally to influence the behavior of individual bureaucrats. Ultimately he must work through intermediaries. The range and complexity of the tasks carried on throughout the executive branch are far beyond the capacity of one man to supervise. "The President needs help," the Brownlow Commission once wrote, and nowhere is that help more sorely needed than in the task of grappling with the bureaucracy (President's Committee on Administrative Management 1937).

There are no more critical choices facing a president when he takes office than his decisions on how best to use intermediaries in handling his relations with the bureaucracy. In the pages that follow we shall present some of the cardinal rules that recent history suggests should guide these decisions. Each of these rules requires the president to ensure that his intermediaries monitor the performance of executive agencies, identify problems they have neglected, and try to compensate for their mistakes.

Presidents should rely primarily on the people they appoint to run executive agencies rather than on their own staff

One immediate decision every new president must make is whether to channel his principal efforts to control bureaucracy through his own staff aides at the White House and in the Executive Office of the President (EOP) or through the people he has put directly in charge of the various agencies. Recent administrations have oscillated between those alternatives, and power has moved back and forth between the White House and the cabinet.

Relying on White House or EOP officials has often appealed to the president in office. These officials are people he trusts. Often they have fought side by side with him through the political campaign that brought them to the White House.

It is less common for the president's appointees to the executive agencies to have such close personal ties with him. When they do, it has been the prevailing belief at the White House that they very quickly "marry the natives," adopting the narrower perspective of their agencies, largely as a result of indoctrination by senior career officials. Rather than influencing the agencies, they become protagonists of the latter's points of view.

Consequently, since the presidency of Franklin D. Roosevelt, the White House staff has expanded and taken on a widening range of activities, a development which reached its high-water mark in President Nixon's first term and which has since receded somewhat.

The experience of the Nixon presidency is instructive. Early in the term there was an atmosphere of hostility between the White House and the executive bureaucracy. As one close observer described it (Nathan 1975, p. 31):

Nixon's New Federalism policies involved taking power away from specialized bureaucracies of the federal government. . . . Tensions between the White House and the bureaucracy grew rapidly as Nixon's domestic policies were spelled out. Increasingly, and as a logical outgrowth of the New Federalism, the Nixon presidency was marked by animosity on both sides between the White House and the domestic bureaucracy.

Nixon's initial strategy for dealing with the bureaucracy was to centralize control over domestic policymaking in the White House. Ultimately, however, this strategy failed, and by the time Nixon's presidency was aborted by the Watergate scandal, the White House had shifted to an alternative plan of putting Nixon loyalists in key positions in executive agencies.

A review of the factors leading to this reversal will provide any president with ample warning against the extravagant expectation that the White House staff can lead the way in controlling the bureaucracy. As Nixon soon discovered, staff members' involvement quickly overloads White House circuits. Presidential aides begin dealing with second- and third-order problems that could better be handled within executive agencies.

Moreover, excessive intervention in the details of bureaucratic decision-making diverts the attention of White House aides from general policy questions that are more legitimate matters of presidential concern. These aides are best suited for identifying and calling presidential attention to fundamental issues that the bureaucracy has neglected because they transcend the jurisdiction of any single agency.

It is as generalists that White House aides can work most effectively. They cannot compete on equal terms with the infinite variety of specialists in the federal bureaucracy. When specialists are needed at the White House for work on task forces or for other joint ventures, they can be recruited on a temporary basis from executive agencies. There have been frequent occasions in the past when White House generalists have collaborated fruitfully with bureaucratic specialists in the development of national policy, especially with respect to problems that span the jurisdictions of more than one agency.

It is important also to remember that while the White House staff may be very good at designing broad-gauge programs, those programs must be carried out by some bureaucratic organization. In recent years students of executive policymaking have called attention to the fact that it is hard to translate policies enunciated by presidents and other high officials into tangible results. The problem arises, it is commonly agreed, because the difficulties of implementing policies are not fully anticipated at the time of formulation. Hence, many policies fail because not enough attention is given in their design to the development of effective ways of carrying them out.[5]

The intermediaries best able to assist the White House in overcoming this implementation gap are the men and women the president names to executive posts in the bureaucracy. Once they become familiar with their agency and its programs, these appointees are in a better position to advise the president on what will and will not work than White House aides can ever hope to be. And once a new program is established, these appointees are best able to steer it towards its objectives. It is the agencies they direct that have the technical capacity to do the things the White House wants done.

Presidents should not try to control all agencies in the same way

On the campaign trail all bureaucrats may look alike to a

prospective president. In office, however, he quickly discovers that the bureaucracy is a varied set of organizations with distinct traditions and powers. If he is not sensitive to these differences, a president may easily blunder into embarrassing political or legal surprises.

The independent regulatory commissions, for instance, require very different treatment than do ordinary executive departments. Regulatory agencies function in part as administrative courts. While they are doing so—hearing and handing down rulings in individual cases—the White House is legally precluded from trying to influence their decisions. Any attempt by a White House aide to intervene in the judicial phase of a regulatory commission's activity can have adverse consequences, as Sherman Adams discovered during the Eisenhower presidency.

At the same time, a president can make a significant impact on the overall direction of policy through his power to name regulatory commissioners as their staggered terms expire during the course of his administration. This is a potent source of influence, especially the right to name the chairmen. One recent study of regulatory agencies concludes that the ability of a president to select their chairmen, and the acceptance of the chairmen's leadership within the commissions, enables the policies of these theoretically independent agencies to be "brought into concert with national policies in important economic areas" (see Welborn 1977, p. 146).

Modern presidents have usually confined to the appointment process their efforts to influence these independent agencies. President Nixon, however, established a White House organization, the Office of Telecommunications Policy (OTP), which tried to address policy issues that had long lain within the jurisdiction of one of these independent agencies, the Federal Communications Commission. The OTP fell into disrepute because of its alleged involvement in efforts to intimidate the news media, and it was abolished as a White House unit during the Carter presidency.

It is not the independent regulatory commissions, however, but the executive departments that represent the bulk of the bureaucratic apparatus the new president confronts. As with regulatory commissions, his ability to control these mammoth organizations turns largely on his power to name their top officials. The president also has some power to determine their organizational structure and the size of their budgets.

During recent years the president's ability to influence executive agencies through his appointing power has often been seen as weakened by the growing need to find technically qualified people to fill high executive posts. This need for top-level technocrats obviously diminishes a president's capacity to control the bureaucracy by appointing members of his own party as cabinet officials. But it is questionable whether the opportunity to make partisan appointments would increase the president's influence over the bureaucracy. For one thing, it requires technical experience to play an effective part in a department's everyday activities. Unless an executive has it, he will not be able to help the president to extend his influence very far down into departmental decisions. Also, a common party allegiance does not guarantee loyalty to the president. It may provide executives with a political base enabling them to pursue policies in conflict with the president's goal. It is for these reasons that modern presidents have paid less attention to partisan considerations in making appointments as they have acquired experience in office (see, for example, Stanley et al. 1967).

While the Nixon administration's experience with OTP suggests that a president would be ill advised to use White House staff to influence decisions within independent regulatory tribunals, the same does not apply to executive departments. Starting with Franklin Roosevelt, presidents have used their staffs very effectively to monitor departmental activities.

This use of White House staff has been particularly prominent and successful in foreign affairs and national security
policy. The establishment of the National Security Council
(NSC) under President Truman and the ascendancy of its
staff director, the special assistant for national security
affairs, under President Kennedy has given the White House
a capacity for oversight in the arena of foreign policy that is
notably lacking in the domestic sector. To be sure, the NSC's
activities have triggered considerable controversy in recent
years. National security advisors seem to have an irresistible
appetite for a larger role in national security policymaking
than was originally intended. This has brought the NSC staff
into frequent conflict with the State Department—a confrontation that has taken a good deal of presidential time
and energy to mediate.

But the White House national security operation has
served presidential interests in spite of these occasional
difficulties, and it is difficult to imagine any president dis-
pensing with it. It would be impossible for a president to meet
public expectations of White House leadership in international affairs without such help. The range of agencies in the
executive branch whose activities have a foreign affairs
dimension is so broad that White House staff intervention is
necessary to maintain coherence of purpose. The State
Department long ago demonstrated that it was not versatile
enough to keep on top of foreign policy in a day when such
topics as international trade, telecommunications, nuclear
development, and space exploration rival traditional diplomatic problems for a place on the president's foreign affairs
agenda.

The apparent success of the NSC staff led many to believe
that a similar organization could be created on the domestic
side, and President Nixon established a Domestic Council in
the White House in 1970. Its goal was to achieve for domestic
issues the kind of oversight, coordination, and leadership in

policy development that Nixon felt the NSC staff had secured in foreign affairs under Henry Kissinger.

Our brief experience with this administrative analogy between foreign and domestic affairs suggests that it is a bad one. The Domestic Council never lived up to expectations, and it was reformed by President Carter. The domestic arena evidently does not lend itself to mastery by any high-level, behind-the-scenes, White House staff operation. It is a highly variegated policy area in which a wide range of groups pursue disparate goals. The domestic bureaucracies are closely tied to—and often dominated by—the groups they serve or seek to regulate. They are not hospitable to comprehensive control along the lines of the NSC model. And even if the political environment were more auspicious, Congress is hardly likely to accept the kind of central direction of domestic policymaking by the White House that it tolerates—not always happily—in foreign affairs.

Presidents must lower their expectations when they move from the foreign to the domestic arena. A president has to limit his agenda by identifying what the "big ticket" items are and neglecting the rest. He should do his best to see that the White House staff follows his example. Otherwise, the White House will wind up with no impact at all. From this perspective, the conversion of the Domestic Council into a Domestic Policy Staff by the Carter administration was a step in the right direction. Worth noting is a strategy of decision attributed to President Eisenhower, who argued that in his administration "no presidential decisions were made by anyone save the President and as few as possible nonpresidential decisions were made by the President" (see Hess 1976).

But while the White House needs to restrain its appetite for direct involvement in the affairs of domestic agencies, it should nonetheless keep itself well informed about their activities. Even if presidents have to confine themselves to dealing with what they regard as the major issues in the domestic sector, they must continue to be well briefed on what is happening throughout the executive branch so that they can identify what these major issues are.

A major task of any White House staff thus is to keep the president informed. Most presidents dislike surprises that are not of their own making, so at its best a White House information system should have a forecasting dimension. Executive agencies should be routinely required to provide the White House with information on their plans for the immediate future, a practice followed in recent administrations, in order that the president can receive early warning of developments taking place in any policy arena that will require his intervention.

In addition to receiving periodic reports from executive agencies on their activities, White House officials can also pick up a great deal of information through informal contacts with top agency officials. The reach of the staff s information system should be broader than the scope of the president's formal legal responsibilities, for it is often developments in areas not under its direct control that have the most far-reaching consequences for the White House; President Roosevelt discovered this when Albert Einstein alerted him to research in nuclear physics that presaged the development of the atomic bomb.

While controlling the bureaucracy has been a perennial challenge for every president, there is no reason to believe that the White House cannot do it

So much has been written and said about the intransigence of the Washington establishment that a new president—like Ronald Reagan in 1981—might well despair of ever having any impact on it. Such pessimism is not supported by the recent history of White House relationships with executive agencies. Friction has been a common characteristic of these relationships, but it has not prevented the White House from accomplishing a great deal through joint action. President Reagan would be well advised to anticipate conflict, but not to expect it to preclude cooperation any more than it does in his relations with Congress.

As noted earlier, suspicion of bureaucracy was particularly pronounced when President Nixon took over the White House in 1969. Members of his immediate staff were firmly convinced that the bureaucracy would be incapable of carrying out the programs of a Republican administration and would, in fact, make every effort to sabotage them. From the White House perspective, this bureaucratic resistance was rooted in ideological differences—liberal bureaucrats were incapable of faithfully serving a conservative president.

But the evidence to support these White House suspicions is less than compelling. To be sure, one study based on data gathered in 1970 does show that a high proportion of senior career officials working for domestic agencies were Democrats and supported a higher level of government spending for social services than a Republican president might be expected to propose (Aberbach and Rockman 1976, pp. 456–68). This study, however, did not show that these differences led to any active resistance by bureaucrats. All it revealed was that "the federal bureaucracy was not fertile soil in which to plant the most conservative of the Nixon administration's social policies" (Aberbach and Rockman 1976, p. 467).

Moreover, a subsequent study of the Nixon presidency based on data gathered in 1976 demonstrated that the "clashing beliefs" between political officials and career administrators receded as time went by (Cole and Caputo 1979, pp. 399–413). The White House appointed additional Republicans to supergrade positions in the bureaucracy, and an increasing number of independents in the senior civil service began to lean toward a Republican political identification.

What the latter investigation suggests is that senior bureaucrats, like Supreme Court justices, "follow the election returns." They will in fact defer to a president and support his programs even when they are not happy with either. This was certainly the case during the Nixon years with respect to programs enacted by Congress that had the full authority of law behind them. Where the White House got into trouble in its dealings with the bureaucracy was when it tried to pursue objectives that seemed illegitimate. An example of this was the impoundment strategy—the Nixon administration's denial of funds for activities that agencies had been duly authorized by law to carry out. While there was legal foundation at the time for the limited use of the impoundment power by presidents, there was no precedent for the scale on which it was employed by the Nixon administration for the purpose of wiping out existing government programs.

In any case, the 1976 investigation of the Nixon bureaucracy clearly showed that the "pull" of the presidency is very strong as far as civil servants are concerned (Cole and Caputo 1979, pp. 412–13):

By 1976 we find substantial proportions of all party identifiers (Democrats, Republicans, Independents) sympathetic to Nixon's proposals. In fact Independents as a group were found to be almost indistinguishable from Republicans in their support of Nixon's policies and programs. Independents and party identifiers combined assure either a Republican or Democratic president substantial support at the senior career levels of the federal bureaucracy. . . . While maintaining its formal independence (and perhaps even basic philosophic differences), the bureaucracy still responds to specific presidential initiatives.

This shift on the part of senior bureaucrats toward support of White House policies while Nixon was president may reflect a strong commitment to the traditional ideal of administrative neutrality on their part—a willingness to serve presidents of all political persuasions with equal loyalty. Or it may reveal an inclination to tilt in the direction of prevailing political winds. In either case, it bodes well for the ability of presidents to control bureaucracy.

In policy matters, moreover, where presidents have encountered not so much resistance as lack of support among bureaucrats, the White House has proved to be very effective at developing management strategies to achieve its goals. And both Democratic and Republican presidents have successfully targeted on bureaucracies where they most expected to encounter foot-dragging: Democrats, on the military; Republicans, on welfare agencies.

Whatever faith a Democrat such as President Kennedy had in his military advisors was quickly dissipated by the Bay of Pigs fiasco during the first year of his administration. Thereafter he relied, not on the Joint Chiefs of Staff, but on White House national security advisors. During the Cuban missile crisis in 1963 he maintained operational control over the American naval blockade. His Democratic successor, President Johnson, used an instrument of budgetary management—program budgeting—as a technique for controlling weapons decisions and set up a variety of task forces designed to break the executive departments' grip on policy development.

On the Republican side, President Nixon relied on management techniques to bring down welfare expenditures—an objective dear to his political party. A system of monitoring decisions on welfare claims was established in the Department of Health, Education, and Welfare that significantly reduced the rate of growth in the number of welfare recipients (see Randall 1979, pp. 795–810). Indeed, had Nixon's second term not been aborted by the Watergate scandal, it is likely he would have blazed a number of new management trails for succeeding presidents to follow in their efforts to tame the bureaucracy, so determined was he to achieve this objective.

HELPFUL TRENDS

Presidents are thus assisted in grappling with bureaucracy by both a general predisposition on the part of career bureaucrats to cooperate and the availability of management techniques that enable the White House to push them in directions it sets. An incoming president anxious to establish ascendancy over the bureaucratic apparatus can take heart from the fact that several trends are now visible which can materially assist him. These trends suggest that the task of controlling the bureaucracy may be less difficult in the future than it has been in the recent past. (For a discussion of these trends, see Heclo 1978.)

One such trend is a decline of public faith in the ability of experts to solve the nation's most pressing problems, including stagflation, the continuing decay of major cities, and our diminished capacity to shape developments in the international arena. Bureaucratic organizations have traditionally derived their status in the political system from their presumed expertise. When expertise loses its credibility, bureaucracy becomes less formidable as a competitor of the White House.

Secondly, as government programs have multiplied, there has been a growing tendency for agency jurisdictions to overlap. When many agencies have a voice in resolving a policy issue, none can exercise monopoly power over the decision-making process. And as bureaucratic organizations acquire the capacity to stalemate each other, issues inevitably move upward to the White House for resolution. During the New Deal era, FDR deliberately contrived overlapping jurisdictions in order to keep the power of decision in his own hands. Modern presidents do not need to engage in such artificial contrivances. Today's agencies have a statutory mandate to compete for power.

Finally, there has been a considerable expansion in the number of groups that take an interest in the activities of each executive agency and regard themselves as part of its constituency. In the past a fairly narrow constellation of groups directly affected by an agency's activities made up its constituency. A variety of previously submerged interests have now emerged—consumers, feminists, and environmentalists, for example. Groups like these have moved into many agencies' constituencies and have greatly changed their character.

When constituencies become more diverse, they no longer provide executive agencies with the single-minded support that they were long accustomed to receive. In conflicts with the White House, for instance, the Corps of Engineers may find that environmental groups align themselves with the president. So the increasingly variegated nature of their constituencies erodes the political base on which agencies once depended to evade presidential control.

What these trends add up to is the fact that bureaucracies have been weakened in their capacity to obstruct the president. In addition, certain newly introduced management changes in the executive branch reinforce the president's ability to control the bureaucracy. Principal among them is the establishment of the Senior Executive Service under President Carter—an innovation that greatly increases the president's ability to select and assign civil servants to senior positions (the GS 16–18 supergrades; see Singer 1980, pp. 2028–31). So the tide of change is not moving against a president bent on augmenting his control over bureaucracy. On the contrary, it is moving in his favor.

8

MARTIN M. SHAPIRO

The Presidency and the Federal Courts

Judicial influence on policymaking. The legitimacy of the Supreme Court. The New Deal theory and its chinks. Eisenhower, the Constitution, and the Court. Concepts of the judicial role in government. Congressional delegation of power. Courts and the agencies. Two "iron triangles" and the presidency.

Political scientists generally accept that recent presidents have been losing control over executive agencies and budget decisions. The current wisdom is that presidential power — certainly in the domestic arena — is seriously constrained by the existence of "iron triangles," or alliances between Congress, an agency, and an interest group. This may be so. But

an equally important development has been less widely
recognized, and that is the increasingly active participation
of the courts in policymaking since the early 1960s.

The courts have been steadily reducing the discretionary
power of executive agencies and rewriting their regulations.
At the same time, a new iron triangle has appeared consisting of agency, court, and interest group. Congress initiates
the triangle by creating a statutory right, but then it with-
draws. The triangle perpetuates itself. The president is effectively excluded from its policy actions, since he has almost no
influence over judges (once appointed) as contrasted with his
power over members of congressional subcommittees. Just
as a president faces a mass of past spending commitments
that obligate much of his budgetary resources, he now faces
an increasing number of statutorily created rights which
arm the courts to obligate even more commitments and to
mandate that the executive branch pursue implementation
policies that run counter to those it favors.

The president now faces courts which are his rival in agenda setting and in the formulation of public goals and values.
How did this happen, and what can he do to protect his
authority?

POLITICAL SUASION AND
JUDICIAL POWER

A new president faces not only political institutions but also
contemporary attitudes about those institutions. This is
nowhere more important than for the Supreme Court.
Deprived of direct control over both the purse and the sword,
the Court's political effectiveness depends largely on voluntary compliance with its commands by other political institutions and by the people. Historically, the Supreme Court has
suffered more than the other two branches from problems of

legitimacy. If the meaning of our Constitution were absolutely clear and the Court simply acted to enforce it, then the Court's actions would be perfectly legitimate. If the Constitution had no fixed meanings, so that the Supreme Court simply wrote its own policy preferences into the Constitution as it went along, then its actions would be perfectly illegitimate. But because the Constitution has some fixity and some flexibility, and because actions of the justices mix law and policy, the Supreme Court has always lived in a state of uncertain legitimacy. Americans have always asked how much the president and Congress should govern, but they have not questioned their right to govern. There is no more characteristic question of American political discourse, however, than the question of whether the Court should govern at all.

There is a New Deal theory of the Supreme Court just as there are New Deal theories of the presidency and Congress, and like those theories it has honorable roots. The three theories are, of course, interdependent. New Deal proponents of the strong presidency argued that the president, rather than Congress, should act as chief lawmaker because the presidency was more unified and because it more truly represented the national majority will. At the same time, a New Deal school of judicial self-restraint was busy subordinating the Supreme Court to Congress. If the Court's judgments on the constitutionality of federal legislation merely substituted judicial policy preferences for legislative ones, then the Court ought to stop reviewing and to leave policy decisions to Congress (see Hand 1958; Mendelson 1961).

While New Deal commentators never openly put the two streams of thought together, the political arithmetic was clear. Congress ought to defer to the lawmaking of the president. The Supreme Court ought to defer to the lawmaking of Congress. Therefore, the Supreme Court ought to defer to the president. QED. The only legitimate role for the Supreme Court was that of whipping the state legal systems into line with the Constitution and federal statutes (see Schmidhauser 1958).

This attitude predominated during the presidencies of Roosevelt, Truman, and Eisenhower. A chink in the New Deal theory, however, allowed the Supreme Court to reemerge as a rival to and manipulator of the presidency. For if the Court were still free to whip the states into line, it might whip them into a different line or require different modes of whipping than the president would have chosen.

Eisenhower's experience with Little Rock is instructive. Clearly, at the time of *Brown* v. *Board of Education* (347 U.S. 483 [1954]) there was a national majority against Jim Crow laws, but it was a marginal majority both in breadth and depth of sentiment—not the kind of majority that would find expression through Congress or the presidency. Once the Supreme Court had put the new anti–Jim Crow policy in place, however, the president's power stakes changed rapidly. Because his military background had led to "man on horseback" fears, Eisenhower was particularly reluctant to use the military to enforce the law. Yet he found himself using the army to do the Supreme Court's bidding—a bidding for which he had no great personal enthusiasm. He did so because the Court had built a coalition that he could not resist. It had added the constituency which believed that the law must be obeyed to the constituency which believed that Jim Crow was a national disgrace. He need not have sent troops to end Jim Crow. He had no choice but to send troops to enforce the Constitution as interpreted by the Court (see Wilkinson 1978).

The New Deal theory of judicial restraint did not die with *Brown* v. *Board of Education* and Little Rock. Indeed, it continued to flourish in the academy long after the Warren Court had passed it by. Nevertheless, it became increasingly difficult to insist that the Court could and should do nothing when it was doing a great deal and when much of what it was doing seemed good. President Nixon could still seize upon judicial self-restraint as a campaign issue—both intellectually alive and emotionally appealing—but it is unlikely that any president or presidential candidate will be able to do so in the near future.

JUDICIAL ACTIVISM

In part, of course, the decline of judicial self-restraint as a political slogan results from the change from the Warren to the Burger Court. The Burger Court is less given to dramatic gestures. Yet this is not the whole story. Even in the bitter controversy over the Burger Court's abortion decisions, the "pro-life" forces have never asserted that the Court had no right to make public policy, only that the Court made an immoral policy.

The major new fact about the Supreme Court is that there has been a fundamental change in the predominant conception of its appropriate role. While some remnants of New Deal theory remain, there is now a strong consensus that the Court should *either* support minority interests not adequately represented elsewhere in the political process *or* defend fundamental public values (Choper 1980; Fiss 1979, pp. 1–58; Ely 1980). Whichever way judicial activism is justified, it reduces the New Deal role of the president. It was Roosevelt who was supposed to protect minorities; Roosevelt, not his Court, who announced the Four Freedoms.

Today's most fashionable school of constitutional thought argues that one great purpose of government is to provide an arena in which men and women can come together to debate and thus to create public values. The courts are ideal for this, every bit as good as Congress and the presidency. Indeed, they are better, because the reasoned argument and elaboration of litigational procedures are particularly good vehicles for ethical/political discourse (Fiss 1979; Tribe 1980, pp. 1063–80).

This new school of thought may be seen as part of the contemporary revolt of the intellectuals against popular majorities. For it asserts that public values are best discovered, not by the messy processes of politics, but by a group of Harvard and Yale lawyers arguing with one another according to a ritual that only they understand in front of a judge drawn from their own ranks.

From a slightly different perspective, the new movement can be seen as part of the rights fetishism that has become a principal tool of the left for extracting what it wants from the political system no matter what the majority or its elected representatives want (see, e.g., Michelman 1969, pp. 7–56). When an interest — what somebody wants — is transformed into a right, it goes to the head of the line. The normal political processes by which legislatures and agencies establish priorities among competing interests are set aside (Shapiro 1979, pp. 126–31). Thus if a court decides that mental patients in state hospitals have a right to treatment, more state money must be spent on psychiatrists even if the state legislature would have preferred to spend the money on fire inspectors. The principal problem that judges pose for other politicians is that recently they have been using their rights-declaring powers liberally and thus asserting ultimate, even if only sporadically exercised, control over the distributional politics that are the focus of the legislative process.

Political executives confronted with their own unpopularity often take comfort in the widespread disparagement of legislatures. It has become a commonplace that many congressmen seek reelection by campaigning against Congress (Fenno 1978). The creation of judicial rights is another form of that disdain. For when a court converts an interest into a right, it is declaring that it does not trust the legislature to be fair. The ultimate defense of judicial rights creation is the belief that if some people in a society are being badly treated, someone must step in if the legislature fails to do so. While forty years ago the someone was typically thought to be the president, today the most frequently nominated someone is the judge (Horowitz 1977).

It would be excessive to suggest that judges have replaced elected officials as our dominant political leaders or that presidential leadership has been replaced by Supreme Court leadership. The president's problem is that the courts may create rights which bring issues to the fore that he might prefer not to confront—desegregation, school busing, abortion. By creating rights, the courts set themselves up as rivals with the president in national agenda setting. Moreover, the particular charm of rights creation is that it can ignore the relational aspects of politics and treat each right as totally independent. As a result, the ability to create rights encourages the single-issue politics that are so troublesome to presidents who are necessarily concerned with coalition building. The Supreme Court can and does promote single-issue movements, leaving the president to deal with them.

STATUTORY RIGHTS

Courts today participate vigorously in announcing values, establishing priorities, and setting agendas, all of which in the days of the Imperial Presidency seemed to be increasingly the preserve of the executive branch. But to appreciate the dynamics of executive/judicial interaction, we must go beyond judicial rights creation to the legislative process. While the Supreme Court has dramatically announced new constitutional rights like the "right" to abortion, Congress has also added to our law an amazing new assortment of statutory rights.

During the Roosevelt administration it became the habit of
Congress to pass very broadly worded statutes delegating
large chunks of its lawmaking power either directly to the
president, to exercise by executive order, or to the federal
agencies, to be exercised by administrative regulations.
Many of these regulations amounted to major pieces of legislation. The Supreme Court has long since approved such
delegations to the executive branch[1] and has held that its
regulations have the same force of law as statutes enacted by
Congress itself.[2]

In New Deal days such delegation followed the New Deal
theory of separation of powers. Congress was deferring to the
executive branch, and the Supreme Court was nominally
deferring to Congress but was actually deferring to the presidency. Delegation was an unmixed blessing to the president,
however, only for so long as certain conditions were met.
First, the president had to control the bureaucracy. Second,
the delegations had to create wide-ranging administrative
discretion rather than vesting legal rights in individuals. A
statute that says agency X may do whatever it pleases to
alleviate problem Y strengthens the president if he controls
agency X. A statute that says agency X is entitled to enforce
the right Y of citizen Z may delegate wide rule-making power
to the agency. It also enables citizen Z to make demands
upon the agency, no matter what the president wants. Third,
the delegation had to be unreviewable by the courts. Where
delegation is accompanied by active judicial review, then,
even if he controls the agency the president must share the
lawmaking power with the courts that do the reviewing. For
whatever the pretense, judicial review of agency lawmaking
amounts to judicial participation in lawmaking.

All three conditions for presidential control have been
eroded. President Roosevelt enjoyed a suddenly enormously
expanded bureaucracy staffed largely by people attracted to
Washington by the promise of the New Deal. Presidents
since Eisenhower have faced an entrenched New Deal

bureaucracy. Thus, delegation of lawmaking power to the agencies has strengthened another rival to presidential authority.

At the same time, Congress and the courts have interacted to produce a shift from administrative discretion to statutory rights. A 1940 statute called the "National Transportation Policy" may provide the ultimate New Deal model of administrative discretion. This act simply empowered the Interstate Commerce Commission to regulate modes of transportation "so . . . as to . . . preserve the inherent advantages of each; to promote . . . efficient service and foster sound economic conditions." In more recent years, however, Congress has tended to conceive the task of solving massive social and economic problems in terms of creating statutory rights vested in individuals, with broad delegations to administrative agencies to implement those rights. For instance, the Education for Handicapped Children Act invests handicapped children with a right to an adequate education and their parents with a right to participate in determining their education. It goes on to delegate to the agency broad discretion to write regulations defining standards of adequacy as well as processes necessary to ensure participation.

Rights are not negotiable. Faced with a handicapped child who has a right to an adequate education, we are unlikely to say that any education that the president says is adequate is adequate or that some bureaucrat should have the discretion to decide that injured athletes rather than handicapped children should have first crack at the hydrotherapy equipment. Rights—whether statutory or constitutional—are assertions of absolute entitlement.

A mere change in statutory rhetoric from agency discretion to citizens' rights would not, in itself, greatly limit the discretion of the executive branch. But the change in rhetoric *plus* the growth of judicial review has done so. In the late 1930s and 1940s the Supreme Court was not only busy providing constitutional legitimacy for vast delegations of congressional lawmaking power to the executive branch, but was also working hard to construct a theory under which administrators wielding that power would be insulated from judicial review. The Court argued that the executive branch constituted a reservoir of technical expertise upon which most administrative decisions depended. It followed that judges, who were not experts, should defer to the decisions of administrators, who were. This general doctrine was supplemented by a special doctrine which called for judicial deference to administrators even in the one area in which it might be argued that judges were the more expert: questions of the meaning of the delegating statute. Even though freeing agencies to interpret these statutes as they pleased would enable them to expand their powers indefinitely, the Supreme Court held that such regulations had the same force of law as if Congress itself had enacted them. The courts would not review them, and the agencies became the final authority on questions of the legal meaning of the statutory provisions under which they operated.[3]

During the 1960s and 1970s, however, this insulation from judicial review broke down. Led by the District of Columbia and 2nd Circuits, judges began to challenge the expertise of the agencies, sometimes directly, but mostly by procedural indirection. The courts came to hold that the agencies must listen to all sides of questions and that failure to do so, and to provide a record proving that they had done so, would lead to judicial invalidation of their regulations.[4] Under the guise of inspecting whether the agency had followed consultative procedures, judges came more and more to second-guess agency policy decisions and to at least delay those they didn't like. At the same time, standing doctrines were liberalized so that not only were courts more willing to review, but also more people were enabled to ask for review. Despite some unease,[5] the Supreme Court has basically accepted this trend. So while the doctrine that agency regulations have the force of law has not changed, courts have again set themselves up as rival interpreters of the congressional language under which the agencies' delegated lawmaking powers are exercised (see Freedman 1978; Stewart 1975, pp. 1667–1784).

This change in the courts' behavior has been seconded by Congress. Many recent statutes delegating lawmaking authority require agencies to engage in the kinds of elaborate consultative procedures that the courts have been requiring. And many of those same statutes give rights to individuals and allow them to vindicate those rights in court.

THE NEW IRON TRIANGLE

What does all this mean for the president? The original New Deal delegations increased his power because they gave full policy discretion to agencies that he controlled. Today the president exercises less control over the federal agencies; the agencies have less discretion in that they cannot refuse to implement statutorily created rights, and the courts have triumphantly reentered the policy arena.

Congressionally created individual rights have been rigidified through agency regulations and judicial review to the point of constraining the president's discretion in vast areas of federal regulation. In addition, networks—"iron triangles"—of congressional subcommittee, executive bureau, and interest group alliances make their own public policy and resist outside control. Now there is the new triangle, consisting of agency, court, and interest group, which is bringing about a new diminution of presidential authority.

Congress or the courts or both give the interest group standing to lobby the agency and the courts. The agency knows that, unless it satisfies the group, the group will sue, thus increasing the cost and delaying the implementation of

the proposed policy. The agency also knows that unless it an-
ticipates the policy views of the courts, the judges will find
some way to reverse or at least delay the proposed policy if a
suit takes place. The interest group knows that the cheapest
thing to do is to persuade the agency. It also knows that, if
properly approached, courts may strengthen its statutory entitlements, thus providing a stronger base for negotiation
with the agency. And the courts know that all they can do is
to increase the time and money costs to the agency, which
can eventually win if it is willing to pay those costs. The
courts also know that if they attempt to build a barrier to
some agency policy by announcing a statutory right debar-
ring it, Congress may reverse them. It follows that the agencies, interest groups, and courts live by mutual accommodation over relatively long periods of time, effectively excluding
the president.

The new triangle is worse for the president than the old.
An alert president might discover ways to reward or punish
individual members of the congressional subcommittee involved. He could reward or punish the agency at budget time.
And most interest groups would prefer presidential
patronage to presidential animosity. But there is little he can
do for—or to—the federal judges who now participate in the
"administration" of statutes.

A brief example will illustrate these points. In the Age Discrimination Act of 1975 Congress prohibited discrimination
on the basis of age in all federally assisted programs. It also
provided several broadly worded exceptions to the prohibi-
tion which allow "reasonable" use of age as a criterion in
assigning jobs and benefits. As Peter Schuck (1979, pp.
27–93) has pointed out in his illuminating case study of the
statute, it looks toward two policy goals: bettering the social
and economic status of the aged and improving economic
efficiency. It creates specific statutory rights for the aged
and delegates lawmaking power to the Department of Labor
to effectuate them. Because the two goals conflict, and the

trade-offs between them are not clearly specified in the statute, the Department of Labor has enormous discretion in writing the real law—its own detailed regulations. In doing so, however, it must follow the protracted procedures required by the courts. Moreover, once the regulations are enacted, aged people who feel they do not adequately protect their rights as established by the statute will challenge them in court. Courts may or may not be tempted into writing their own version of the statute. Congress having acted, the law on age discrimination is now being written. It will take a long time to write, and it will be the product of a great deal of discretion. But almost none of that discretion will be wielded by the president.

THE PRESIDENT'S RESOURCES

In summary, the president now faces a Supreme Court which rivals his authority in formulating public goals and values and in agenda setting. And in formulating values, the Court often contributes to the single-issue politics that make it difficult for the president to form and lead a winning national coalition. Furthermore, the Court has the power to implicate the president in the achievement of the goals *it* chooses, thus diverting presidential energies and creating expectations about presidential performance that the president may be unable to satisfy. The Supreme Court and the other federal courts have also returned to a major role in day-to-day, detailed lawmaking. That return has helped to create an agency/interest group/court triangle which dominates much of the routine decision-making of government and is largely impervious to presidential intervention.

What resources does the president command to meet his judicial rivals? Unfortunately for him, the answer is more than enough resources to meet the micro problems and

almost none to meet the macro developments I have just outlined. Compared to these macro phenomena, the various
points of microtension between president and Supreme Court
which appear so dramatically to threaten his power are
really trivial.

The microlevel problems are "point" problems that tend to
come to a head in a single case or a short series of cases
which bring to constitutional issue the legitimacy of some
particular claim of presidential authority. The batting
average of the presidency in such disputes is high. The president's massive constitutional authority has been increased
rather than decreased by successive Supreme Court decisions, even those of the Nixon years. In these areas, the
president is fully armed with the executive mystique and has
the power both to fine-tune his claims to the political exigencies and to adopt alternative means of achieving his goals
(Scigliano 1972).

It is one of the small ironies of history that a Republican
president, Nixon, was smashed in the process of attempting
to push the New Deal theory of the presidency to its logical
extreme. His insistence on the absolute power to impound
funds appropriated by Congress and to be the sole judge of
when the exigencies of national security required him to exercise an executive privilege to withhold whatever information he pleased from Congress, the courts, and the people was
met by an alliance of Congress and the courts. Nevertheless,
the presidency emerged with legal recognition of both the
impoundment power and executive privilege, recognition
that had not existed before. Similarly, President Nixon
suffered congressional refusal to accept two consecutive
presidential nominations to the Supreme Court, but the appointment power remained firmly in his hands. The Nixon
administration was repulsed in an attempt to restrain
publication of the Pentagon Papers in the name of national
security, but the security classification system is still with us
(Fisher 1978).

At the macro level, the causes of the president's problems are beyond his control. The increase in judicial willingness to intervene in administrative lawmaking was caused by a basic increase in judicial self-confidence resulting from changing public attitudes toward technocratic government. As Americans lost faith in the technocrat, the judge emerged as the lay hero riding forth to curb his arbitrary power. Because American attitudes toward technocracy are fundamentally ambivalent, we may shortly experience another swing in favor of the expert and a consequent decline in judicial activity. But there is little that any given president can do to bring this about except, perhaps, to learn that denouncing the bureaucracy strengthens the hands of judges.

On another front, however, each new president can contribute something to an increase in presidential discretion. Presidents have probably already learned that massive congressional delegations of lawmaking power to the bureaucracy are not necessarily delegations to them. They must also recognize that massive congressional creations of new statutory rights obligate administrative resources just as massive spending programs obligate financial resources. And along with the obligation come higher levels of judicial intervention. To counter this, the president can be careful about the kinds of legislation he proposes. A bill authorizing the federal government to spend X billion to improve education for the handicapped has far different consequences for presidential authority than one that gives the handicapped a right to adequate education and requires the Department of Education to write regulations sustaining that right. Presidents can control spending far more readily than rights once they have been let loose in the rights triangle. Presidents must learn to draft their statutes so as to promise government programs, not to guarantee legal rights. The movement toward rights legislation has been so strong, however, that any given president seems likely to make only limited headway against it.

What about the power of appointment? This is a very weak resource. As recent history shows, the voting of justices on matters of immediate constitutional concern.to the president does not depend on who appointed them. No president is likely to be so insightful about the twin mysteries of human personality and future events as to appoint just the right person for just those constitutional issues of presidential power that will arise during his term (Abraham 1974).

Nor is a president likely to find appointees who exactly share his value preferences. Justices appointed because they are tough on crime or pro-busing will turn out to have values different from his in other areas such as welfare or presidential power or economic regulation.

Even more important, the new iron triangle does not depend on the Supreme Court alone, but also on certain key courts of appeal and district courts. In many areas of law, appointments to the District of Columbia and 2nd Circuits are as crucial as those to the Supreme Court. Nevertheless, when so many judges sitting for life share judicial power, no single president's appointments make much immediate difference. There is no doubt that the five Democratic terms after 1932 filled the federal bench with judges whose ideology made the judicial activism of the 1960s and 1970s possible, but no single president could have achieved that result, nor did presidents Roosevelt and Truman intend the results they achieved.

Presidents ought to take their judicial appointments seriously as an opportunity to influence long-range policy directions and perhaps to have a more immediate impact on one or two areas of policymaking with which they are particularly concerned. The appointment power can do little, however, to bring the judicial rivals of the president to heel.

We must conclude that the federal judiciary plays a substantial role in the fragmentation of political authority that confronts the president. From time to time it can and does seize the initiative from him in setting the issue agenda and

proclaiming dominant values. And it can and does participate in the mass of low-level incremental decision-making
that fixes most of the policies of government in channels that
the president can do little about. Should we continue to pile
up statutes that mandate legal duties to public and private
authorities and assign rights to individuals and groups to obtain judicial enforcement of those mandates, we will not only
greatly increase the power of the nonelected branch to inter-
fere in our individual lives and set our national priorities, but
we will arrive at a stage of legal overkill that will reduce the
president's options in domestic policy to the vanishing point.
The president's best defense is to seize the initiative in
proclaiming values, but to avoid the rhetoric of rights that invites both judicial intervention and policy rigidity.

III

The Office

9

HUGH HECLO

The Changing
Presidential Office *

The crowded presidency. The Executive Office—its structure, programs, pressures. Constraints on internal management. The presidential party and the media. Diffusion of policymaking power. Government regulation or market competition? Presidential maneuvering within the White House bureaucracy. Five hazards in administering, president, and managing.

*This paper was prepared as part of a larger research project on the presidency supported by the National Academy of Public Administration.

The office of the president has become so complex, so pro-
pelled by its own internal bureaucratic dynamics, that it now
presents every new president with a major problem of internal management. Without a conscious effort to the contrary,
he may not even perceive the prison that his helpers erect
around him.

To tackle this problem successfully, a president must be
aware of how "his" office can constrain him and must use
"his" staff at least as effectively as they use him. He must be
aware of the management impact of everything he does. He
must choose his priorities carefully and pursue them
tenaciously lest he become dependent on the priorities of
everyone else around him. He must have a good sense of how
his staff act and interact. He must maintain a delicate balance between the Executive Office and his appointees in the
departments and agencies. Above all, he must set himself at
the center of a web of pressures and counterpressures that
ultimately serves his purposes.

THE INTERNAL MANAGEMENT PROBLEM
OF THE PRESIDENCY

Our most familiar image of the presidency finds a man, sitting alone, in the dimly lit Oval Office. Against this shadowy
background the familiar face ponders that ultimate expression of power, a presidential decision.

It is a compelling and profoundly misleading picture. Presidential decisions are obviously important. But a more accurate image would show a presidency composed of at least a
thousand people—a jumble of personal loyalists, professional technocrats, and bureaucratic staff with one man
struggling, often vainly, to stay abreast of it all. What that
familiar face ponders in the Oval Office is likely to be a series
of conversations with advisors or a few pages of paper con-

taining several options. These represent the last distillates produced from immense rivers of information flowing from sources—and condensed in ways—about which the president probably knows little. The great irony is that, as more and more forces combine to program the president, he sees only people who are trying to help him do what he wants.

In 1980 the Executive Office of the President (EOP) is composed of ten disparate major units, including a White House Office with its own two dozen or so basic subdivisions (see Figure 1). The number of people involved is subject to a variety of inventive accounting methods, but a reasonable approximation would be 500 or so people attached to the White House and another roughly 1,500 people in the rest of the EOP.[1] There seems little doubt that a trimmer, more rational, staffing arrangement would help a president meet national needs as well as substantially simplify any president's job of managing his own office. Thinking through that redesign problem is the burden of Chapter 10.

Yet, however the presidency is equipped with staffs and processes, the president's personal management problem remains. His choice is to run or to be run by his office. No conceivable staffing arrangement will meet all his needs, and yet every arrangement carries the potential of submerging his interests into those of his helpers and their machinery. All the trends suggest that the grip of this well-intentioned machinery on the president is likely to grow, just as it has grown in the past two decades. The president's great danger lies in thinking that by making decisions he is actually managing. His internal management problem—the underside of the presidency—is to use those who serve him without becoming dependent on them. He must avoid being victimized by their loyalty to him or by his loyalty to them. To put it most directly, I do not see how, given contemporary demands on the office, a president can exercise leadership without being quietly manipulative within that office.

Figure 1
The Executive Office of the President 1980

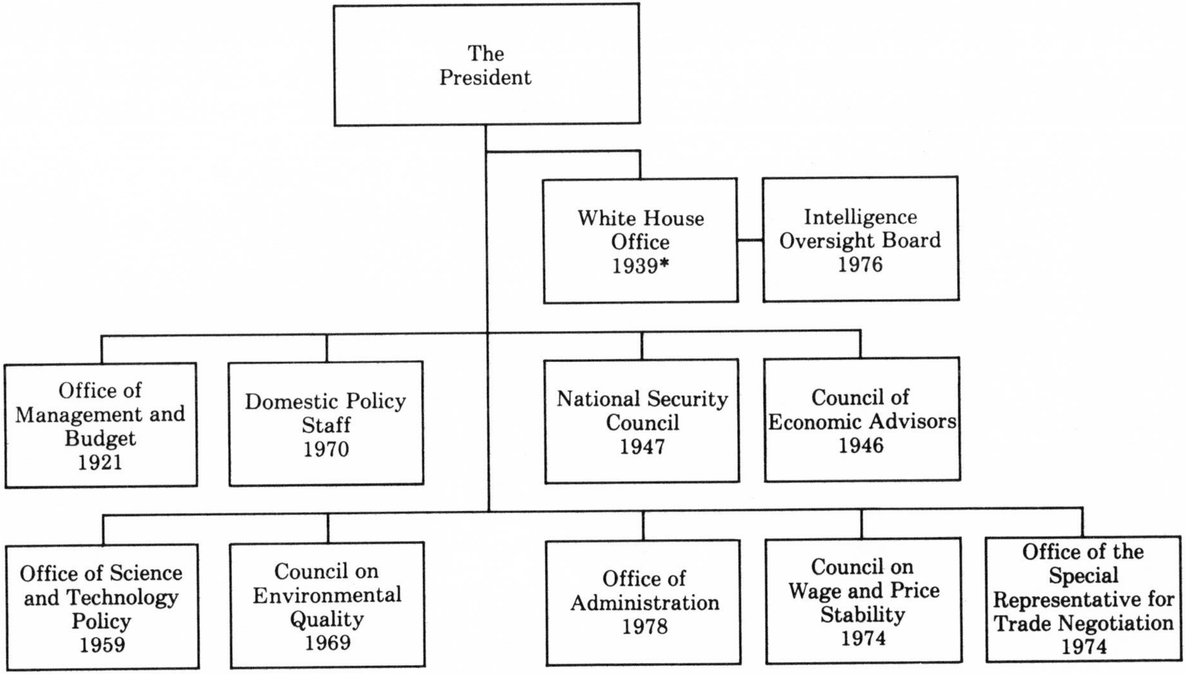

```
                              ┌──────────────┐
                              │     The      │
                              │  President   │
                              └──────────────┘

┌──────────────┐  ┌──────────────┐  ┌──────────────┐  ┌──────────────────┐
│  Office of   │  │   Domestic   │  │ White House  │  │  Intelligence    │
│ Management   │  │ Policy Staff │  │   Office      │  │ Oversight Board  │
│ and Budget   │  │    1970      │  │   1939*       │  │      1976        │
│    1921      │  └──────────────┘  └──────────────┘  └──────────────────┘
└──────────────┘

┌──────────────┐  ┌──────────────┐  ┌──────────────┐  ┌──────────────────┐
│  Office of   │  │ Council on   │  │  National    │  │   Council of     │
│ Science and  │  │Environmental │  │  Security    │  │   Economic       │
│ Technology   │  │  Quality     │  │  Council     │  │   Advisors       │
│  Policy      │  │   1969       │  │   1947       │  │     1946         │
│   1959       │  └──────────────┘  └──────────────┘  └──────────────────┘
└──────────────┘

                  ┌──────────────┐  ┌──────────────┐  ┌──────────────────┐
                  │  Office of   │  │ Council on   │  │   Office of the  │
                  │Administration│  │ Wage and     │  │     Special      │
                  │    1978      │  │ Price        │  │ Representative   │
                  └──────────────┘  │ Stability    │  │ for Trade        │
                                    │   1974       │  │ Negotiation      │
                                    └──────────────┘  │     1974         │
                                                      └──────────────────┘
```

CONSTRAINTS ON INTERNAL MANAGEMENT

At first blush, it would seem that the internal arrangements of his own office are simply a matter of presidential taste. And so they are in most unimportant respects. Apart from matters of style, the president's main area of discretion is the choice as to what personalities he will deal with directly in the everyday running of his office. Even this choice is likely to be constrained by personal commitments to familiar aides, particularly since no modern candidate can hope to negotiate the long-drawn-out campaign process without a bevy of loyal aides. Those who manage the campaign bureaucracy inevitably have a claim on the White House bureaucracy.

In terms of its *deep structure*, however, the office is largely a given that a president can change slowly if at all. This structure is a web of other people's expectations and needs. On the surface, the new president seems to inherit an empty house. In fact, he enters an office already shaped and crowded by other people's desires. What the would-be presidents seem to be reaching for on the nightly news is simply the top prize in our ultimate contest as a competitive society. What the winner grasps is an office that is the raw, exposed ganglion of government where immense lines of force come together in ways that no single person can control. The total effect is to program the modern president.

Legal and political pressures

One set of constraints arises from a growing number of statutory requirements placed on the office. Core advisory units of the presidency (Council of Economic Advisors, National Security Council, Domestic Council) were established by laws passed by Congress and can be altered only by persuading Congress to change these laws. A president can, of course, use or bypass this formal machinery, but the fact is that over the years these units have generally been accepted as important parts of the presidency and have generated expectations that presidents will not simply ride roughshod over their operations. For example, as President-elect Reagan prepared to take office, a key issue discussed was who would bring to him the work of staffs from the national security and domestic councils, not whether to have and to use these units in the first place.

Legal constraints also arise from statutory requirements which tell a president what he must do. At last count there were forty-three separate requirements for annually recurring presidential reports (environmental impacts, foreign arms sales, and so on). None of these reports are things about which a president bothers himself personally except in the rarest of circumstances. What they require are more staff work, more specialists, and more routines within the presidency. Each process gives someone a proprietary interest in that process—in other words, someone other than the president with a claim on what must get done in the presidency.

A second part of the web preventing a president from designing his own office is the political interest of outsiders. Many people, it turns out, have a stake in the internal arrangements of the presidency. Even a hint of major increases in presidential staff arouses immediate and intense congressional criticism. Thus President Carter in his first few months in office, for example, in order to avoid future trouble with his reorganization plans, had to informally promise a leading congressional committee chairman that he would not increase the size of the EOP even though important, nonpolitical parts of the presidency were seriously undermanned.

Congressional committees hold the purse strings for every major unit in the EOP; they can and have made life miserable for the head of a unit such as the president's Office of Management and Budget (OMB), requiring exhaustive and exhausting testimony, cutting funds for unfavored projects, and adding staff for functions bearing no relation to a president's interests. Since the Nixon administration, moreover, Congress has been far more reluctant to grant funds in special emergency or "management improvement" accounts which presidents could formerly use largely at their discretion. Even a president's papers are no longer his. Under a recent congressional enactment, President Reagan will be the first chief executive in our history who will not be able to take his papers away with him when he leaves office.

Congress is only the most obvious of the political constituencies constraining presidential management of the presidency. Various specialized communities have an interest in staking out claims to particular pieces of the Executive Office. This applies, for example, to the Office of Science and Technology Policy (disbanded in 1973 and reinstated in 1976 at the demand of the scientific community), environmentalists (Council on Environmental Quality), and many others in the recent past. More subtly, the Council of Economic Advisors serves as the voice of the economics profession and the National Security Council does likewise for professional students of foreign and military affairs. Even though each of these communities contains different viewpoints from which a president can pick and choose, he is not free to deny someone from these professional groups a major advisory role in the highest councils of his administration.[2]

Legal constraints and political constituencies in the presidency have grown in the past two decades, but a president can try to "manage around" them by observing the formalities. Whatever the statutory requirements, a president's real management system consists of whom he consults, where he bestows trust, and how he polices those in his trust. There are two remaining sets of constraints that have grown in recent years and that strike at the very heart of this real-life management system. Because they spring from deep-seated social and political trends, these two forces are not elements that can be managed around. Indeed, presidents under the necessity of responding to these twin pressures become the agents for programming their own office. The more that recent presidents have thought they were putting their personal stamp on the office and events, the more they have affirmed a larger design that they cannot control and can rarely comprehend.

The requisites of a presidential party

As far as one can tell from the historical record, the five presidents since Eisenhower did not consciously plan to create their own political parties. Yet that, in embryo, is what has come to exist in the White House. Consider for a moment some of the specialized subdivisions that existed in the Carter White House *before* the active start of the 1980 presidential campaign:

- Assistant to the President (Women's Affairs)
- Assistant to the President (Organizational Liaison)
- Special Assistant for Hispanic Affairs
- Special Assistant for Ethnic Affairs
- Special Assistant for Civil Rights
- Counselor to the President on Aging [ours, not his]
- Special Assistant for Consumer Affairs
- Assistant for Intergovernmental Affairs
- Assistant for Congressional Liaison
- Special Assistant to the President (Press and Public Relations)

Taken as a whole, the list indicates something more important than the desire of particular groups to have their representatives at the president's elbow. What these and similar political operatives for other presidents suggest is an attempt to reach out from the White House and to build at least some lines of reliable political support for presidents. If one were inventing a political party, these are exactly the types of office at branch headquarters that one would want to create. What is lacking is only the local cells that would give such an organization feet and hands. As President Carter discovered, fireside chats, town meetings, and convocations with local publishers and editors are no substitute for *that*.

The fact is that each president during the last twenty years has felt increasingly compelled to mobilize the White House to build the equivalent of a presidential party for governing. To some presidents (such as Johnson or Nixon) the inclination comes naturally but, whatever the vagaries of personality, every contemporary president has been under pressure to move in the same direction. The reason is clear, and it constitutes the substance of Part I of this book: a more politically volatile public, a less-manageable Congress, a disappearing party hierarchy, proliferating groups of single-minded activists which merge with the networks of policy experts discussed later. All these add up to a shifting political base of support for presidents. This is not atomization — a breaking down of our political life into tiny elemental particles (see King 1978). It is rampant pluralism, with groups crosscutting the political landscape into incoherent patterns. Atomization would produce anomie and anarchy. Rampant pluralism produces what we in fact have: unnegotiable demands, political stagnation, and stalemate.

People in the White House have had little choice but to try and cope with this trend by shoring up the president's own base of support. Given the succession of one-term presidents since the Kennedy assassination, no one would want to claim great success for these efforts, but that is not the point. What modern president could reasonably be expected to give up the attempt at using the White House to build a presidential party?

Once that fact is admitted, we can begin to see how even the most loyal aides and the presidents themselves cooperate in the programming of the modern presidency. When mayors or governors have problems, it is not enough to refer their

calls to some departmental appointee or bureaucrat. Doing
that will not build the strong relations which a president
needs. Hence, someone in the White House is tasked to keep
an eye on "intergovernmental relations." A small staff
develops. The mayors' and governors' telephone calls are
returned from the White House, their entrée to the
bureaucracy smoothed a little. By helping them, the president helps himself. In the longer run, however, the president
acquires a staff with a vested interest in continuing to process such problems, and he confirms the larger expectation
that he is somehow responsible for seeing to it that a fiend-
ishly complex federal system works to the satisfaction of all
concerned.

There is no need to belabor the point. The same dynamic
applies in one area of presidential activity after another. Will
the president work exclusively through top congressional
leaders, none of whom can control the actions of the legislature? Or will the president try to string together the many
pieces of Congress that are in business for themselves? All
the pressures of the moment dictate the latter course. Ac-
cordingly, the president acquires an extensive congressional
liaison staff, doing favors and attracting demands for more.
President Carter in his first year showed little willingness to
be programmed as a builder of his own party in Congress,
and he paid dearly for following his preferences. Can a president rest content in channeling relations he needs with all
the interest groups in our mobilized society through his party's national committee or a federal department? The
answer began to come clear as early as 1940 when Franklin
Delano Roosevelt, in seeking a third term, had one aide
working part-time on relations with ethnics and unions and
another preparing materials on what the New Deal had done
"for the benefit of Negroes."[3] Since then a veritable political
technocracy of such people has developed, entangling the
presidential office in extensive networks of activists interested in this and that issue.

There is — or seems to be — a way out of all these entanglements produced by the need of presidents to create a quasi-party for themselves. Richard Neustadt (1980, p. 238) described it in late 1979:

> While national party organizations fall away, while congressional party discipline relaxes, while interest groups proliferate and issue networks rise, a President who wishes to compete for leadership in framing policy and shaping coalitions has to make the most he can out of his popular connection. Anticipating home reactions, Washingtonians . . . are vulnerable to any breeze from home that presidential words and sights can stir. . . . The President with television talent will be likely to put his very talent at the center of his hopes when he takes office.

As viewers of the past four presidents can attest, even chief executives with a definite untalent for television are likely to seize on the tube to deploy their leadership. Unfortunately, by trying to do a little programming of their own on TV, presidents do not escape their personal management problem and may (especially if talented) only add to it by mistaking a successful screen image for the substance of leadership.

The tube is a blunt instrument. It allows a president to explain himself, catch a mood, create a persona. These are important, but they are not things through which a president escapes the programming that crowds in on his leadership. On the contrary. The generalized utility of television for the president has a counterpart in the media's need for its own kind of presidency. The increasingly powerful news media need stories, preferably with a White House backdrop. They need presidential statements to help create the story, favored access and background information from the White House staff to give them an edge in the competition for stories. When all else fails, the media need care and feeding by the White House press office with a steady stream of handouts to those who cannot find a story. This communications industry complex of the presidency is a far cry from the early off-the-record chats that presidents used in order to give the "boys in the press" an idea of their thinking and activities. The media's expectations run against the grain of the president's managerial needs for private deliberations, for discretion as to when to get into or out of the news, and for an administration that appears united. Television language accurately captures the disutility of the medium for presidential management purposes. The tube *follows* stories, but the president must first manage a process for choosing where *he* wants to go. TV *covers* events in general, but the president's office needs to give sustained attention to specific, often technical, matters where there is never a clear story line.

The requisites for a presidential party, including television, are probably with the White House to stay. The members of his political technocracy will be a constraint or an opportunity—usually some weighting of both—for a president, depending on how he maneuvers among them. But if they are not to be pure constraint, the watchword must be active presidential maneuvering, not lying in repose or trusting in his aides' undoubtedly sincere professions of loyalty. Yet this section has referred only to the political base of the president's office. Another trend strikes even deeper into the presidency than has our growing political fragmentation and volatility. This is a massive social diffusion of policymaking powers.

The hemorrhage of presidential power

The classic question to ask about the presidential office is what has happened to its power. It is a question that invites a thumbs up or thumbs down vote: increasing or decreasing? More imperial or more post-Watergate? The developments of the last twenty years call for a more complicated answer. Presidential power has increased by becoming more extended, scattered, and shared; it has decreased by becoming less of a prerogative, less unilateral, and less closely held by the man himself. The right word for what has happened to the power of the office is diffusion, not dissipation. This condition exists, not basically because Congress or other groups have made successful grabs at the president's power, but because of the very nature of modern policymaking and the growth of federal activity.

Consider for a moment the antibureaucracy Reagan transition bureaucracy. This effort, writ small, is a good snapshot of what has happened to presidential power. The president-elect begins before inauguration with a $2 million, taxpayer-funded, budget, a building, a motor pool, a minimum of seven dozen advisory committees, a communications system, and official stationery for the "Office of the President-Elect." If one imposed more formality than ever exists in practice, an organization chart early in the transition effort would look roughly as shown in Figure 2.

What, a person may well ask, is going on here? Certainly some of this is intended only for public consumption, some as a political liaison job for building the relations necessary to a presidential party. But there is more than that, and it shows up in the substantive work of the various policy groups and "issue clusters." The president-elect may have a few general themes in mind, but to have any impact on complex modern policies he needs to have specific, usually highly technical, proposals. Moreover, whatever he might want to do to increase *or* to decrease federal government activity, he is automatically entangled in a web of relations with other people who can have a decisive impact on the same issue—not just congressmen, but a bureaucracy of congressional staffs numbering well over 13,000 professionals; not just mayors and governors, but analysts and lobbyists to represent these elected officials in Washington; not just grasping interest groups, but a mini-industry in the nation's capital employing 15,000 or more full-time professionals.

The exact numbers are less important than the fact that the federal government has acquired responsibilities requir-

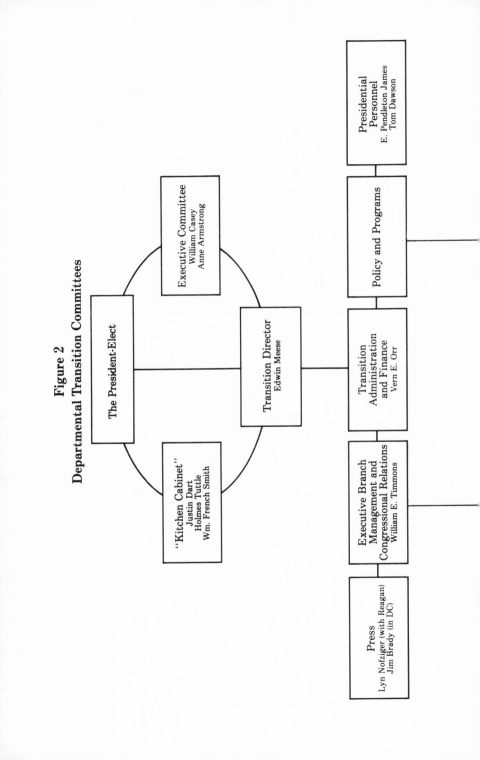

Figure 2
Departmental Transition Committees

The President-Elect

"Kitchen Cabinet"
Justin Dart
Holmes Tuttle
Wm. French Smith

Executive Committee
William Casey
Anne Armstrong

Transition Director
Edwin Meese

Presidential Personnel
E. Pendleton James
Tom Dawson

Policy and Programs

Transition Administration and Finance
Vern E. Orr

Executive Branch Management and Congressional Relations
William E. Timmons

Press
Lyn Nofziger (with Reagan)
Jim Brady (in DC)

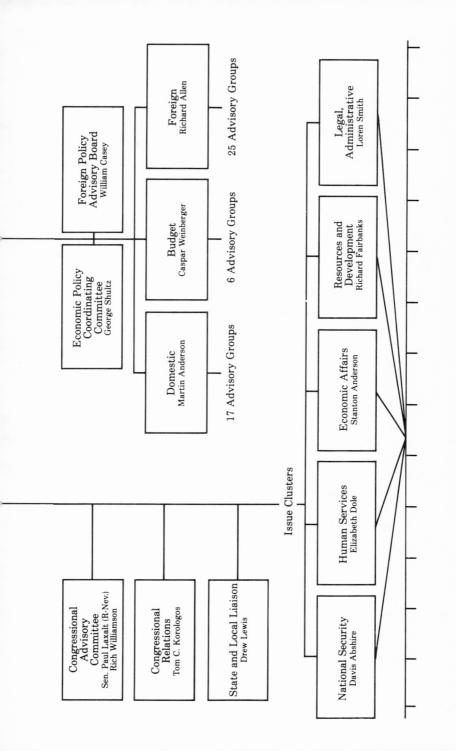

Congressional Advisory Committee
Sen. Paul Laxalt (R-Nev.)
Rich Williamson

Congressional Relations
Tom C. Korologos

State and Local Liaison
Drew Lewis

Economic Policy Coordinating Committee
George Shultz

Foreign Policy Advisory Board
William Casey

Domestic
Martin Anderson

Budget
Caspar Weinberger

Foreign
Richard Allen

17 Advisory Groups

6 Advisory Groups

25 Advisory Groups

Issue Clusters

National Security
Davis Abshire

Human Services
Elizabeth Dole

Economic Affairs
Stanton Anderson

Resources and Development
Richard Fairbanks

Legal, Administrative
Loren Smith

ing successful linkages between all manner of public, semi-public, and private groups. This applies not only to functions acquired in the last two decades—consumer protection, medical and school financing, mass transportation, and so on—but also to older tasks enhanced with more demanding goals: occupational safety, natural resource use and protection, economic management and industrial revitalization, and so on. Can the president, with a few themes and a handful of aides, negotiate his ideas through these linkages and past the many other knowledgeable participants with a stake in what he is doing? Not likely. And so the helpers, offices, and briefing books pile up on the president-elect no less than on the presidency.

The United States does not have a high-level, government-wide, civil service that could (as in European countries) help a new chief executive and his top team turn their ideas into administrative realities; there is scarcely even a low-level civil service in the White House to help with the paperwork. The increasing resort to transition bureaucracies is one accommodation to this fact, thereby loading onto the presidency more of the responsibility for turning themes into playable scores than would otherwise be the case. But with or without a competent civil service, the very nature of federal activity impels the presidency to become a predictable bureaucracy so that other participants can play their parts.

Imagine, for example, a president committed to replacing government regulation with market competition and incentives in various policy areas. Having grown accustomed to the old regulations and possessing the power to make or break any proposed "market solution" that affects them, people in Congress, the departments, interest groups, and subnational governments need to know what, in detail, the president proposes to do. To create a market where none has been implies some forethought about how far it will extend, what transitional arrangements with the affected groups will be made, how this will affect programs in related areas,

what rules of competition will be enforced, and who will enforce them. Since markets typically impose some costs and
spill-overs that many people consider unfair, thought must
also be given to compensations, subsidies, and other kinds of
protections (more regulations!). All of this implies presidential helpers who can work knowledgeably with planners,
analysts, economists, administrators, inspectors, lawyers,
not to mention all the political legwork involved. To survive
in this kind of world, the president needs to be surrounded by
policy technocrats no less than by the political technocrats of
his quasi-party. But how can the president know that all
these bright, committed, and (like the rest of us) self-
interested people are doing what *he* would want?

THE PRESIDENT AS MANAGER

Whoever the president and whatever his style, the political
and policy bureaucracies crowd in on him. They are there in
his office to help, but their needs are not necessarily his
needs. Delegation is unavoidable; yet no one aide or combination of aides has his responsibilities or takes his oath of
office. However much the president trusts personal friends,
political loyalists, or technocrats, he is the person that the
average citizen and history will hold accountable.

If this diagnosis of the presidential office is close to the
truth, then there is one big prescription. The president must
take responsibility for deprogramming himself. Since the
deep structure of the office is shaped by trends well outside
his control, the president must try to preserve his
maneuverability within this structure—a maneuverability
not just in the images of personal style, but in the substance
of work that gets done around him. Trusting a chief of staff
or a few senior aides is not enough. Behind the scenes, the
president must manage and manipulate if he is not to be

suffocated by the political and policy technocrats of Washington.

To manage is something that falls between administering in detail and merely presiding in general. At most, the president himself can directly administer one or two major issues and half a dozen or so senior aides. And to preside is a dangerous abdication to the momentum of forces around him. It is difficult to put the president's management chore into words without seeming to be cynical or sinister. To speak of the president's manipulation of the people in his office should not summon up Nixonian memories, for if ever there was a president cut off from (though criminally responsible for) what was going on in his own office, it was Richard Nixon. The appropriate mentor is still the first inhabitant of the modern presidency, Franklin Roosevelt. For a paraplegic president, his appreciation for the primary task of internal management came almost instinctively: to use those who waited on him without becoming dependent on them.

Roosevelt had his tactics; other presidents will have theirs. But the basic necessity for personal management remains and grows as modern presidents become increasingly penned in. Programmed more than paralyzed, today's president needs many different eyes and ears for the things he should know, legs to take him where he should be, and protective devices to avoid situations that leave him vulnerable.

How to do all this? The exact structure and personalities are less important than sometimes thought. Given the record of recent administrations, there are some useful guidelines to be drawn from experience, usually of the painful variety.

1. Self-awareness is the place to begin. The president, by his own actions and even more by the anticipations of his actions that he creates in other people, generates a kind of de facto management system. The more he is willing to do, the more he will be asked to do. The more questions he will take rather than passing them to others, the more he will be

asked. The more unconditional his support of his staff seems, the less the incentive for good performance. The more widely spread his trust, the less its value. These are obvious points familiar to any executive, but under the crush of daily emergencies and decisions in the presidency they become more important and easier to overlook.

2. Selectivity needs to be a part of self-awareness. Since the president can personally administer only a few issues and can manage only a handful of aides, he needs to know the one or two things that matter to him most, subject to changing circumstances. Without this selectivity, there are no goals to work towards and disorientation quickly spreads throughout his office and administration. Most of the rest of his presidency, to put it bluntly, will consist of managing for damage control in the history books.

3. Self-awareness and selectivity have to be linked to a consciousness of the bureaucratic terrain in his own office through which the president is moving. A presidential bureaucracy—rather, a collection of bureaucracies—seems to be with us to stay, and its workings pose special hazards for the president. The following are perhaps the most common hazards:

● Presidential staffs tend to bring into the presidency conflicts and controversies raging among departments, congressional committees, and interest groups. This means that the president, unless he makes a conscious effort to the contrary, is likely to be closely identified with the inevitable ebb and flow of debate that occurs on complex policy matters—a tentative finding this way, an interim decision that way. Even the most firm-minded president is bound to appear indecisive in this situation. Perhaps the best safeguard is for the president to allow a great deal of "precooking" of policies some distance away from him, with low-visibility participation by presidential staff members to protect his interests. This approach seems most appropriate for the bulk of issues that are not among his few priority concerns.

● Each presidential staff, in order to carry weight inside the office and with outsiders, seeks to invent ways that allow it to claim that its members are acting "at the direction of the president." And each such invention ties the president more closely to the work of unfamiliar helpers. Because all these people have a stake in generating presidential decisions, his influence and public standing are likely to be on the line in more places than he might wish. A president can help himself by making sure that issues coming to him really are matters on which he, rather than someone else, has to make a formal decision. The exact machinery is less important than the need for the president to choose some particular system—an administrative secretary, a chief of staff, a secretariat, a formal procedure of decision memoranda—for disciplining the way he gets into decisions and for keeping tabs on what he, rather than anyone else, wants done. It is only the president who, by his own actions, can enforce and sustain any such system.

● The presidential bureaucracy has a natural desire for self-preservation. Internal conflicts which would convey more information to the president by being openly fought out tend to be submerged in sub rosa court politics inside the White House and the rest of the EOP. Rather than a free-for-all among presidential staffs, what typically exists is a kind of truce by which each staff settles for a piece of the president's attention and decision-making. This hardly helps the president to know what is going on. To overcome this tendency the president, again by his own behavior, needs to make it clear that he expects in-house disagreements, that suppression of contrary views is punished, and that all can live to fight another day—as long as the battle does not continue once the president has made up his own mind. The same staff procedures used to keep the president out of unnecessary decisions can probably be used to create a fair hearing and due process for such internal conflicts.

● Because of the trends identified earlier, the presidential office tends to be divided into two large hemispheres: a political technocracy and a policy technocracy. On almost every conceivable issue the president needs to hear, unvarnished, the facts from both sides. In general, the competition between the two hemispheres for presidential attention has tended to become unequal as media attention has increased and political fragmentation grown. Political staff work tends to drive out longer-term, institutional interests in policy and administration. This tendency is amplified if the president makes it clear that he gives serious attention only to his short-term personal stakes in the issues coming before him.

4. Paradoxically, one of the most effective ways for the president to manage his own office is through the use of his appointees in the departments and agencies. If these department heads are known to have intimate knowledge of the president's thinking, and therefore seem likely to be backed by the president in disputes with White House staffers, White House aides will likely be kept in their proper place as assistants to the president rather than as assistant presidents.

Unfortunately, every new administration seems to raise false expectations by proclaiming that the president intends to manage through his cabinet officers, or words to that effect. In fact, their individual frames of reference are too narrow to give the president all the perspective he needs, and their collective interests are a fiction without active presidential support and guidance. Hence the president must manage through both his own office's bureaucracies *and* his department and agency heads. In general, the cabinet is a communication—not a decision-making—device. It carries information to and from the president. At their best, cabinet officers help the president by telling him things he would not otherwise hear, by conveying his sense of a unified administration, by keeping presidential staff in line. It is the president's management job to see that when department and agency heads fight among themselves—as they inevitably will—it is done in front of him and tells him something worth knowing.

5. In addition to his political staffs, policy offices, and cabinet officers, the president typically has access to his closest personal friends: the Kitchen Cabinet. Experience suggests that it is safest to keep these advisors outside his office staffs or official departmental family. The reason is simple and practical. If the president is to protect himself as he manages, any other person must be dispensable. Because not everyone wishes the president well, putting a close personal friend in an official position leaves both that person, and through him, the president, vulnerable. Informal advisors attract less attention, are changed more easily, and perform their greatest services precisely because they are not caught up in the daily grind of government machinery. Exceptions can, of course, be found; President Eisenhower and President Kennedy made effective use of their brothers in official positions, as did President Truman of his friend John Snyder. But for every Snyder there is a Bert Lance, and it is just as well to recognize the risks at the outset. Only the president can decide whether it is worth having someone so close that his presidency will be gravely wounded through that person's loss to scandal, the appearance of scandal, or larger policy ends.

Cautions about these five hazards add up to an approach to presidential management that tries to use the various tensions and counterpressures inherent in the job. The counterpressures within his own office staffs, between them and cabinet officers, and between all these and the president's

closest personal loyalists are opportunities as well as constraints. A president with some self-awareness can use this
cat's cradle of tensions to help see to it that he is at the
center of things when he wants to be and "out of it" when he
needs to be. The management aim cannot, therefore, simply
be to create a unified team; it must be to create the counterpressures that will be useful to him, lest he become victimized by his own helpers.

Others, no doubt, will see things differently, but this much
seems clear: a modern president who cannot govern his own
office is unlikely to be able to govern anything else.

10

PETER L. SZANTON

Reconstructing the Presidency

The need for coherence and direction in national policy. Single-issue constituencies as a threat. Distributed sacrifice. Integrating a plural society. The role of presidential staffs. Tasks of the president and of the presidency. Program effectiveness. Interdepartmental conflict. Cabinet responsibilities; an inner cabinet, a reorganized EOP.

The crisis of confidence in our leadership is a recurring theme of this book, as it is of much current political commentary. There seems to be widespread understanding now that our institutions are quick to create disputes and slow to resolve them, adept at representing special interests and poor at insisting on common ones, and far more sensitive to pressures of the moment than to longer-term national needs.

If the problem, in part, is a dispersal of power from the center, then a main remedy must be to strengthen our central institutions and to tighten the links among them. To any such effort a strengthening of the presidency must be central.

The obstacles to such a course—obstacles emplaced by the president's competitors for political influence, by legitimate and deep-seated concerns for pluralism, and by the size and difficulty of the nation's tasks—are formidable. After reviewing the arguments for wishing to strengthen the presidency as an instrument for the coordination of federal government, this chapter outlines three linked means of accomplishing this. These involve using key cabinet officers to manage a broader range of interdepartmental issues, including those officers far more deeply than has been recent practice in the president's own decision-making, and restructuring presidential staffs so as to make them better able to view problems as the president is obliged to see them, not as political (but not administrative), foreign (but not domestic), or substantive (but not symbolic)—or vice versa—but whole.

During the century that ended in 1960 only two American presidents who sought a second term failed to win it. Since 1960 one president has entered a second term; none has completed one. Many factors, accident among them, help account for that change. But surely the major cause is this: as public expectations of the president ballooned during the last two decades, the capacities of the presidency shrank.

If the problem were simply a disparity between the expected and the possible, a change of expectations could resolve it. President Reagan might take advantage of current skepticism about government to teach the country that presidential power should be limited, and that it is. But the matter is much harder. Current expectations of the presidency are mainly reasonable; our politics requires what only the president can lead in providing: coherence and direction in national policy. Indeed, at least three recent trends appear to have made a strong presidency more important than ever before.

One development is simply the steady expansion in both the number and complexity of the responsibilities assigned to the federal government. As recently as 1940 the federal government was, by current standards, tiny. Its total budget that year for the first time exceeded $10 billion; its purposes were limited, its functions specialized and relatively self-contained. The federal budget is now roughly fifteen times that amount in real dollars, and the government undertakes vastly more than its inherent and irreducible jobs—maintaining order, dispensing justice, conducting relations with other states, defending the nation from external threat. It now takes responsibility for stable prices, full employment, environmental quality, equal opportunity, consumer protection, safety in the work place, and so on. It is a measure of the complexity of these newer objectives that they transcend the scope of any single federal department. Each, therefore, requires goal-setting, decision-making, coordination of actions, and the evaluation of results at some level above the departments. Indeed, none are fully within the power of the federal government as a whole. Many require coordinated or at least consistent actions, not only among federal agencies, but with state and local governments and a range of private interests as well. Some require collaborative arrangements with other nations.

A second development has been the now widely recognized erosion of authority in exactly those central institutions of American society that might help accomplish such consistent action. Not merely the presidency, but many of the institutions that have inculcated common values, mediated differences, and helped strike broad acceptable compromises have lost their authority over the last two decades. Congressional leadership no longer imposes the discipline of even ten years ago. The ability of candidates at every level to raise money and to achieve recognition in their own names means that elected officials no longer owe strong loyalty to political parties. Abuses of power, mistakes of policy, a more sophisticated citizenry, a far less deferential press have worn away the presumption of rightness that formerly accompanied most official action. The complexity of the external world and the absence, for almost twenty years, of any clear-cut challenge from abroad have permitted the relaxation of common bonds.

And as integrating forces have weakened, the power of particular interests has grown. Whether devoted to the right to life or to bear small arms, or to ERA or Israel, single-issue constituencies now threaten any dissenting officeholder whose seat is not absolutely secure. The result is that the power of our political institutions to mediate between contending interests and to impose a measure of discipline on our pluralistic politics has eroded just as it has become more important.

The third development compounds the problem. In a period of falling comparative productivity in the United States, rising raw materials prices, persistent inflation, and requirements for increased defense expenditures, many of the major political issues of the near future will involve not the allocation of benefits but, as in the current case of energy, the distribution of sacrifice. In no political system are losses accepted readily. In a system whose integrating institutions are weak and whose authority is widely diffused, they may not be accepted at all. Faced with the need to allocate costs, a system of diffused authority tends toward paralysis. The energy issue again illustrates the point.

So for those concerned about the effectiveness of the American government in the last decades of the 20th century, a main task—perhaps the overriding task—is to attempt to reconstruct those institutions that tend to resolve disputes rather than to create them, that represent common interests rather than special ones, that look to the longer term rather than to the pressures of the moment. More precisely, the task is to strengthen both those institutions individually and the connections among them—connections like those that previously linked the majority party, congressional leadership, and the presidency.

The presidency is the key. It always has been.

Energy in the executive is a leading character in the definition of good government. It is essential to the protection of the community against foreign attacks; it is not less essential to the steady administration of the laws ... to the security of liberty against the enterprises and assaults of ambition, of faction, and of anarchy.

So did *The Federalist*, No. 70, put it. All the more so now. Of the three branches of government, only one has a chief. Only one official is elected by the nation as a whole; only one is expected to seek the welfare of the whole; only one speaks for the whole. The president is the single point in our system at which civil and military, foreign and domestic, legislative and executive, administrative and political, come together. One point, of course, is not enough. No matter how skillfully used, the powers of the presidency alone cannot manage all the integrative tasks of a plural society. The Congress, governors' and mayors' associations, political parties, labor and business leadership, umbrella organizations of every kind, must share in that work. So the larger task is not simply to strengthen the presidency; it is to revive all the integrating institutions and to create more collaborative relations among them.[1] That, I believe, is the context in which rethinking the office of the presidency should be approached.

But it is worth noting that this view conflicts with both doctrine and practice. Americans have long believed that, except in time of national emergency, the authority of the president should be sharply limited and, correspondingly, that the office of the presidency should be modest in size and responsibility. The aim of our constitutional arrangements, as Justice Brandeis succinctly put it, was "not to promote efficiency but to preclude the exercise of arbitrary power." The widespread view that government is too big has forced all recent presidents to try to hold down the size of the White House and of the Executive Office of the President (EOP) — the only entities they themselves control. The truth that good management means delegation has been read to mean that the presidential staff must be specialized and limited — as though its tasks were technical and few. And, interestingly, nowhere in the executive branch is there an institutional advocate for a contrary view. Cabinet officers wish to maximize their own autonomy and, while individual EOP offices may propose a modest expansion for themselves, none has either the incentive or the breadth of concern to propose a more comprehensive or better integrated overall staff to the president.

Other pressures have also applied. The Congress is inherently hostile to strong presidential direction in programmatic areas. It prefers independent bureaux to well-integrated cabinet departments, and autonomous departments to tightly run administrations; the resulting autonomy leaves the executive branch more accessible to congressional influence. So the larger and more influential the EOP has become, the stronger the congressional impulse to formalize and constrain it. Thus in recent years the director of the Office of Management and Budget (OMB) has become subject to Senate confirmation and is called more and more frequently to testify. And whether the president's national security assistant should not similarly be confirmed has recently been the subject of Senate hearings.

The last two decades have, moreover, appeared to show that presidents were not excessively weak but dangerously strong. Vietnam seemed to demonstrate that even in the realm in which the Congress and the country have traditionally deferred to presidential leadership — that of national security policy — presidents could not be trusted. And Watergate displayed a president attempting illegally to weaken his domestic opposition.

Finally, the notion that the president's staff should be small has also drawn strength from several bureaucratic truths. Large staffs are not simply extensions of the president's will; they express views and biases of their own. And the bigger they are, the more remote from the president and the less accurately they speak for him. Presidential staffs, moreover, like staffs generally, tend to skew policy. Free of the discipline that program management imposes, often lacking much experience in government, they are typically quick to suggest initiatives and slow to recognize the weight of prior commitments and the constraints of law or custom. Unable to implement the policies they propose, they are not likely to know whether others can implement them or not. And close to the seat of power and typically frustrated, as presidents are, by the slow pace of governmental action, presidential staffs often misconceive their role. They are tempted to redo rather than review, to engage in "micromanagement" from afar.

Taken together, these are potent reasons—constitutional, political, and bureaucratic—for concern about a more capable EOP. They account for the fact that, while the Executive Office has grown substantially since its establishment in 1939, it is still small and, more important, disparate and poorly structured. At the end of the Carter administration the EOP, as counted by a panel on presidential management of the National Academy of Public Administration (1980), consisted of 1,700 people organized into ten principal units:[2] the Office of Management and Budget, by far the largest with a staff of almost 600; the Domestic Policy Staff of approximately 50; a National Security Council staff of 80; the Council of Economic Advisers, the Council on Environmental Quality, the Office of Science and Technology, and the Office of the Special Representative for Trade Negotiation, each employing fewer than 50 people; a Council on Wage and Price Stability of some 90 employees; and some 200 support personnel in an Office of Administration. Finally, there were lumped into the White House Office some 400 additional persons—assistants to the president for various functions, the press secretary, the counsel, congressional liaison office, advisers on consumer, Hispanic, aging and ethnic affairs, appointment secretaries, speech writers and their staffs, and a first lady's staff. It is an Executive Office formed by accretion, impressive neither for the logic of its design nor for its recent performance.

WHAT NEEDS DOING?

What tasks need to be performed above the level of the cabinet departments, at what level of detail, and how close to the president? The answers to these three questions should control the design of the White House and the EOP. It may be useful to think of those tasks in terms of the simple four-cell matrix in Figure 1.

The tasks of the president mean here those he must perform personally even though they may require substantial staff support. Tasks of the presidency are those that no president should ordinarily perform himself but that must be accomplished at some level above the departments, and in his name. Each of these categories can be, in turn, divided into relatively routine tasks on the one hand and critical ones on the other.

These simple categories seem useful because they highlight an interesting fact. The relatively routine functions of both the president and the presidency have changed little in recent years, and both are now passably staffed. But the high priority tasks of both the president and the presidency have changed substantially. It is they that seem now beyond the capacity of the president or the EOP to perform at the level their importance requires.

Figure 1

Tasks of the President and Presidency

	Routine	Critical
President	Maintaining relationships	High politics
Presidency	Oversight and review	Coordination

Let us glance briefly at the more routine jobs. Those of the president himself are concerned mainly with the maintenance of various relationships: with the public, special constituencies, and political colleagues. They involve steady contact with the Congress, the media, governors and mayors, and with particular constituencies of high political importance. With the atomization of Congress it has become necessary to deal with a very large number of individual members of Congress rather than simply focussing, as presidents as recent as Lyndon Johnson could do, on the leaders and key committee chairmen in each house. Similarly, with the growth of special-interest politics, the president is probably obliged to show personal concern for a wide range of particular sensitivities and, as federal, state, and local responsibilities have intertwined, the White House needs better working relationships with governors and mayors. The president must therefore now maintain a large congressional relations office and smaller staffs for liaison with particular private-interest groups and with state and local officials. But these offices now exist, and their functions are more or less adequately performed. The president's problem, as the previous chapter has argued, is to avoid becoming their captive.

The more routine functions of the presidency, basically those of oversight and review, need strengthening. Like any executive who delegates responsibilities, the president must see to it that the performance of his agents is monitored and assessed. Two questions should dominate such reviews: Are programs working? Are discretionary actions of the departments broadly consistent with presidential policies?

Program effectiveness has recently drawn little sustained attention—largely, one suspects, because many questionable programs have built up a daunting degree of political support. It is in the relatively rare cases where a program is not yet in place (and thus lacks many of the supporter-dependents it will later acquire) but its future is of such public interest as to deeply engage the president himself that serious reviews of probable effectiveness are undertaken in the EOP. President Carter's decision on the B−1 bomber had this character, and was supported by substantial staff work. But where these conditions are not met, the question of program effectiveness is normally so far avoided that even sustained and large-scale corruption, taking place just where one would expect to find it (in a vast central purchasing agency like the General Services Administration, for example), goes unnoticed. But a competently led OMB, energetically exercising its management mandate in conjunction with annual budgetary reviews, would probably be sufficient to perform this function.

Similarly, departmental action is rarely reviewed for consistency with presidential policy except when the departments propose explicit new policy measures—where their legislative proposals, for example, are subjected to the standard OMB legislative clearance process. But again, current OMB and domestic policy and national security staffs could readily undertake this task. Only presidential insistence that they do so, and the development of simple notice and clearance processes, would be required.

It is in the two crucial right-hand boxes that presidential capacities need real renovation. The highest priority tasks of the president himself—labeled here "high politics"— involve that limited number of hard decisions in which the president himself must be personally decisive. Classically, these are decisions of three kinds: the ten or twenty politically toughest trade-offs in each year's budget; the resolution of persistent disputes among cabinet-level officials on key issues of foreign relations or of domestic policy; and the design of major new policy initiatives—the Great Society programs that defined the Johnson administration, for example, or Nixon's revenue sharing.

The president is currently well staffed for only one of these responsibilities, that of the budget. To help him understand, assess, and resolve nonbudgetary disputes among cabinet officials, existing EOP offices may be adequate in size but they are poorly structured. The separate national security, domestic policy, and economic staffs operate largely in isolation. They thus tend not to clarify but to obscure exactly what makes major issues so hard to fully understand or sensibly resolve, namely, that most such issues have "foreign" *and* "economic" *and* "domestic" causes and that decisions about them will have "foreign" and "economic" and "domestic" consequences. Neither immigration policy nor the choice of anti-inflation measures, nor grain sales to the Soviet Union, nor the tolerable rate of import of Japanese automobiles, nor the size of the U.S. budget deficit, can usefully be placed within any one of those three categories. Like all major issues of national policy, they must be assessed in all three dimensions. Often, of course, they are so broadly assessed even under current arrangements. The fact that Treasury's responsibilities involve portions of each of the three realms proves helpful. So, in the Carter National Security Council, did the presence of an assistant to the president for the economic summit conferences who exercised his charter broadly. But the inherent tendency of the separate staffs is to view matters simply in light of their own expertise, and the occasional tendency of their chiefs is to seek the triumph of their own policy views rather than the completion of a balanced process of decision.

And for designing major new policy initiatives there is now no remotely adequate mechanism for imaginatively considering questions involving more than one department. What staff could be assigned, say, the rethinking of U.S. policy toward Mexico in the light of the full range of U.S. concerns at play—a range that (to say nothing of Mexican concerns) includes Mexican oil and gas, the costs and benefits of "undocumented" aliens, the sentiments of Hispanic voters in the United States, fishing rights in Mexican waters, the political evolution of Central America, the control of U.S. drug traffic, black-Hispanic tensions in the United States? There is no need, of course, to staff such an enterprise predominantly from the Executive Office; indeed, it would be essential to deeply involve each of the many affected departments. But any such broad reassessment requires strong direction and some staff support from persons whose responsibilities are broader and whose concerns are less parochial than can typically be true of departmental officials. Normally that breadth, and the needed sensitivity to the president's perspective, can only come from the EOP. Uncontrolled trial by combat among the affected departments will produce, as it did in the Carter administration's intense but unavailing effort to frame a new urban strategy, only bitter feelings and bad policy.

Despite its bland label, "coordination," the final cell contains the hardest challenge. The reason, as noted earlier, is that the purposes of the federal government are now vastly larger in scale and more ambitious in intent than ever before. Stable prices, full employment, conservation of the environment, maintenance of international influence—each important national goal is beyond the reach of any single cabinet department. The agencies responsible for portions of those goals must therefore be guided by some design that is larger than any department can itself create. Establishing that design, and coordinating departmental actions to insure that they conform to it, must be mainly performed in the Executive Office.

That is all the more true now because major federal objectives not only transcend departmental goals; those objectives may now be inconsistent. When this is so, the potential agents of coordination outside the Executive Office can no longer function as they once did. Historically, there have been at least two such agents. For domestic programs, they were state, city, and county governments. Local governments could previously—if laboriously—assemble for themselves more or less coherent packages of federal programs (housing subsidies, road construction, waste treatment) that would serve their own ends (renovation of an urban core). Federal programs were funded and managed by separate agencies. They called for different information, set varying standards, operated on unrelated schedules, and were therefore difficult to pull together. But they were not flatly inconsistent. Frequently that is no longer the case; an industrial development program, for example, may seek what an environmental agency forbids. Such a conflict can be resolved only by federal authority.

Similarly, when international affairs involved mainly treaty rights, the recognition of states, the type and amounts of foreign aid, and the like, the departments of state and defense could between them sort out the competing considerations and, with a minimum of presidential conflict-resolution, take the necessary actions. But where the substance of foreign relations, as now, includes such domestically significant and politically sensitive matters as insuring energy supplies, limiting the impact of foreign manufacturers, and controlling inflation, those two departments are only two of many—many, moreover, whose goals may sharply conflict.

The military analogy is clear. Until almost the end of World War II U.S. military services fought essentially separate wars. The army managed its own campaigns on land, the navy independently secured the sea lanes, and their command arrangements were separate. Since at least 1943, however, it has been clear that most important campaigns involve "combined arms," and command arrangements have adapted to that reality. All U.S. military units overseas now operate under a single "joint" or "unified" commander who has operational authority over ground, naval, and air units assigned to his command. Important domestic goals, no less than military ones, now require "combined arms" campaigns. But domestic policy conflict lacks the vivid tests of success or failure that warfare imposes. So command arrangements for domestic agencies still resemble the weak and shifting arrangements of committees, voluntary consultative bodies, and ad hoc task forces that characterized the attempts to coordinate military effort forty years ago.

At bottom, of course, this is not a problem of organizational design but of politics. Neither the EOP nor any other entity can wield a power that political forces deny it. That is why a general reconstruction of the integrating institutions of American political life is likely to be necessary to an effective presidency. But that larger purpose has implications for the reform of the EOP itself. It sets one of the twin goals of that reform: to strengthen the EOP as a force for coherence in policy and action, and to broaden the connections among the various institutions that balance, moderate, and force trade-offs among competing social claims.

WHAT WILL IT TAKE?

The exact design of the White House and EOP must depend, in any administration, on the temperament and operating style of the president and on the capacities and interests of his chief lieutenants. No permanently appropriate blueprint can therefore be drawn and even ad hoc plans, if proposed by an outsider, are not likely to be helpful. But the directions of required reform are clear, and the principles that should guide those reforms can readily be outlined.

For all the reasons already discussed, the dominant goal of these reforms must be to expand the capacity of the EOP, and of the administration as a whole, to integrate policy and coordinate action. Every other political institution in our system—the Congress, the courts, the extraordinary range of special-interest organizations—will continue to represent, to one degree or another, the centrifugal forces in American society. Only the presidency can organize and lead the defense of the center.

There are many ways to strengthen its capacity to do so. Those most likely to prove feasible and effective are three: broadening the responsibilities of key cabinet members, making those cabinet officers collegial participants in presidential decision-making, and insuring that EOP and White House staffs assist both the president and the inner cabinet to see problems whole rather than in partial and particular terms.

Broadening the responsibilities of cabinet officers

To the extent that integration can be accomplished below the level of the presidency, it should be. The principal means is to broaden the authority (and perspective) of a limited number of cabinet members and to rely upon them to settle some issues that otherwise would be forced up to the EOP or the White House. There are several ways to attempt this. The most formal are almost certainly the least useful.

The ultimate expression of this principle is to formally restructure the executive branch into a much smaller number of cabinet departments, each with broader jurisdiction. Movement toward such "super-cabinet" agencies was much discussed among critics of government in the 1960s and early 1970s. It was recommended by President Nixon's Ash Council and was actually tried in a number of state and local governments. But as President Johnson had found when he could not secure even a congressional hearing for his 1967 proposal to consolidate the departments of commerce and labor and as Nixon rediscovered when the Ash consolidation proposals gained no ground, the political pressures to preserve separate federal organizations are powerful and bureaucratic resistance to such consolidation is fierce.[3] The costs, therefore, of achieving such wholesale reorganization would be massive. They would almost certainly outweigh the benefits, especially since many of the benefits can be garnered in far less contentious ways.

An intermediate method, easier to achieve and similar to that adopted by Nixon at the opening of his second term, would be to expressly designate the secretaries of key departments as assistants to the president for broad areas—social policy, natural resources, economic affairs, and the like. Thus, clearly equipped with two hats and a special relationship to the president, such inner cabinet members could attempt to assume jurisdiction over many issues that fell only partly within the authority of their departments.

There is a still less formal and almost equally effective way to achieve the same end, however. It is simply to use, persistently and visibly, a well-selected set of particularly able and responsible cabinet officers in the same way without special titles. The power of any EOP official over cabinet officers resides simply in the expectation that, should the cabinet officer appeal the EOP position to the president directly, the president would be likely to back his own staff member. The same calculation affects the influence of cabinet members themselves. Those known to have the confidence of the president will be deferred to by their colleagues. This will be all the more true if they are persons of breadth and judgment, and if the president uses them as suggested immediately below.

Creating an inner cabinet[4]

Both to reinforce the integrating power of senior cabinet officials and to sharply improve the quality of his own decision-making, the president should establish, formally or otherwise, an inner cabinet of four to six members whose perspectives are broad, whose presidential loyalties are strong, and whose departments are heavyweights. These senior line officials should be drawn into collegial consideration of virtually all key presidential issues, whether their departments seem deeply affected or not.

All recent presidents have come into office announcing that they intended to rely heavily on their cabinet secretaries; some have spoken of "cabinet government." As traditionally understood, neither can work. Unless strong counterpressure is applied, cabinet officers become captive advocates of the departments they head, and a cabinet of twelve or fourteen members is too large, too miscellaneous, and too leaky a forum for working discussions of sensitive issues. But regularly drawing a limited number of well-chosen secretaries into presidential decision-making is a different matter. Their regular exposure to the president's needs should tend to broaden their views and their small number will permit serious debate. Such a group can weigh both presidential and departmental prospects and operational as well as policy concerns. And the diversity of their responsibilities will help insure that the full ramifications—domestic, foreign, economic—of complex issues are recognized. To both symbolize and facilitate their special status, these officials should probably be given small offices in the White House or the adjoining Executive Office Building.[5]

A more helpful EOP

Both to support such a collegial inner cabinet and to provide him personally with more useful staff work, the president should reshape the EOP. The main criteria of this redesign should be to facilitate linkages between the EOP's now compartmentalized foreign, domestic, and economic units, and between analytic skill and political sensitivity, and policymaking and knowledge of operations. Again, there are many ways to achieve the end. Staffs now separate might be combined—the national security and domestic policy staffs, together with some added economic competence, could be made part of a single presidential or "cabinet" staff. Less formal changes—rotation of assignments among separate staffs, joint staff meetings, co-location of offices, joint referral of issues—might be used instead. In either event, the direction of movement should be toward EOP units fewer in number, larger in scope, looser in structure and, most important, under unified direction from someone—preferably a wisely chosen chief of staff—short of the president himself. The overriding point is that the EOP must not reproduce the pattern of special expertise and particular concerns that necessarily divide and segment the rest of government. It must contain highly specialized competence, but its distinctive task is to assist the president to see things whole. It must therefore be so organized, staffed, and managed as to insure that it will regularly and reliably bring to bear on major issues, before they arrive on the president's desk, an understanding of their myriad dimensions—symbolic, substantive, administrative, fiscal, foreign, and domestic. If it fails in that, then that hardest of integrating tasks will be undertaken by the president alone, an impossible and unnecessary burden.[6]

And as suggested earlier, the EOP needs strengthening in other ways as well. In particular, those small portions of the various EOP staffs devoted to planning future initiatives, to managing the processes of coordination, or to monitoring the implementation of presidential decisions should be strengthened—by evidence of sustained presidential concern for those functions—and somewhat enlarged. This is not a matter of politicizing the EOP or filling it with presidential hatchet men. For each of the presidential staffing tasks discussed, the most valuable quality is not political loyalty but knowledgeable responsiveness.

STRENGTHENING THE INTEGRATORS

As to how integrating institutions outside the executive might be strengthened and linked to the president, this essay must be even more sketchy. But the major points seem clear. In dealing with Congress, the president should try to channel his influence through party and committee leadership, and to consult with that leadership as executive positions are being formulated. This is a hard prescription, but not impossible: in both the development of U.S. positions for the Tokyo Round Trade Agreements in 1978 and 1979 and in the recasting of the Carter administration's FY 1981 budget it had remarkably productive effects.[7]

Similarly, the president should attempt to relate to associations of governors and mayors rather than to individuals, and to umbrella organizations of private interests rather than to single entities or leaders, genuinely consulting them wherever possible rather than informing them after the fact. The key point is this: he must be a wholesaler of influence, not a retailer. This conception of his role both economizes on his time—the national resource in shortest supply—and strengthens the collective leadership of other integrating institutions, thus enlarging their own capacity to mediate differences and to enforce some measure of internal discipline.

Finally, of course, the president must himself attempt to mobilize public opinion in support of the general interest as against particular or special concerns in those few cases where the issue is truly transcendent. There seems good evidence that such mobilization—like many of the other proposals offered here—will be somewhat easier to accomplish in the 1980s than they might have been in the 1960s and 1970s. The "me" decades appear to be ending; leaders able to articulate the nation's common and enduring interests may well find it easier than their immediate predecessors did to advance them.

IV

The Current Policy
Agenda

11

ROBERT E. HALL

Lowering Inflation and Stimulating Economic Growth

Wages, prices, and the use of resources. Disinflation effects. The failure of taxation. Interest rates— savings, mortgages, annuities. Monetary policy, inflation, and the Federal Reserve. Pegging nominal GNP: a simple procedure. Fiscal policy and output. Taxes— payroll, commodity, income—and the labor supply. A presidential program.

The macroeconomic task facing the new president is so obvious as to require little discussion: end inflation and stimulate real activity at the same time. This chapter outlines a strategy to accomplish these goals. Under this strategy, the federal government commits itself irrevocably to a predetermined growth path for the dollar value of the total output of the economy. Monetary policy is assigned the single task of stabilizing nominal gross national product (GNP). Fiscal instruments are then used to stimulate real output and lower inflation. Because monetary policy pegs the value of output, every percent of extra real output obtained from fiscal stimulus is automatically matched by a one percent reduction in prices. Fiscal expansion cannot set off unwanted inflation under the strategy proposed.

The president of the United States has enormous power over the prime instruments of macroeconomic power, though there are few over which he has unilateral legal power. Monetary policy is conducted by the independent Federal Reserve System, but history has shown that the Fed listens carefully to the president and, in any case, the president appoints the chairman of the Federal Reserve Board after less than two years in office. Congressional approval is required for fiscal moves, but again, the persuasion of the president has proven decisive. Very substantial support exists in Congress today for responsible tax cuts that are part of a comprehensive program of economic renewal. If the president comes forward with such a program, he should be able to enlist the enthusiastic cooperation of the Federal Reserve Board and the enactment of the fiscal side by Congress after considerable debate and perhaps some modification.

STRUCTURAL CONSTRAINTS ON MACROECONOMIC POLICY

There is little question about the ability of monetary policy to peg nominal GNP. Both economic logic and the historical performance of the economy agree on a close association between the money stock and the value of output. What is much more controversial and uncertain is the division of the value of output into real output and inflation, especially in response to a stimulus to supply.

Within orthodox economics, monetarist and Keynesian, favorable shifts in supply do not have an immediate or strong anti-inflationary effect and do not lead to large increases in output when nominal GNP is being pegged. Rather, the price level and the utilization of resources are governed by the wage level. Even well after an anti-inflationary drive begins, wage inflation continues at its customary rate. If nominal GNP is held back through monetary pegging, labor begins to price itself out of the market. Employment is limited not by the willingness of workers to offer their services, but by the willingness of employers to offer work when wages are excessive. It is the irrational momentum of wage inflation that makes employment shrink during the process of disinflation. Stimulus to labor supply may help accelerate the eventual accommodation of wages to lower inflation, but only in the longer run. A prolonged period of slack accompanies disinflation whether or not supply is stimulated. In the early years of a nominal GNP peg it is real GNP, not prices, that is held back by restrictive monetary policy. This orthodox position is widely accepted by American macroeconomists. The experiences with disinflation in continental Europe and Japan over the past decade do not contradict it—all nations who successfully overcame the inflation of the early 1970s went through periods of slack at the same time. Current British experience also seems to support the orthodox view.

The orthodox view rests on the momentum of wage inflation, a phenomenon which has so far resisted successful explanation in terms of basic economic postulates. Orthodox macroeconomics is not orthodox microeconomics. For this reason, we cannot be confident in our statements about the real consequences of disinflation. Unlike the momentum of a moving object, it is possible that the momentum of wages can be dissipated without any real effort by invoking a suitably convincing government dictum. Many orthodox economists feel that wages will fall in line once the government convinces the public that this time it really means that inflation is coming to an end. But others argue that this advice leads to prolonged, deep recession—that the irrationality of wage determination cannot be overcome just by making convincing announcements.

Because the real effects of disinflation cannot be predicted reliably, it is essential to frame the goals of macroeconomic policy over the next few years in terms of slowing the growth of nominal GNP. A convincing statement by the government that it is determined to achieve this goal, together with maximal use of the types of fiscal policy that are most favorable for disinflation, should yield a substantial reduction in inflation, even in the early years of the policy. We must avoid specific promises, however, about ending inflation. The quantitative goals and promises of the government should be stated in terms of variables it actually controls—nominal GNP and taxes.

WHY INFLATION IS COSTLY

Economists disagree sharply on the economic benefits of ending inflation. Many argue the virtues of learning to live with inflation rather than incurring the costs of ending it. Others feel that, while there is no compelling economic argument for price stability, the public is so strongly committed to stability as a goal of public policy that the proper role of the economist is to point out the best way to end inflation, not to question its desirability. A great many economists feel the public suffers from an illusion that overstates the benefits of price stability—they think their dollar incomes would continue to rise rapidly after the end of inflation, so they would achieve rapid real income growth. Or, to put it the other way around, recent inflation has deprived them of real income gains they would otherwise have received.

Whatever the merits of this view, it seems to me that price stability has some very substantial economic benefits that justify a considerable investment in the design and execution of anti-inflationary programs. The social value of a stable monetary unit is amply demonstrated by the remarkable inability of public and private economic institutions to adapt to inflation over the past decade. The most conspicuous failure is in taxation. Inflation has diverted resources into government's hands in a way that never would have passed in a national referendum, simply because tax schedules are written in U.S. dollars, not in abstract dollars of constant purchasing power. Not only have individual taxpayers been driven into higher marginal brackets by inflation, but the taxation of income from capital has been raised to unacceptable levels because of the declining real value of depreciation deductions under continuing inflation. The income from the typical corporate investment in plant and equipment is taxed at rates of between 60 and 70 percent, counting both the corporate and personal income taxes and after allowing for the favorable effects of the investment credit. Taxation at this rate is a pure artifact of inflation. It was never intended by Congress; still, no action has yet been taken to lower effective tax rates on capital.

There is no reasonable prospect that the inertia of the federal government will change. Even if we introduce enough acceleration of depreciation to bring down capital taxation to a reasonable level today, the tax system will adjust with the same lag to future changes in inflation. If we do end inflation, we are likely to wind up with a tax system designed to perform efficiently at 10 percent inflation which will be seriously distortionary at low inflation. The lesson I draw from this experience is the desirability of writing a tax system which assumes a constant value of the dollar. Our experience to date convinces me that indexing the tax system so that it will adapt to changing inflation is beyond our reach.

Other public institutions besides taxes have had trouble adapting to inflation. For example, interest-rate controls that victimize the small saver have hardly been raised at all as the general level of interest rates has risen under inflation. Again, it was not the regulators' intent to increase the gap between the rates earned by sophisticated investors and those who rely on passbook savings accounts, but this was the unintended effect of the transition to high inflation.

Less frequently noted is the problem of adapting private economic arrangements to inflation. The level-payment mortgage, which is a desirable way to spread the burden of a house purchase over the future when prices are stable, is quite perverse under 10 percent inflation—it calls for a very high fraction of a family's income in the early years and a low fraction later, after inflation has swollen the family's earnings. Only very recently have graduated-payment mortgages become available to solve this problem. Further, graduated mortgages have been widely misunderstood and mistrusted. They are frequently thought to be suitable only for young earners whose income is expected to rise rapidly in real terms. Though a graduated mortgage is particularly suited to these families, it is a desirable accommodation to inflation for families who expect their real incomes to remain constant over the future. A recent article in the *Wall Street Journal* on graduated mortgages convinced me that almost nobody, including the author of the article, understands their benefits. Graduated mortgages apparently sell at a considerable discount in the secondary market because they are so poorly understood.

A related and more troublesome failure of private arrangements to adapt to inflation arises in the case of annuities. Annuities provide fixed-dollar payments for the remaining lifetimes of their purchasers and are a common form of retirement benefit. Under stable prices, they are the ideal way for the retired to smooth their resources over the period of retirement. With significant inflation, fixed-dollar annuities pay generously in the early years of retirement and almost nothing at the end of ten or twenty years. The typical retiree today lives for about twenty years after retirement. At 10 percent inflation, the purchasing power of a dollar falls to about 14 cents over twenty years. Fixed-dollar annuities provide almost no support to people who survive fifteen years or longer. The answer, as in the case of mortgages, is a graduated annuity in which the dollar payment rises by, say, 10 percent per year. Of course, the early payments would be much less than in a fixed-dollar annuity in order to finance the later payments. As far as I am aware, no insurance company or retirement fund offers a graduated annuity. Even if they did, few retirees would choose it over the seemingly more generous fixed-payment annuity.

Mortgages and annuities are very significant financial instruments in the lives of most Americans. Under 10 percent inflation they have lost much of their convenience and usefulness, yet the move to restore the function they originally provided with stable prices by graduating their payments has been greeted with suspicion and rejection. The lesson I take from this experience is that the public still relies very heavily on the idea that the dollar functions as an indicator of future value. People strongly resist modification of economic institutions which recognizes that the purchasing power of the dollar is declining over time, so that future payments should involve more dollars than the corresponding current payments. Rather than trying to reform the institutions and to teach the public how to deal with secular inflation, I think we should give serious consideration to preserving the dollar as a meaningful way to make financial plans well into the future. In short, we should stabilize the purchasing power of the dollar. The government should make a binding commitment to price stability. The gains from such a move are substantial. Exactly because we have made so little progress in revising economic institutions to handle inflation, the time is ripe to end inflation.

THE UNFAVORABLE COURSE OF THE AMERICAN ECONOMY

The new administration inherits an economy with depressed real economic activity and continuing inflation near 10 percent. According to reasonable forecasts made at the time I write (December 1980), real GNP will not regain its peak level of late 1979 until the very end of 1981, and might still be well below even into 1982. Very modest attempts by the Federal Reserve to control money growth have raised interest rates to record levels. Though output is well below potential, employment has remained remarkably high and unemployment is only slightly above currently accepted ideas of full employment. Correspondingly, productivity is in a sad state.

In such an economy, nothing could be less welcome than anti-inflationary policies involving further restraint on real activity. The pressure to expand the economy will be intense. Yet it is essential to take immediate anti-inflationary steps. The situation is ripe for radical policy moves. Our history of emergency economic measures, however, is completely discouraging. Drastic actions taken by President Roosevelt in 1933 to 1935 appear in retrospect as damaging the recovery from the Great Depression. President Nixon's emergency invocation of wage and price controls in 1971, in circumstances similar to current ones but not as adverse, laid many of the foundations of today's inflation and depressed real activity. Economic emergencies have not made a positive contribution to macroeconomic policymaking in the United States.

Still, a major change in macro policy needs to be formulated and put in place in the early months of the new administration. It must pay close attention to the calls for vigorous real activity as well as the end of inflation.

MONETARY POLICY TO PEG NOMINAL GNP

Monetary policy is the core of any reasonable anti-inflation policy. Most of the errors of monetary policy in the United States in the past two decades came from the inadequate and contradictory instructions given to the Federal Reserve. The Fed has accepted too much responsibility for interest rates and real economic activity, and far too little responsibility for the dollar value of output and for the quantity of money. At the very outset of the new macro policy the Fed should be told to do exactly one thing and to do it well: its one task should be the pegging of nominal GNP to a prescribed target. Interest rates, employment, and real output should be determined by free markets operating under the influence of appropriate fiscal policy. Good macro policy does not ignore high interest rates or inadequate levels of real activity. But monetary policy should deal with them only through the stabilization of the value of output. An economy on a smooth path of nominal GNP growth will not have the wild fluctuations of output and interest rates characteristic of the recent U.S. economy.

Why peg nominal GNP rather than some other nominal quantity? The choice of nominal GNP is the logical middle ground between pegging prices directly (the most ambitious goal) and simply pegging the money stock (a goal long advocated by monetarists). Pegging prices makes the economy highly susceptible to price shocks. If the Fed is instructed to contract whenever an oil price increase or other outside shock occurs, the prices of other products will have to fall to maintain the price peg. We are unable to predict the magnitude of the corresponding decline in real activity; some economists think it may be as large as 2 or 3 percentage points of real output for each percent of inflation suppressed. In any case, strict pegging of prices is not particularly desirable. The social benefits of price stability come from reliable planning in dollars over a ten- or twenty-year period, not so much from year to year. The goal of price stability is well met if prices fluctuate above and below a stable long-run level. There are no substantial benefits from ironing out fluctuations of a few percent, and there may be important real costs.

Instructing the Fed to do no more than stabilize money growth at a low level is equally inappropriate. Stable money growth does not necessarily bring stable prices in the long run. Changes in monetary institutions and in the economic role of the assets we rather arbitrarily label as money take place at variable rates. The current decade is one of particularly rapid change. With the passage of the Depository Institutions Deregulation and Monetary Control Act of 1980, the legal right to issue money will be extended to new classes of institutions. Financial innovations like the money market fund and the debit card will proliferate, with the encouragement of the federal government. As a result, experts are in wide disagreement on the definition and measurement of money. Further, disinflation itself will stimulate the demand for money—with lower interest rates, the financial incentive to hold assets in nonmonetary form will diminish and the public will want to hold larger money balances in relation to income.

All of these changes will alter the relation between the rate of money growth and the rate of inflation. The goal of price stability will not be met by setting an arbitrary definition of money and requiring that the Fed peg the quantity of money. Monetarists who have called for policies of predetermined money growth have generally done so in despair of any better policy, fearing that, if given the opportunity, the Fed would do something even worse. Within a general overhaul of macro policy, however, many monetarists would agree on the superiority of pegging nominal GNP to pegging the money stock.

In the longer run, pegging nominal GNP stabilizes prices. Real output fluctuates around its full-employment level, and so the price level—which is the ratio of nominal to real GNP—must grow at a rate equal to the difference between the growth of nominal GNP and the growth of full-employment real GNP. Pegging nominal GNP thus will eliminate secular inflation. Within this noninflationary, long-run setting, it permits monetary policy to lean against the wind in a desirable way—expansion is called for during a recession, when nominal GNP falls because real GNP falls, and contraction during a boom. Pegging the money stock prohibits these responses, and pegging prices creates unreliable stabilization—recessions are not invariably accompanied by falling prices, nor are booms accompanied by rising prices in all cases.

A simple operating procedure would enable the Fed to keep nominal GNP on target. First, it should select a readily controllable monetary aggregate as the basis for its daily operations. This could be one or another measure of the monetary base or it could be a narrow concept of money itself. Then the monetary aggregate should be manipulated to offset any deviations of nominal GNP from its prescribed growth path. Though the actual operating policy need not be so formal, the following rule would work well: each quarter, if nominal GNP is on target, raise the monetary aggregate at a prescribed annual rate (2 to 3 percent per year after an initial period at higher rates). If GNP is above target, reduce the annual growth rate of the aggregate by the number of percentage points that GNP exceeds the target. If GNP is below the target, raise the rate in the same way. The Fed should be permitted to develop its own operating procedure and modify it with experience. It should avoid extreme movements in the money stock and corresponding movements in interest rates. But its overriding goal should be achieving the nominal GNP peg as closely as possible. Longer-term drift of actual from target nominal GNP should not be tolerated. Whenever nominal GNP departs from the target set at the outset of the program by more than 3 percent, the Fed should be required to make a specific accounting and to show that it plans to return nominal GNP to its prescribed level.

Under my proposal, the Fed's operating procedure would be something like the following: Each month the Commerce Department prepares a new estimate of the level of nominal GNP in the most recently completed calendar quarter. The Fed would then formulate the next month's instructions to its trading desk about the necessary rate of growth or contraction of the volume of currency and reserves. Normally the growth rate would be about 2.0 percent at annual rates, but if nominal GNP were, say, 1.5 percent above the target, the next month's instructions would call for only 0.5 percent growth at annual rates.

Through this kind of procedure, the Fed is readily capable of controlling nominal GNP. Quite a number of researchers have documented a strong quantitative relationship between monetary aggregates and nominal GNP. They have found that this quarter's nominal GNP is proportional to a moving average of the base in this quarter and in the three preceding quarters. There is a lag, but it lasts no more than a year. The relationship is reliable in terms of changes—a vigorous expansion of monetary aggregates in one quarter will almost always be followed by a comparable boom in nominal GNP over the ensuing year—but the relationship tends to wander as years pass. The accretion of random, permanent shifts means that stabilizing the aggregates does not stabilize nominal GNP in the long run. The Fed must adapt to these shifts by raising and lowering growth in the aggregate in response to departures of nominal GNP from the target.

In summary, pegging nominal GNP has the following virtues:

1.   Above all else, it essentially removes uncertainty about the future value of the dollar. It will reestablish the dollar as the sensible way for businesses and households to make financial plans.

2.   The policy is highly robust under changes in monetary institutions and money demand that could be dangerously inflationary or deflationary under rules of constant money growth. Its key feature is to link the *growth rate* of a monetary aggregate to the *level* of nominal GNP. Because of this link, the level of the aggregate adjusts in an uninflationary way to all permanent changes in the relation of the monetary aggregate to nominal GNP.

3.   The policy does not rest on detailed assumptions about the characteristics or behavior of the U.S. economy. It does not require that inflation respond quickly to changes in the money stock, though it does perform well if the response is speedy. It relies on the well-documented and noncontroversial relationship between nominal GNP and monetary aggregates. Economists of widely differing persuasions are agreed on the strength of this relationship.

4.   Within a noninflationary long-run setting, it calls upon the Fed to lean against the wind in a desirable way—the money stock would grow a little less than normal during booms and a little more than normal during recessions.

FISCAL POLICY TO STIMULATE REAL ACTIVITY

With monetary policy pegging nominal GNP along a path of diminishing growth, the task of fiscal policy is to sustain and encourage real output and employment. By construction, fiscal policy does not influence nominal GNP. Whatever impact a fiscal move might have is offset by the response of monetary policy in maintaining the nominal GNP peg. Fiscal policy operates under a key constraint: *it can raise real output only to the extent that it lowers prices.* Fiscal moves that might seem to be stimulative will be fully offset by monetary contraction unless they succeed in lowering prices. If one takes the extreme (and unsupportable) view that fiscal policy is powerless to affect prices, then it is equally powerless to affect total real output. In such an economy, fiscal policy determines only the composition of real output, not its level. Fortunately, fiscal instruments can diminish inflation and so can stimulate output in the contemporary U.S. economy.

Anti-inflationary fiscal policies reduce prices by reducing costs of production. Labor costs can be lowered through reduced payroll taxation or through reduced wages. Wages will fall if labor supply increases. Capital costs can be lowered through reduced taxation of capital income for corporations and households. This quick summary suggests three types of stimulative, anti-inflationary tax cuts: payroll taxes, personal income taxes, corporate income taxes.

Before considering these in more detail, it is necessary to say something about government expenditures and the deficit. Expenditure policy and tax policy are not really separate fiscal instruments. When it spends money, the government must sooner or later finance the expenditure with taxes. Deficits can only be temporary. Further, there is little indication that expenditures are or should be manipulated for macroeconomic stabilization purposes. The most logical way to think about fiscal policy from the macro perspective is the following: expenditures are determined from non-macroeconomic considerations of national defense, public welfare, and the like. Macro policymakers choose tax rates to meet stabilization objectives and to finance total expenditures on the average over time. If they choose rates that generate less revenue than expenditures during a year, they are implicitly choosing higher rates and excess revenue in some future year.

Cuts in the employer payroll tax are the single most attractive stimulative fiscal measure available today. Currently, employers face a tax of a little over 6 percent on the bulk of their payrolls. Immediate elimination of this tax would reduce payroll costs by almost 5 percent and would reduce total costs of production by about 3.5 percent. Prices would fall by the same 3.5 percent. With nominal output pegged by monetary policy, real output would rise by 3.5 percent. This adds up to an extremely healthy economy, compared to current forecasts. Though eliminating the tax provides only a one-time decline in prices and stimulus to real output, it would be a highly favorable way to launch a long-term macro policy.

The employer payroll tax will yield about $90 billion in the forthcoming year, all of it earmarked for the social security system. Simple elimination of the tax is infeasible, both because it would raise the total federal deficit to an alarming level and because it would bankrupt social security in a matter of months. Increasing personal income taxes would be a necessary accompaniment to the elimination of the employer payroll tax. The magnitude of the increase is difficult to calculate, but it would be on the order of 2 percent of total personal income. This makes some allowance for the reduction in federal expenditures that occurs automatically through cost-of-living escalation of benefits and wages.

The disinflationary power of moving from commodity taxation to income taxation has been demonstrated in reverse by recent British experience. An early move of the Thatcher government was to cut income taxes and raise value-added taxes (whose economic impact is almost exactly the same as our payroll tax). British inflation surged as a result. Contractionary monetary policy has been struggling to contain high rates of inflation both from this source and from the history of past rapid money growth and inflation. Real output has declined alarmingly.

I recognize that cutting employer taxes by 5 percentage

points and raising income taxes by 2 percentage points is not a politically attractive move. Labor will see it as a giveaway to business and will regard the 3.5 percent increase in real incomes it promises as no more than a conjecture. Still, it is the most promising dramatic move in the direction of lower prices and higher real output that I can identify.

The other fiscal policy that operates through labor costs is reducing the taxation of labor income to stimulate labor supply. Proponents of this "supply-side" strategy say the following: Make truly significant cuts in the taxation of labor income. Labor will be attracted out of the household (and, possibly, out of an underground economy some feel is substantial) into the market economy where competition with existing wage earners will limit wage inflation, costs of production will rise less rapidly, and price inflation will moderate.

Evidence on the magnitude of the supply response is mixed. The recent trend in the population has been toward spending an increased fraction of time in market work, even though inflation has pushed marginal tax rates upward. The fraction of the population aged sixteen and over who are in the labor force rose from 60.1 percent in 1969 to 63.7 percent in 1979. But the labor force participation rate fell for men from 79.8 percent to 77.9 percent. The rise came from women—from 42.7 percent to 51.0. If the behavior of women is attributable to noneconomic forces, then one could argue that the decline in work among men reveals the response to rising taxation. Further, much of the decline among men occurred in the age groups above sixty-two, where the availability of increasingly generous social security benefits should be thought of as a decline in the economic reward to work.

Comparisons of the work performed by people facing different wages and belonging to families with different incomes also sheds some light on the labor supply response to lower taxes. Differences here between men and women are very conspicuous. Men tend to work approximately full time over wide ranges of wages and incomes. On this account, there is little reason to expect a large increase in their work effort if income taxes are cut. On the other hand, high-wage women are much more likely to work than are those facing low wages. If the likely behavior of women in the face of a tax cut can be inferred by comparing different women with different wages today (which may not be a reliable basis for inference, for a number of reasons), then at least a one percent increase in labor supply should be stimulated by a one percentage point cut in tax rates.

For low-wage workers, direct evidence on the impact of taxes on labor supply is available from a number of negative income tax experiments. The typical experimental subject was given a substantial income grant and was then taxed on earnings at a rate of around 50 percent. Hours of work fell noticeably for both men and women. Unfortunately, experts analyzing the results have not reliably separated the effects of the income grant from the earnings tax. A very rough guess from the experimental evidence is that men reduce their labor supply by about 0.1 percent for each extra percent of wage tax, while women react about ten times as strongly.

None of this evidence remotely justifies a definitive statement that policymakers can rely on a particular magnitude of labor supply response to tax reductions. Equally, it does not clearly refute the new school's view that an important anti-inflationary response is available from labor supply. It is interesting to ask what a rough estimate of the actual magnitude of the effect is. Suppose that each percent reduction in marginal tax rates stimulates labor supply by 0.4 percent. The 30 percent reduction in total revenue from the personal income tax proposed by the new school could finance a reduction of about 5 percentage points in the marginal tax rates of all taxpayers. Labor supply would rise by 2 percent.

Under a monetary policy that pegs nominal GNP, an increase in labor supply can stimulate employment only if it succeeds in depressing wages. There is wide disagreement on the immediate effect on wages of increases in labor supply. Economists who have studied the empirical relation between wages and unemployment universally reached the conclusion that an increase in unemployment of one percentage point reduces wage inflation by no more than half a percent over the first full year. Further, an increase in labor supply of 2 percent probably increases unemployment by only one percentage point. Thus the empirical relation between labor supply and wages seems weak. However, this interpretation of the evidence has been challenged on theoretical grounds from a number of directions. The most that can be said today is that policymakers should not rely on a vigorous anti-inflationary effect of an increase in labor supply in the early years after a tax cut.

Economists are on somewhat surer footing in asserting that an increase in labor supply increases employment and output and decreases wages and prices in the longer run. In this respect, personal tax cuts are a desirable policy for the long run. Of course, federal expenditures have to be financed one way or the other. Among the various taxes in use today, the personal income tax is one of the more desirable ones. If total revenue has to be kept at roughly its present level, it would be best to cut payroll and corporate taxes and to raise personal income taxes. If total revenue can be cut substantially, then some cuts in personal income taxes would make sense.

Before launching large reductions in the personal income tax, the new administration should be aware of how low effective rates of taxation are in the United States today. Personal income tax payments in 1979 were only 11.3 percent of total personal income. One way or another, most families are able to arrange their income receipts to pay quite low marginal tax rates. There is no crisis of disincentives from income taxes. What is most badly needed is not a reduction in average taxation, but reductions in top marginal rates. The case for this reform is primarily microeconomic, however. There are not enough people in the United States who are actually taxed at high marginal rates and whose labor supply is sufficiently sensitive to the taxation to bring about a large immediate increase in work effort when top marginal rates are cut.

The third line of fiscal attack on costs of production involves lowering the taxation of capital income. Here there is very much a crisis of disincentives. Most capital income is taxed twice, once at the corporate level and again when it flows to households. Even without inflation, high effective tax rates have discouraged investment in plant and equipment, channeling savings instead into real estate and personal tax shelters. Inflation has worsened the disincentive by lowering the real value of depreciation deductions. The overall efficiency of the American economy has been seriously degraded by heavy taxation of capital income. Any plan for economic renewal must involve substantial tax relief for investment.

Higher rates of investment stimulated by lower taxes will bring only modest improvements in productivity in the first few years. The benefits of lower prices and higher real output will accumulate as time passes in proportion to the rising capital stock. It is important that President Reagan not promise any immediate transformation of the economy after enactment of tax reductions for capital income.

WHAT THE PRESIDENT SHOULD DO

The core of a new program for managing the U.S. economy should be a commitment to a specific growth path for nominal GNP. The full weight of presidential authority should be put behind an announcement that the growth of the value of output will be brought down to noninflationary levels over the course of the next four years. This should be the only specific promise, but it should be a binding one. The support of the Federal Reserve Board should be enlisted for restating the goals of monetary policy in terms of the nominal GNP target. The chairman of the Federal Reserve Board should join with the president in announcing that achieving the nominal GNP peg will be the sole responsibility of monetary policy. The public should be left with no doubt that the value of output will be stabilized under the new policy.

At the same time, the president should submit to Congress a comprehensive fiscal package for stimulating real growth during and after the period of disinflation. The goal of the program should be real growth of 3 to 4 percent per year starting in 1982, but it should be made clear that this level of performance cannot be guaranteed.

The first element of the fiscal package should be a substantial reduction in the employer payroll tax. This is the surest anti-inflationary stimulus to real economic activity. This move alone should transform the current gloomy outlook for 1981–1982 into one of strong real growth. By demonstrating at the very outset of the program that the nominal GNP peg and associated fiscal reforms are together capable of cooling inflation while restoring real growth, the program will derive the maximum benefit from improved expectations about the long-run performance of the economy.

The second element should be a reform of capital taxation. A sharp reduction in asset lifetimes for tax purposes, along the lines of the Conable-Jones 10–5–3 proposal, is a rough and ready move. In the longer run, a complete elimination of the corporate income tax through integration with the personal income tax should be the goal.

The third element should be a combination of cuts in federal expenditures and increases, if necessary, in personal income taxes. Here the goal should be a balanced budget in the long run. The choice between expenditure reductions and personal tax increases should reflect judgments about the relative values of public and private spending and about income redistribution. It does not have important macroeconomic implications beyond the obvious connection between today's private investment and future productive capacity. Even without large reductions in existing programs, prospective federal expenditures will be substantially smaller under the rapid real growth promised by the cuts in payroll and capital taxes.

No element of this program is radical or impractical, though some of them would encounter important political obstacles. As a whole, it promises the end of inflation during a single presidential term together with the restoration of high employment and real growth. This accomplishment would stand in remarkable contrast to the inflation and stagnation of the past decade.

12

ROBERT S. PINDYCK

An Agenda for American Energy Policy*

The divisiveness of U.S. energy policies. Misguided regulation of oil and natural gas. The Natural Gas Policy Act. The crude oil price controls–entitlements system. Synthetic fuels and the Carter program. New technologies. Designing a new energy policy — decontrol; food stamps; private implementation of government research findings; an import tariff; the strategic oil reserve.

*The work leading to this paper was supported by the Center for Energy Policy Research of the MIT Energy Laboratory, and that support is gratefully acknowledged.

It is not surprising that over the last several years the American public has begun to question the ability of any administration and any Congress to deal effectively with the major problems facing the country. There has been a growing sense that in areas ranging from foreign policy to defense policy to economic policy our government lacks direction, and perhaps competence.

This crisis of leadership and governmental competence is most striking in energy policy. For a decade government has tried to grapple with pricing policies, domestic shortages, foreign dependence, tax policy, and the development of alternative energy sources. No subject in recent years has been debated in more hearings of congressional committees and subcommittees, filled more pages of the *Congressional Record*, and occupied more time of the president and his staff.

Although some progress has occurred, the overall record in energy policy has been dismal. As this is being written, the cuntry is more dependent than ever on foreign sources of oil that are more insecure than ever.[1] Natural gas exploration and production is being unnecessarily limited by the 1978 Natural Gas Policy Act that lets wellhead prices slowly increase, but under a maze of new bureaucratic regulations that will benefit only the lawyers paid to litigate their interpretation. And finally, at a time when both inflation and the government budget are out of control, we have undertaken an $88 billion synthetic fuels program—which is bound to be one of the most costly and wasteful government programs ever, which is acknowledged to provide *no* reduction in oil imports before 1990, and which is likely to provide only minimal benefits after 1990. In sum, the record only reinforces the public's sense of government paralysis.

Now the old problems of energy policy will confront a new administration and a new Congress. They will have a unique opportunity to take a fresh approach to the problem that in the past has divided public opinion and paralyzed government. If they can seize it, it may help to restore some of the public's lost confidence in their leadership. However, success will depend on understanding why energy policy has been so intractable in the past as well as on some economic "facts of life" that must provide the foundation of any sensible energy policy in the future.

My objectives in this paper are threefold. First, I will discuss why energy policy has been such a divisive issue in the United States during the past decade. This will help us understand why past administrations and Congresses have been unable and/or unwilling to formulate, legislate, and implement an overall energy policy that is rational and economically sound.

Second, I will discuss the specific ways in which recent and current energy policy measures have been misguided and why they are likely to be counterproductive in the future if they continue to be pursued. Here I will focus largely on two particular aspects of recent energy policy: price controls on natural gas and oil, and the government's synthetic fuels program. Although there have been other aspects of energy policy that were equally misguided, these two are most important in terms of their cost to the American economy.

Third, and most important, I will outline the specific changes in energy policy that are needed today and that I believe should appear on the new administration's agenda.

THE CONFLICT OVER ENERGY POLICY

The debate over American energy policy began well before the Organization of Petroleum Exporting Countries (OPEC) oil price increase of 1973–1974, and focused initially on the regulation of natural gas wellhead prices as spot shortages of gas began occurring in 1971 and 1972. Why has that debate been so intense, so enduring, and so divisive? Why has the

formulation of a coherent energy policy seemed so intractable?

In 1977 Robert Hall and I described a fundamental conflict
in the objectives of energy policy: on the one hand, a desire to
keep the price of energy down and, on the other hand, a
desire to stem what appeared to be an uncontrolled growth in
oil imports (see Hall and Pindyck 1980). The former was not
surprising; consumers are displeased to see the price of *anything* rise, and in this case they could express that dis-
pleasure through their votes. At the same time, the desire to
limit the growth of oil imports was understandable; these imports made us politically and economically vulnerable to the
demands and decisions of a small number of oil-exporting
countries, and they contributed to inflation by reducing the
international value of the dollar through their impact on our
trade balance.

The basic conflict is simple. Do we let the domestic price of
energy rise so that consumers have the incentive to consume
less and producers have the incentive to produce more—so
that our growing dependence on imported oil can be
stemmed and spot shortages of fuels averted? Or do we keep
the price of energy low and try to reduce imports with a
patchwork of expensive subsidies for alternative energy
sources and, when shortages occur, ration supplies?

American energy policy favored the low-price option
throughout the 1970s. Price controls on natural gas remained in effect despite growing shortages of that fuel. In
1974 we saw the introduction of the price controls—entitlements system for crude oil, which in effect subsidizes OPEC
imports. And price controls have remained in force for
gasoline, with small national shortages greatly exacerbated
by the "regional allocation" system—as imposed by the
Federal Energy Administration in the winter of 1974 and by
the Department of Energy in the summer of 1979.

In recent years the United States has begun slowly to turn
away from its low-price policies. The Natural Gas Policy Act

of 1978, although extending regulation to intrastate gas and creating a bureaucratic nightmare by separately regulating some twenty-odd categories of gas, at least moves us toward the eventual deregulation of most categories of gas by the middle or late 1980s. And thanks to an important step in the right direction taken by the Carter administration, the price controls—entitlements system for crude oil is currently scheduled to end by October 1981.

Nonetheless, the basic conflict still remains, and what is most disturbing is that the approach taken to resolve that conflict during the last year and a half of the Carter administration is bound to be counterproductive in the long run. There has been a great temptation to find a "cheap fix" to the energy problem—cheap in terms of *political cost*, if not in terms of *real economic cost*. The Carter administration's far-reaching program to provide government subsidies for a plethora of nonconventional energy supplies is exactly the kind of cheap fix that is politically attractive but that should be avoided.

By now most Americans realize that energy has become much more costly, and that it is likely to become more costly still. But it is important to understand that there are two alternative ways that Americans can pay for the higher cost of their energy. One way is to pay *directly*, through higher prices. The other is to pay *indirectly*, through increased tax revenues that are then allocated to synthetic fuel production or conservation subsidies, through increased general inflation generated in part through an artificially induced growth of OPEC imports, and sometimes through the cost of lost time spent waiting in lines resulting from outright shortages of fuels.

Paying for energy *directly* is by far the more efficient way. It gives consumers a direct incentive to conserve. There is less incentive to lower the thermostat or to drive a smaller car if part of each consumer's energy bill is paid for through taxes or through general inflation, since no one can reduce that portion of the bill by consuming less.

Similarly, when consumers pay directly, producers receive payment directly, and this gives them the incentive to *minimize the cost of production*, producing lower-cost fuels today and moving toward higher-cost fuels only as it becomes necessary in the future. And when energy is paid for directly, the fuel mix of the future—whether it will include shale oil, liquified coal, solar energy, wind power, or whatever—is determined on *economic* grounds, so that its long-run cost is minimized. If instead we pay for our energy through our taxes, the fuel mix of the future will be determined on *political* grounds, with projects financed by the government based on the congressional districts in which they are to be built, the political connections of the particular corporations seeking subsidies, etc. This is bound to lead to a wasteful allocation of resources and to a much higher cost of energy.

But why, then, did the Carter administration—and the Congress—create the synthetic fuels program? The reason is a simple one—*it is politically cheaper to have the public pay for its energy indirectly*. In this way the public (or at least part of it) *thinks* it is getting cheap energy—something for nothing. And congressmen *know* they will be getting large-scale construction projects for their districts and that they will *appear* to be "doing something" about the energy problem. In fact, the public will end up paying even more for its energy, although the payments will be disguised because they will take the form of higher taxes and greater inflation.

This is an important lesson which has yet to be fully learned by the government and, perhaps more important, by the American public. In energy policy, perhaps more than in any other area, presidential governance will require an ability to effectively explain to the public the basic facts of life of energy economics. This ability was sorely lacking in the Carter administration; perhaps they did not even understand the lesson.

MISTAKES TO LEARN FROM: PRICE CONTROLS ON NATURAL GAS AND OIL

Today's energy problems result in part from the misguided policies of the past. If we are to develop a sensible energy policy for the future, it is important to fully understand these mistakes. We will focus on the two most serious mistakes: the systems of price controls that were imposed on natural gas and oil markets, and the large and costly synthetic fuels program set up in the last year of the Carter administration.

It is useful to stress again that both of these mistakes resulted from a set of conflicting policy goals — to keep prices to consumers low, and at the same time to reduce dependence on foreign oil. And it is useful to stress again that both mistakes were based on the incorrect belief that the government could somehow "legislate" a low cost of energy so that consumers would be protected from the cost implications of growing resource scarcity combined with a cartel that controls the world price of oil. In short, both mistakes resulted from the failure to recognize that one way or another — directly or indirectly—Americans must pay more for energy, and that it is more efficient to pay directly.

Let us begin with price controls, since this was the major instrument used to keep the price of energy to American consumers — and American producers — well below world market levels and was therefore a major cause of the growth of oil imports in the 1970s. Two separate price control policies have been in force in the United States — the longstanding regulation of the price of natural gas by the Federal Power Commission (FPC) and later by the Federal Energy Regulatory Commission (FERC) of the Department of Energy (DOE), and the more recent crude oil price controls—entitlements program.

The average price of natural gas at the wellhead has been regulated since 1954, but those regulations became "effective" (in the sense that regulated prices were below prices that would have prevailed had the market not been regulated) beginning only around 1962.[2] From 1962 to 1970 natural gas prices continued to deviate more and more from world market prices and from the thermal-equivalent prices of competing fuels (such as home heating oil) in the United States.

Not surprisingly, the demand for natural gas was artificially stimulated and the supply of natural gas was artificially repressed, so that from 1962 to 1970 the average reserve/production ratio for natural gas fields in the United States fell from about 20 to about 12. The deviations of regulated natural gas prices from free market prices became even greater in the 1970s, and by 1971 the United States began to experience outright shortages of natural gas in different regions of the country. At first those shortages were limited to agricultural and industrial consumers in the North Central part of the country; but over time they grew, and during January and February 1976 natural gas shortages caused plant shutdowns which resulted in the layoff of some 1.1 million workers.

As we saw in the winter of 1976, major energy shortages can have a much more severe impact on an industrial economy than even large increases in energy prices. By restricting the production of other goods and creating supply bottlenecks throughout the economy, energy shortages can cause considerable economic damage.

In addition to the cost of shortages, the regulation of natural gas markets imposed other indirect costs on the American economy. Because natural gas price controls substantially subsidized the consumption of gas by those who were able to obtain it (mainly households, but also industries in some parts of the country), it artificially increased the level of their consumption. Since those unable to obtain natural gas had to shift their demands to oil or electricity, price controls likewise artificially increased the demands for these alternative fuels. Over the 1974–1978 period the net effect was to increase the demand for energy in the United States by about 1 or 2 million barrels of oil-equivalents per day (Hall and Pindyck 1980). In addition, price controls severely limited the supply of natural gas, since even the prices for new contracts were held well below world levels. The net result was to artificially increase oil imports in the United States by at least 2 million barrels per day. The indirect cost becomes clear if one remembers that those higher imports had to be paid for —through a reduction in the international value of the dollar and corresponding increases in the prices of all other imported goods. Indeed, it is ironic that critics of deregulation argued that it would be inflationary, whereas in fact, in the long run, regulation itself was far more inflationary.

The Natural Gas Policy Act of 1978 was a step in the right direction. It significantly increased the regulated wellhead prices of many categories of natural gas and provided for further increases in the future, leading to the deregulation of most categories of gas by the middle or late 1980s.

But while it moves in the right direction, the act contains some significant flaws. First, by delaying deregulation of certain categories of gas, it may actually cause natural gas production (at least for those categories) to be *less* over the next five years than might otherwise have been the case. Second, by creating some twenty-odd categories of natural gas and subjecting each category to separate regulations, the act is a bureaucratic nightmare that is likely to depress gas production. Finally, the act does not provide the incentive necessary for the exploitation of potential high-cost gas reserves —i.e., those at great depths or in formations otherwise hard to tap. These flaws in the act should be kept in mind should it again come before the Congress during the next year.

Let us now turn to the crude oil price controls—entitlements system. First of all, it is important to understand that this policy not only reduces the domestic price of crude oil and refined oil products, but that it acts in addition as a *tax* on domestic oil production and as a *subsidy* for imported oil. Under this system domestic producers receive an average price below the price paid by refiners, which is in turn below the world market price set by OPEC. In order to refine a barrel of domestic crude oil, producers must purchase an "entitlement," so that this is in effect a tax on domestic production. At the same time, refiners who import crude oil at the world price *receive* entitlements which are financed by the payments from domestic producers and which, in effect, provide a subsidy for imported oil. Ironically enough, our crude oil regulatory policy has put the United States government in the business of subsidizing oil imports, most of which come from OPEC!

And what has been the effect of this policy? In the winter of 1974 and the summer of 1979—occasions when OPEC sharply increased world oil prices—crude oil price controls, combined with price controls on retail product markets, led to outright shortages of gasoline. Those shortages, furthermore, which were only about 5 or 10 percent of total demand on a nationwide basis, were made still worse by additional government regulatory activity. In an attempt to "allocate" the shortages around the country, the FEA (in 1974) and the DOE (1979) simply concentrated the shortages and shifted them across the country, so that at any one time some regions of the country had large *surpluses* of gasoline while others had shortages on the order of 30 or 40 percent of demand.

Gasoline lines were both obvious and aggravating, but the more serious effect of crude oil regulatory policy was less obvious. That effect, as in the case of natural gas regulation, was to artificially stimulate demand and to artificially repress crude oil exploration, development, and production. In other words, crude oil regulatory policy artificially increased our level of oil imports—by about 3 million barrels per day between 1976 and 1978. And once again, that increase in imports put downward pressure on the international value of the dollar, which in turn led to increases in the prices of all imported goods and contributed to general inflation.

We see, then, that price controls on natural gas and oil have resulted in shortages, increased dependence on oil imports, and increased inflation. In addition, they have resulted in the wasteful consumption of energy resources that have been artificially priced below their true value. Finally, they have created an incentive for the government to adopt subsidization programs—such as the synthetic fuels program to be discussed below—which themselves increase long-run energy costs unnecessarily and contribute still more to inflation.

MISTAKES TO LEARN FROM: THE SYNTHETIC FUELS PROGRAM

On 15 July 1979 President Carter explained in a televised energy address that the United States had become intolerably dependent on insecure supplies of imported oil. This assessment was correct, but the president's prescription— an enormous government synthetic fuels program—was dead wrong. By any rational economic criteria, this program is bound to be inefficient and wasteful; it is unlikely to contribute significantly to the solution of our energy problems even by 1990, and it could seriously harm the country's economic health. Such a program is particularly undesirable today, when the need to limit government expenditures will impose severe restrictions on other important areas of government activity.

It is important to stress that the problem is not that there

is no future for synthetic fuels and other nonconventional
energy supplies. It is highly likely that, as energy prices continue to rise, some of these new sources will become commercially viable and will eventually displace conventional oil and
natural gas as major fuels. But, as they become economical,
they can be—and should be—produced by private companies without government subsidies.

The Carter administration's synthetic fuels program is undesirable for six basic reasons.

First, and perhaps most important, there is simply no need
for subsidies. The arguments raised in favor of the synthetic
fuels program usually relate to claims that these energy
sources have certain special characteristics—such as calling
for advanced technology, heavy capital requirements, and
long lead times, and being subject to various uncertainties—
and that these characteristics make private sector commercialization difficult or impossible without government assistance. But these claims are false.[3] While it is true that large
capital expenditures are required to produce some of these
energy sources on a commercial scale, this has also been the
case for many other projects undertaken by the private sector. It is also true that the lead times involved in the construction and licensing of operating plants for some of these
energy sources is large, perhaps five to ten years, but this
has commonly been the case in many other private ventures.

There are indeed uncertainties associated with the private
commercialization of new energy technologies, but only two
form a real impediment to commercialization. These are the
uncertainties associated with possible future price regulation
and taxation and the uncertainties about environmental
restrictions. It should not be surprising that companies are
unwilling to take risks in developing new energy technologies when they perceive a probable government ceiling
on their upside profit potential. Similarly, the industry fears
an unpredictable revision of current environmental regulations. *But these are uncertainties that the government created
and that the government can remove.*

The government should remove controls on the current and future prices of energy supplies and should commit itself to allowing energy markets to operate freely in the future. In addition, the government should revise unnecessary environmental regulations and should clarify what regulations will apply in the future. If these things were done, private companies would be in an excellent position to develop economical synthetic fuels efficiently and without subsidies.

The second reason that the synthetic fuels program is undesirable has to do with the inefficiency and waste associated with having energy consumers pay indirectly for their energy. As I explained earlier in this paper, by converting direct energy purchases into purchases paid for through taxes, a subsidy program will artificially inflate energy consumption. There is now a growing body of statistical evidence indicating that price increases would significantly reduce energy demand, particularly after several years.[4] A subsidy program would remove this price incentive and would thereby contribute to the growth of energy consumption. By subsidizing the commercialization of synthetic fuels, the government would in effect be asking taxpayers to finance the difference between the high cost of producing synthetic fuel supplies and the lower price that consumers would pay.

The third reason is that large cost overruns are more likely in a government-subsidized program, and *much* more likely in a government-managed program. This means that the final cost of synthetic fuels could easily turn out to be several times higher than recent estimates suggest. It is ironic that President Carter, who was so critical about cost overruns in government agencies, supported a program that provides large incentives for cost overruns. Under this program, the size and form of the subsidy will be linked to the costs of synthetic fuel production and to the differences between those costs and the world prices of conventional energy supplies. This will give companies contemplating synthetic fuel projects every incentive to inflate their cost estimates.

The fourth reason relates to the sheer size of the expenditures planned for the synthetic fuels program. In his same televised address to the nation on 15 July, President Carter said that Americans do not save enough and that the average savings rate in this country is lower than in almost any other industrialized country. His concern for the growth of productive capacity in this country is quite warranted. Yet the proposed expenditures for the synthetic fuels program could crowd out other much-needed investment, and could thereby depress the future economic growth of the country. It hardly seems sensible to implement an energy program that could seriously exacerbate this very problem.

Fifth, if we are going to use subsidies to reduce our dependence on foreign oil, we should at least use them where they are likely to be most cost-effective. There are a number of alternatives which do not sound as glamorous as a large synthetic fuels program but do not cost as much. On the demand side, for example, tax credits could be used more extensively for home insulation and storm windows, and subsidies could be used to encourage purchases of more fuel-efficient cars (through a credit paid to the consumer or the car dealer). On the supply side, subsidies could be used to promote enhanced recovery of oil and gas along with the production of heavy oil. These alternatives offer a higher and more certain rate of return than do large synthetic fuels projects.

The sixth reason is that the synthetic fuels program runs the risk of locking us in to the wrong synthetic fuel technologies. Private industry, not the Department of Energy, is best placed to determine which new energy technologies are most economical and most promising and to manage their commercial development most effectively. Private industry is best able to respond quickly and efficiently to future technological and economic developments. And private industry is better able than any government bureaucracy to stop work on a particular project if it turns out that it is not as promising as it once appeared to be. Unlike a government agency, a private company is usually unwilling to continue to pour money into an unprofitable project because of its location in a particular congressional district or to "save face."

But despite its wastefulness, its inefficiency, and its ineffectiveness, it is not surprising that the synthetic fuels program received the support it did from the administration and the Congress. Unfortunately, the program's very nature makes it attractive politically. The program gives the appearance that the government is "doing something" about the energy problem and, at least initially, the true cost of the program is hidden from the public and only begins to be perceived later as taxes increase and inflation continues to grow.

THE FRAMEWORK FOR A NEW ENERGY POLICY

Let us now review the particular "do"s and "don't"s that should be the guiding rules in the design and implementation of a new American energy policy. This list is not intended to be all-inclusive, but focuses on the *most important* issues that need to be addressed in the near future.[5]

Decontrol energy prices. The new administration should be committed to the complete decontrol of energy prices. This includes oil and gas prices at the wellhead as well as retail product prices. Furthermore, there should be a commitment to refrain from regulation in the future, so that developers of new high-cost and high-risk energy supplies need not fear that their profits will be regulated or taxed away if energy prices continue to rise.

It is widely feared in the United States that production cutbacks in certain OPEC countries might lead to fuel shortages in this country. But it is important to remember that short-

ages in retail markets can result from *only one thing*—
government attempts to control the prices of fuels below
market-clearing levels. It is exactly such controls (combined
with government attempts to allocate regional supplies) that
have caused gasoline lines in the United States. Because
they allowed prices to rise to market-clearing levels, the
other major industrial nations escaped this problem, even
though some of them are far more dependent on imports
than the United States.

Remember that the crude oil price controls—entitlements
system came into being in 1974 as a response to the OPEC oil
price increases. Should major cutbacks in OPEC production
occur in the future, the very thing *not* to do is to impose price
controls. On the contrary, maximum price flexibility should
be maintained.

Related to a policy of decontrol, the United States should
be committed to free trade in energy markets. This means
that importers of crude oil should never be "urged" not to
purchase on the spot market as they were in the spring and
early summer of 1979 (which contributed to our gasoline
shortages that year). Similarly, importers of natural gas
should be free to strike any contract they wish with Mexican
or Canadian suppliers.

Protect the poor. While the permanent decontrol of
energy prices is essential, we must recognize that this will
impose a significant burden on the poor. In our 1977 article,
Robert Hall and I suggested expanding the present food-
stamp program to cover fuel expenditures as the most
promising way of helping the poor in this area. Food-stamp
allotments could be increased and home heating bills (or that
portion of a family's rent allocated to fuels) and gasoline
could be covered under the program. If the expanded food-
stamp program were aimed at the lowest 20 percent of the income distribution, the additional cost to the taxpayer would
be modest—certainly much less than subsidizing all energy
consumption as in the past.

Keep the government out of commercialization. We have already discussed the synthetic fuels program as an example of a misguided policy. The lesson is simple: private companies, and not the government, should undertake the commercialization of new energy technologies. Furthermore, private companies do not need—and should not receive— government subsidies for the production of particular energy supplies. This rule should apply to the full gambit of nonconventional energy sources—shale oil, liquified or gasified coal, solar energy, biomass, wind power, etc. If any of these energy sources are economical or will become economical, private companies will have all the incentive they need to produce them, and there is simply no role for government subsidies.

Do not let the government choose the fuel mix of the future. One of the biggest dangers of large government subsidization of synthetic fuels and other nonconventional energy supplies is that it allows the government to decide which fuels will be produced commercially in the future, and to do so on political and bureaucratic grounds rather than on economic ones.

Today no one can accurately predict what energy sources will turn out to be most economical fifteen or twenty years from now.

For example, some have claimed that oil and natural gas supplies will dwindle over the next fifteen or twenty years, so that these fuels will account for a relatively small proportion of our total energy consumption by the year 2000.[6] This claim may turn out to be correct, but it may also turn out to be totally incorrect. At this point we simply *don't know* what the potential is for further oil and gas discoveries, particularly in the face of rising prices. The statistical, geological, and econometric evidence is unclear, and it indicates that there is considerable uncertainty over supply levels at higher prices. Furthermore, there have been recent indications that those supplies may be very significant and may come from sources that would not have been predicted five years ago.

Again, the point here is a simple one. The fuel mix of the future should be determined by energy producers on economic grounds and should be financed by energy consumers, not by the government. Any fuel mix that is artificially imposed —whether it consists of solar energy, "conservation," or synthetic fuels—can only increase the long-run cost of energy for all of us.

The government should support energy research. Although the government should keep out of the development and production phases of energy supply, government support of basic research is a good economic policy. Technological advance in energy is critical and needs to be encouraged. Government funding is warranted because basic research into new energy technologies has a high social value that is greater than the incentives facing private researchers. The ideas and techniques developed in publicly supported research can and should be made freely available. The private sector can be counted on to commercialize those new technologies that make good economic sense.

Impose a tariff on imported oil. Even with the complete deregulation of energy markets, our dependence on imported oil would probably continue to be higher than is economically, politically, and strategically desirable. It would make good sense to further reduce our dependence on imported energy and thereby reduce the potential economic impact of any sudden increases in world energy prices. The most effective means of reducing this dependence would be to impose a tariff on imported oil. Such a tariff would increase the price of energy to consumers and producers in the United States. By reducing energy consumption and increasing domestic energy production, the tariff would further reduce our imports. Proceeds from the tariff could be—and should be—used to help finance reductions in the payroll tax. This would reduce the overall cost of production in the economy and offset both the recessionary and inflationary impacts of rising energy prices.[7]

Develop the strategic oil reserve. The creation of a strategic oil reserve should be another important component of energy policy. A strategic reserve has two functions. First, in the event of an all-out war or military action that disrupted most shipping and trading of oil, the world oil market might cease to function and imports might be unavailable at any price. Strategic reserves could then be used to prevent such shortages.

Second, short of a major military conflict, strategic reserves are not needed to prevent shortages. But a *sharp* increase in energy prices resulting from an OPEC production cutback could be economically damaging to this country. A strategic reserve could be used to smooth out price increases in the wake of such a production cutback.[8]

It is important, however, to point out that strategic reserves are most effective when they form part of a multilateral agreement. When a stockpile is released, no matter where it happens to be, it adds to the supply of oil in the *world* market and thereby reduces the world price. If *only* the United States released a stockpile in the wake of a crisis, its imports of oil would fall but the impact on world oil prices—and prices faced by American consumers—would be minor. On the other hand, if most of the major OECD (Organization of Economic Cooperation and Development) nations maintained large stockpiles of oil which, as part of an international agreement, were released into the market following a production cutback, this would significantly reduce any resulting economic damage.

CONCLUSION

The agenda discussed above would represent a significant change in American energy policy. Some of these measures can be implemented easily, but others will be difficult to implement because of pressures from certain interest groups and possible resistance from Congress and the public.

Crude oil price controls are scheduled for demise by October 1981, but the president could remove these controls earlier by an executive order. (Congress must be informed of the intention to deregulate and would have thirty days to disapprove.) Deregulation of natural gas prices, on the other hand, would require new legislation. The president should push hard for that legislation and, in particular, should seek to couple complete deregulation of natural gas prices with a 25 percent windfall profits tax on gas produced through conventional means. (Natural gas deregulation would probably lead to a 70 to 100 percent increase in new contract prices, but that would represent only a 10 to 20 percent increase in average field prices and smaller percentage increases in wholesale and retail prices.)

Retail gasoline prices should also be deregulated and the Department of Energy's gasoline "allocation system" (implemented under the Emergency Petroleum Allocation Act) should be dismantled. Both of these actions could be done by executive order. Under normal market conditions deregulation would cause little if any change in retail gasoline prices, although gasoline prices could increase significantly were there to be a sharp increase in world oil prices. But such an increase would then be desirable as a means of restraining consumption and averting shortages—shortages that in 1979 were only exacerbated by the DOE allocation system.

The president should also seek to impose a tariff on imported oil of about $10 per barrel. In the absence of an emergency, it is unclear whether the president could impose this tariff without congressional legislation, so such legislation should be sought.

Twenty billion dollars have already been earmarked for synthetic fuel subsidies and part of that amount has already been disbursed. That figure, however, represents a current ceiling on spending, so that the administration need not continue further disbursements. (Any unspent money would revert back to the Treasury and would reduce any budget deficit.) The president should make a clear commitment to dismantle the synthetic fuels program—which will be difficult, since some of his own political support has come from the large companies that will gain from these subsidies. On the other hand, it is doubtful that the president's intentions to cut government spending will remain credible if this glaring example of government waste on a vast scale is allowed to continue.

As explained at the outset of this chapter, there are good reasons for the past failures of government to develop sensible energy policies. The public and its elected representatives in Congress are not eager to face the reality of expensive energy and all that it implies. The political obstacles are large, and until they are overcome we will continue to flounder.

This country will be dangerously vulnerable to disruptions in the supply of imported oil, particularly that from the Middle East, until sensible energy policies are developed and implemented. The real cost of energy to the American public will continue to rise more than is necessary. Furthermore, we will be handicapped in the fight against inflation and the overall health of our economy could be jeopardized.

But much of the problem may lie in communication. The Carter administration's greatest failure in the area of energy policy was an inability or an unwillingness to explain the problem—and the necessary solutions—to the public in a convincing manner. If President Reagan can make the case to the public clearly, strongly, and consistently, if he can effectively convey an understanding of what must be done, that may turn out to be his most important asset.

13

RICHARD K. BETTS

Managing Foreign and Defense Policy

The drift toward insecurity. Dealing with substance: the diffusion of power. Policy instruments: military, economic, political, diplomatic. Interagency cooperation and coordination—political and professional appointees. The president's leadership style—magistral or activist. Legislative/executive relations. Constraints and trade-offs.

President Reagan will face imposing challenges in the international arena which will be more difficult to meet than ever before, even if all his ideas and choices turn out to be wise. The greater clarity that has emerged in the past few years about the scope of these problems will help him; the foreign policy establishment's unwarranted optimism through much of the 1970s—about superpower détente, stabilization of arms competition, and the trend toward greater international cooperation that should flow from increasing economic interdependence—has been washed away. On the other hand, there is now less room for maneuver and less margin for error than in the first three decades of the postwar era. Moreover, the greater clarity about the general challenges masks a large reservoir of confusion about priorities and the interrelationships between specific problems. There is no reason to let fatalism overwhelm policy, though, because there is much the president *can* do to cope with adversity.

U.S. opinion on foreign policy fluctuates periodically between extremes of alarmism and complacency. The reaction to the Vietnam war after 1970 discredited concern about Soviet military power and the competition for influence in the Third World and led to a frantic counterreaction, congealed at the end of the decade by the kidnapping of U.S. diplomats in Iran and the Soviet invasion of Afghanistan. Dramatic shifts in opinion, which flow from disillusionment with overambitious conceptions rather than from the pragmatic and balanced appreciation of the complex mix of danger and opportunity that always underlies international relations, risk near-hysterical overreactions that breed subsequent reversals. Neither high drama nor nonchalance provide reliable bases for coherent and consistent policy. To arrest the drift toward insecurity without sacrificing enduring improvement to quick cosmetic gains, the president will have to navigate treacherous channels of strategic calculation and domestic management. He will have to identify not only the constraints he faces in rebuilding the country's security, but also the *limits* of the threats which, in some instances, may make low-key adaptation more effective than muscle-flexing that could boomerang in the long term.

Unlike bureaucratic departments, congressional committees, or pundits who can address particular elements of foreign policy while ignoring others that may pose contradictory requirements, the president has to grasp the full range of U.S. imperatives, interests, and ideals, and manage an integrated and viable response. His task can be appreciated logically by breaking it down into two levels: the external *substance* of problems in the international sphere, and the internal *process* through which responses can be developed within the American political system.

SUBSTANCE: POLICY AND STRATEGY

At the peak of the cold war there was little doubt about the nature and scope of U.S. foreign policy. There were uncertainties in the immediate postwar period, reflected in criticisms of Truman's policies from the left (Henry Wallace) and right (Robert Taft) and in the "great debate" on sending U.S. troops to Europe; but two events in 1950 provided the basis for a new consensus on America's role in the world. The first was the drafting of NSC−68, the government study that recommended unprecedented increases in peacetime military power (see Hammond 1962, pp. 267−398; Huntington 1961, pp. 47−64). The second was the shock of the Korean war which made the implementation of NSC−68 feasible, producing massive rearmament and a new plateau of peacetime defense spending (from which defense budgets — exclusive of large increments for the Vietnam war — have since varied up or down, but by no more than 6 percent in any single year). Until the end of the 1960s, when disillusionment over Vietnam fractured the cold-war consensus, U.S. presidents, Congress, and public opinion remained nearly united in commitment to one overriding goal: the containment of Russian and Chinese communist power.

The post-Vietnam interregnum turned out to be short. Today's renewed militancy, however, cannot solve current problems by wholesale resurrection of pre-Vietnam policies. The world has changed in some ways that may ease the demands on American policy, but in many more ways that are likely to increase them.

Global trends

The overarching characteristic of the evolution of the international system from an American perspective has been the diffusion of power. In absolute terms, despite recent economic difficulties, the United States has more resources and power potential than it had at the peak of the cold war. But meaningful power is relative, and it has been steadily slipping away from the United States in three directions.

The first is toward the East. The Soviet Union has an inferior and inefficient economy which is entering a period of severe strain. But over the thirty-five years since the USSR emerged exhausted from World War II, its economic growth has reduced the gap between the superpowers. Moscow still presents no competitive challenge in world trade, but its more autarkic system can translate internal economic progress into the one dimension that *can* threaten the West: military power.

This does not mean that the president has to resign the country to living with a greater threat. Two developments work in the other direction. One is that China, in the past decade, has changed from a threat that Washington must meet into a threat that Moscow must confront. The second is the diffusion of power to U.S. allies in the industrialized world. More dramatically than the Soviet Union, Western Europe and Japan have recovered from the devastation of war to the point that they equal or surpass the United States in many economic respects. When the balance of power is considered in the collective terms of the two alliance systems rather than in terms of the two superpowers alone, Moscow seems less strong. The Soviet Union substantially outspends the United States on defense, for example, but the North Atlantic Treaty Organization (NATO) as a whole outspends the Warsaw Pact.[1]

The growth in allied power potential, however, is a mixed blessing. First, it has not been translated into a commensurate growth in actual military power. No ally devotes as large a proportion of its domestic product to defense as does the United States. Historically this is no problem, because American preeminence after 1945 was so overwhelming that it seemed logical to all that this country would assume a disproportionate burden and responsibility for containment. Now that German and Japanese living standards rival American, however, there is an objective contradiction in a relationship whereby the United States should sacrifice more to defend these countries than they do themselves. Some disproportion can be written off as the price we pay to lead the alliance and to keep most of the nuclear deterrent under U.S. control. If the gap in relative effort remains large, however, the contradiction will become progressively harder to ignore, especially as U.S. desires to improve military capabilities run up against severe domestic fiscal limitations.

The second problem is the divergence between Washington and allied capitals over the emphasis that should be placed on military power as an element in relations with the Soviet Union. Only Britain today comes close to the same view of how to meet the Soviet threat, and the Thatcher government could be replaced by an increasingly leftist Labour Party. West Germany has developed a huge stake in economic cooperation with the East. Japan is increasing military investments, but slowly; as a proportion of gross national product, its defense effort remains barely a quarter of that of the United States. Allies who are more dependent on trade will not welcome confrontationist policies toward the East (or toward unfriendly Arab states). The solidarity of the alliance thus is threatened by both the allies' greater interest in détente and the U.S. interest in distributing military burdens more equitably.

The third direction in which power has diffused is toward the nonindustrial world, most significantly the energy exporters of the Middle East. The decline of American hegemony over the global economy is the most jarring and least remediable of adverse economic trends. Aside from a possibly infeasible and probably counterproductive solution by pure imperialism—the seizure of Persian Gulf oil fields—this is a change that agile American policy may moderate (with more effective energy policies) but will still have to live with. The diffusion of sovereignty to other parts of the nonindustrial world since decolonization in the 1960s is less of a threat to the United States, because the power of these states did not grow substantially with independence. But it still matters. Should American exasperation with poor, leftist, and belligerent Third World countries lead to disdainful hauteur in our policies, Angolas and Ethiopias will proliferate no matter how much we pump up anti-Soviet military forces and covert political action.

Instruments of policy

A foreign policy designed to make the world safe for America depends on power, ideology, and strategies for making the best use of both. The principal dimensions of power are military and economic. To exploit both requires some degree of compromise between draining resources to minimize near-term military risk and conserving them to protect long-term economic advantage. Compared to the Soviet Union, the United States faces the greatest challenge in the military sphere. We must redress the adverse trends of the past decade without further deranging the U.S. economy. The trade-off is by no means delicate, and it becomes severe only at extreme levels of military investment. Determining how much military power is enough requires an appreciation of the limits to how many global interests it can protect. The foreign policy establishment during much of the 1970s veered too sharply toward denigrating the utility of force. The challenge now is to ensure that the pendulum of opinion does not swing too far in the other direction, toward insensitivity to the political and diplomatic aspects of the competition for influence in parts of the world where superpower military confrontation is a smaller danger—or a less useful strategy—than in the highest priority regions. But in any case, force remains the *ultima ratio,* and therefore the highest priority for concern.

Military power

Rapprochement with China has reduced the demands on U.S. military planning from what they were before the 1970s (by facilitating the reduction of forces earmarked for Asian contingencies), but other global developments have, on balance, increased requirements. The emergence of the Persian Gulf—Indian Ocean area as a new third theater of defense commitment, together with the consistent improvement of Soviet military capabilities at all levels, has raised the question of the adequacy of U.S. force posture more insistently than at any time since 1950.

The highest level of threat to the United States is the danger of thermonuclear war. Until the early 1970s Washington always had confidence in American nuclear superiority over the Soviet Union. There were times when fears arose that such superiority was about to be lost, such as that at the end of the 1950s, and there were often doubts that superiority really offered much protection against conventional aggression, given the USSR's capacity to retaliate against American cities. But by the 1970s strategic nuclear parity had definitely arrived, and by 1980 many observers— including virtually all of President Reagan's defense advisors—were convinced that clear Soviet superiority would exist in the early 1980s.

Many analysts would still argue that a numerical advantage in nuclear striking power will not benefit the Russians because many U.S. forces would survive a surprise attack and could devastate Russian civil and industrial targets even if they could not effectively attack Soviet military targets. Even the Carter administration rejected this view as complacent, and President Reagan certainly accepted the counterarguments (see Nitze 1976, 1978).[2] Now he has to decide what to do about it in terms of procurement, strategy, and arms control initiatives.

The principal elements of strategic nuclear force modernization have been in development since before the Carter administration: the MX intercontinental ballistic missile (ICBM), Trident submarines and C−4 and D−5 submarine-launched ballistic missiles (SLBM), a new manned bomber to replace aging B−52s, and advanced long-range cruise missiles. Yet the fruition of many of these programs still lies far on the horizon. Even by optimistic estimates, the MX cannot begin deployment before the middle of the decade, and the most critical aspect of the program's development—the design of a viable mobile basing system—has proved intractable to date. Every scheme devised has posed severe liabilities, either in technical efficacy, cost, environmental impact, or political objections in the localities where the bases would be constructed. The simplest solution would be to put the new missiles in the old silos that housed the Minuteman ICBMs they are to replace, but this would defeat the purpose of making them less vulnerable to attack. Competing demands on shipbuilding capacity limit the rate at which Trident submarines can be deployed, and snags have already put that program behind schedule (Burt 1980, pp. A1, A17). President Carter cancelled production of the B−1 bomber in 1977 on grounds that it would soon be vulnerable to Soviet air defenses and that reliance on cruise missiles launched from B−52s offered a more cost-effective alternative for the 1980s. Constraints on the production of cruise missiles and on the rate at which B−52s can be reconfigured to carry them limit the extent to which they can compensate for lags in other nuclear forces. Returning to the B−1 is not as attractive now even to many air force officers, given the possibility of developing a more capable aircraft.

President Reagan thus faces a trade-off between efficiency and risk. Some of his advisors recommended several "quick fixes"—production or redeployment of weapon systems that already exist rather than waiting for more advanced designs—to reduce weaknesses in the first half of this decade (see Van Cleave et al. 1979). If the possibility of war or a confrontation like the Cuban missile crisis is high in this period, quick fixes may be advisable. But if the president is more concerned with getting the most for each defense dollar over the long haul, such projects appear wasteful. Technical efficiency, though, is more calculable than strategic risk.

Prudence dictates in favor of hedging against risk, but this does not solve the problem of choice because enhancing nuclear power must be balanced against improving conventional forces. And the latter are in an even worse state. While U.S. nuclear striking power declined relative to the Soviets' in the 1970s, it increased absolutely as the number and accuracy of warheads grew. But conventional forces for combat on land and at sea declined *both* relatively and absolutely. Much of the shrinkage can be attributed to the phasing out of the Vietnam war and to the rapprochement with China, but not all. While Soviet forces facing the North Atlantic Treaty Organization (NATO) have not grown quantitatively since 1968, they have improved qualitatively and the Soviet navy has expanded dramatically.

Improving the U.S. position in the conventional balance poses many choices, but four stand out. Most fundamental is the number of simultaneous contingencies which U.S. forces should be able to handle. The most ambitious formulation was the "two-and-a-half wars" notion of the Democratic administrations in the 1960s: the capacity to fight major wars in both Europe and Asia as well as a smaller engagement in some other area such as the Caribbean. The move to a "one-and-a-half war" criterion in the 1970s was justified by the Nixon Doctrine's greater reliance on allied manpower. With the new focus on the Persian Gulf, the Carter administration appeared to be moving toward what some observers see as a "one-and-*two*-half wars" strategy—Europe, Korea, and the Middle East. The only way to rationalize such a strategy without expanding ground and naval forces is to accept a higher level of risk, either by earmarking fewer units for each contingency or by liberalizing the "drawdown rules"— that is, relaxing the assumption that the United States would have to fight on all three fronts at once, and planning to be able to shift some elements of forces for one theater into another.

A second choice, for the navy, is between continuing to invest in a force structure which emphasizes large ships with high unit capabilities or shifting toward a larger number of smaller vessels. The Soviets have far more combat ships than the United States, but the advantage is reversed in terms of total tonnage; the USSR does not, in contrast to the U.S. Navy, organize its fleets around large attack aircraft carriers. The American carrier task force embodies a more impressive dose of striking power, but large ships are increasingly vulnerable to attack.

Another choice is whether to focus on visible combat capabilities (weaponry and manpower) for ground force improvement or to concentrate on increasing transport assets (airlift and sealift) for global mobility. Mobility is more vital to Washington than to Moscow, since the likely arenas of combat are further from the United States. Although our capacity to project power in most parts of the world is superior, it is not sufficient to ensure a comparable interventionary advantage in such specific critical areas as the Persian Gulf.

The fourth and most difficult choice is whether to return to conscription. The All-Volunteer Force is expensive, since pay must be competitive with the civilian economy if the services are to attract competent people. Personnel costs now account for over half of the defense budget. At least at the margins, this constricts investment in hardware. Even with high pay, there is a limit to the numbers of people who can be attracted and thus to the number of labor-intensive components of military power (such as army divisions) that can be fielded. And to the extent that the United States relies on sophisticated weapon systems to compensate for manpower, the premium rises on retaining skilled technicians—which again puts pressure on pay scales.

Strategies

The challenges and choices so far discussed all involve the visible elements of military power, hardware, and personnel. Increases in force levels in themselves, however, will not solve defense problems. Their value depends on the strategies and tactics that would determine their application in war. These considerations complicate choices because some of them mandate investments that might have to be made at the expense of additional materiel or combatant manpower.

In the area of nuclear warfare, for example, the simplest and cheapest strategy in terms of procurement would be to retaliate immediately against any Soviet attack by striking back, with all surviving forces, against Soviet cities and industrial complexes. A consensus has grown, however, that such a plan alone would not maximize deterrence and would be irrational to implement if deterrence failed. If President Reagan intends to follow the counsel of his defense advisors and keep widening the flexibility of U.S. retaliatory options as his predecessors have tried to do, it will be less important to buy additional missiles and bombers than to fortify command, control, and communications facilities, survivable reconnaissance assets, computer systems capable of functioning in nuclear environments, and civil defense infrastructures.

At the conventional level there is also a dilemma in seeking both flexibility and high force levels. One aspect of the problem is the low "teeth-to-tail" (combat to support) ratio in U.S. ground forces. The vast bulk of force structure is devoted to logistics and supply rather than to combat elements. This increases the capacity to fight a long war and to redeploy forces over great distances, but it limits firepower. The trade-off is most evident in the area of readiness, a concern that has grown in salience as the increasing technological complexity of weapon systems has made maintenance progressively more difficult. Congress has regularly preferred buying additional weapons to appropriating funds to keep inventories combat ready. U.S. tactical aircraft such as the F−14 and F−15 are the most sophisticated in the world, but they are unflyable much of the time because of repair and maintenance requirements.

All this points to the increased dubiousness of the traditional American devotion to maximizing the technical quality and versatility of individual weapons. Sophisticated systems raise unit costs, thus reducing the number of weapons that can be procured as well as the readiness of those few that do enter the force structure. A "high-low" mix of high-performance systems and cheaper, less-advanced ones is the solution in principle, but to date it has proved difficult to implement in practice (see White 1974, pp. 3−60).

All of these military problems could be tackled by spending more money, but they are too great to be solved across the board. The president will have to make fundamental choices about strategic priorities that will guide the defense establishment in determining where first to put the patches. In any case, they underline the limits to military power and the importance of looking to other dimensions of influence.

Economic power

Economic power is still our primary advantage in the international arena. The Soviets can offer ideological encouragement and modern weapons to struggling new nations, but they can do comparatively little to solve these countries' development problems. The trilateral allies still dominate international trade, and anti-Soviet oil exporters such as Saudi Arabia are among the most important emerging middle powers. Western economic aid and investment are tools that the USSR cannot match in the global competition for influence. The problematic aspects of international economic policy for the United States lie more in relations with our friends than with our enemies.

The West achieved economic preeminence because of the productive superiority of industrial capitalism, which relies on the pursuit of self-interest by those who hold the capital. In a world where interdependence and competition have been eroding Western power, the temptation is strong to reassert U.S. national self-interest by limiting economic aid and regulating trade flows that appear to favor foreign exporters. If U.S. economic power is to be used to promote a more expansive concept of national interest, however, it may require some sacrifice. Economic aid certainly cannot buy the fealty of Third World countries; considering how marginal the investment is compared to our defense budget, however, even marginal diplomatic gains can justify it. The refusal to assist poor nonaligned countries is no more consistent with enlightened conservatism than is military isolationism.

Similarly, a strict criterion of economic "fairness" in relations with industrial democracies is a logical goal, but if applied peremptorily it could cost more strategically—by threatening alliance cohesion—than it gains economically. One area in which western economic predominance could come back to bite us is that of finance. Cumulatively, the massive indebtedness of Eastern European and nonaligned nations that are potentially insolvent and politically unstable raises the spectre of large defaults and makes it uncertain whether the borrowers or lenders are the real hostages in the world economy. All of these considerations underline the salience of political skills in Washington's approach to international problems.

Diplomacy

Diplomacy is only a process, and aside from variations in the finesse with which it can transmit American messages, it supports national U.S. interests only to the extent that U.S. policies themselves are intrinsically compelling. Style matters, so the decisiveness with which Washington asserts "leadership" with its allies should not be undervalued. But leadership itself does not solve problems unless the president leads where Bonn, Tokyo, London, or other friendly capitals want to go. The differences in the objective interests of the trilateral allies establish a latent tension which poses opportunities and challenges for the president in reinvigorating NATO or harmonizing economic intercourse with Japan. But he will have to be supple, and his leadership will have to include compromise. For example, persuading Western European governments to improve their military forces might entail greater U.S. flexibility on arms control negotiations with Moscow. The December 1979 NATO decision to modernize long-range theater nuclear forces, for example, was premised on U.S. ratification of the SALT II treaty and on additional negotiations with the Russians on theater nuclear deployments.

The principal forum in which negotiations have been pursued as a substitute for unilateral initiatives over the past dozen years is that of the Strategic Arms Limitations Talks (SALT). President Reagan has declared his intention to obtain a more satisfactory agreement than Carter's SALT II treaty. But if the new administration holds out for a *significantly* more advantageous treaty, the Russians are unlikely to agree. The president will then face the difficult prospect that unilateral action to improve the relative U.S. position will not bear fruit until *after* the period covered by Carter's treaty. If the Soviets are unconstrained during that time, *their* programs could offset most of whatever gains Washington could make—or more. (The SALT II treaty requires the USSR to dismantle 250 strategic launchers and limits the number of independently targetable warheads it can place on individual missiles, while the principal U.S. investment programs—MX and Trident—are unconstrained.) Thus the most immediate and important political choice for the president is whether to put the principle of greater equity ahead of pragmatism or to seek minor cosmetic changes in SALT II acceptable to the Soviets in order to impose some restraints on their options in the early 1980s.

An even more delicate political challenge is the exertion of American influence in the Middle East. Historically the United States had little difficulty in treating its political values as part of its national interest because the ratio between our power and the dangers to our security was so high. With two oceans and weak or friendly nations on our borders, there was no need to subordinate the promotion of liberal democracy abroad to objective interests as defined in *Realpolitik* terms—wealth, power, and security. Indeed, supporting and increasing the number of regimes like our own generally contribute to American security. But in the Middle East the consistency between ideals and material interests is in doubt. The principal U.S. interest in the region is guaranteed access to oil, but uncritical support for the one progressive democracy in the area that shares U.S. values— Israel—may not help to secure that interest.

Many would argue that U.S. support for Israel has no bearing on the appeal of Arab radicalism or on the potential for

Soviet influence in the region or on the danger of revolution-
ary regime changes in conservative Persian Gulf states. If
every Arab leader were willing to make the same concessions
as Anwar Sadat, and could stay in power, that might be true.
But heavy U.S. economic subsidization of Israel (the country
has had a national budget higher than its GNP), coincident
with toleration of Israeli occupation of Arab territories, does
not help reduce hostility toward the United States. One problem is that a theoretically reasonable alternative—credibly
guaranteeing the survival of Israel in exchange for the
restoration of conquered Arab lands and some sort of Palestinian state—appeals neither to Americans nor to Israelis.
With a history of persecution and betrayal unparalleled in
the twentieth century, the Jews of Israel have scant reason
to willfully entrust their security to another nation, although
dependence on external economic support and on American
willingness to deter Soviet military intervention illustrates
the limits of sovereignty as a solution to security. To make
the guarantee credible as it is in Europe, at least a "tripwire"
U.S. force would have to be stationed in Israel, explicitly committed to engage any attacker. And even if this solution were
acceptable to Washington and Jerusalem, it would not address the danger of increased terrorism launched from a
"cancer state," as many Israeli characterize a potential
Palestinian entity.

But is stationing American forces in Israel so unpalatable
now that the United States is developing a Rapid Deployment Force designed primarily to intervene in the Persian
Gulf? Jerusalem would probably let Washington use Israeli
territory for that purpose. The issue for the president to
decide is whether there should be any linkage—some political concessions by Israel, perhaps only limited, in exchange
for increased security furnished by U.S. military power—or
whether Arab grievances are so unrelated to U.S. interests
or so insatiable that they should be ignored. The Middle East
presents problems that link American diplomatic, economic,

military, and domestic political interests. If the new administration can function adeptly enough to develop an integrated policy and to shepherd it through external and internal political constraints, then it can probably function successfully on *any* issue.

POLICY: CHOOSING AND IMPLEMENTING

The international system presents the dangers and opportunities with which the United States has to grapple, and poses constraints on the feasible policy alternatives the president can consider. Because these bounds are uncertain, however, and because some domestic goals compete with foreign policy concerns, the range of choice is wide. The president needs a conscious strategy for concerting the intragovernmental processes of assessment, consultation, and generation of options. His problem is to choose policies that are not only sensible in terms of international imperatives and constraints, but are capable of navigating the shoals of a domestic political structure in which power is extraordinarily dispersed. Thus the president must integrate administration, choice, and salesmanship. The starting point is the pattern of organization that he establishes or allows to evolve within the executive branch.

Machinery and procedures for management

The principal administrative alternatives are a hierarchical system in which one or two presidential subordinates are dominant or a collegial cabinet system. The latter appears attractive in principle but has rarely worked in practice. The National Security Council (NSC) was created in the late 1940s to be the primary forum for collective deliberation on foreign and defense policy by cabinet-level officials, but most presidents have relied on less formal processes. Eisenhower gave his secretary of state a strong mandate as his number one spokesman, and mediated between his secretaries of defense and treasury on issues of military spending. Nixon vested power in one assistant—Henry Kissinger. Other presidents have worked with different combinations of authority among top officials, but few have fostered a truly egalitarian process of decision-making.

A major debate in recent years has centered on how much influence White House personnel—specifically, the assistant to the president for national security affairs and his NSC staff—should have. Most observers maintain that such influence should be slight, that the NSC staff should be small and should function as a neutral coordinator of departmental studies and communications, and that the State Department should have the leading role in formulating and executing policies (Destler 1972). This, however, is a matter of presidential preference. Kissinger became dominant not because of any Svengali-like arrogation of power, but because Nixon wanted clout concentrated in the White House. Brzezinski frustrated the bureaucracy not because he usurped power, but because he was the only high-level advocate of hawkish policies in a government weighted with dovish appointees: Cyrus Vance functioned as an ad hoc manager more than an assertive leader, and Carter could not decide definitely which way to tilt in his policies, so Brzezinski's status grew out of his balancing role in the policymaking competition.

Which officials become dominant depends—obviously, but to a degree curiously unappreciated by many critics—on which inspire the most trust in the Oval Office. How much conflict develops among defense and foreign affairs agencies depends on how much Reagan encourages vigorous competition and advocacy, and on the extent to which dissensus is built into the structure of deliberation and decision (for instance, tension between fiscally stringent economic advisors and defense advisors intent on the dramatic expansion of military capabilities). More and more the substance of policy problems themselves, in a world where trade-offs in U.S. goals have become harder to submerge, promotes incoherence in the policymaking process. The president can strive for coherence by two related methods. He can staff his administration with appointees who are all devoted to the same priorities, determining from the outset to favor certain considerations and to slight others, and let the "magistrate" pattern of governance take its course. And he can let the bureaucracy wrangle over issues and resolve them himself in a sequential but consistent manner. Carter failed because he did neither.

In any case, the solution does not lie in the organizational *structure*; changing the organization chart can only modify the *potential* for more coherent decision-making. The solution depends on how the president integrates his own general preferences into the process of specific deliberations. If he appoints people who share the same views and who work well together to the four top foreign affairs positions—the secretaries of state and defense, the assistant to the president for national security, and the director of central intelligence—the system will function well and the president's personal burden will be eased. The risk in such homogeneity lies in excessive certainty about policy priorities and in the danger that basic assumptions not challenged regularly—in a way that only diversity of views at the height of government can ensure—may lead to overcommitment and surprise when specific problems evolve in a manner that fails to conform to expectations. The alternative system—maximizing pragmatism by letting freewheeling disagreement among advisors and agencies highlight uncertainties and policy trade-offs—can also function well. But that alternative places a heavier burden on the president, requiring him to spend longer hours digesting memoranda, adjudicating disputes, and taking responsibility for controversial choices. No theorist can specify which alternative makes better sense, because the option depends on which sort of risks in decision-making are more comfortable to the president personally.

The discussion so far has dealt only with the overarching conception of foreign policy management. Other considerations of more particular inter- and intradepartmental mechanisms for coping with national security problems pose less direct but ultimately important choices. One is the question of interagency cooperation on crosscutting issues which have multiplied since World War II. This is related to the degree to which functional responsibilities are compartmentalized within departments or duplicated between them. For example, the Defense Department has a "little State Department"—the Office of International Security Affairs (ISA) and, since 1977, the Office of the Under Secretary for Policy; the State Department has a "little Defense Department"— the Bureau of Politico-Military Affairs (PM). Both units used to be minor, but Robert McNamara made ISA an important office in the 1960s and Cyrus Vance beefed up PM. A president concerned with streamlining government to make it more efficient might choose to reduce the profile of both organizations and to segregate departmental responsibilities more explicitly. This would place a higher burden on the secretaries of state and defense, however, to sort out overlapping problems themselves, or else risk increasing the chances that some foreign and defense programs might unfold in a disjointed or contradictory fashion. Spartan efficiency and careful coordination do not always go hand in hand.

Coordination, of course, is no simple solution to the conflicting missions of different agencies.[3] A clear example of the problem is the role of the director of central intelligence (DCI) who is responsible not only for his own organization, the Central Intelligence Agency, but also for overseeing other elements of the intelligence "community": principally the Defense Intelligence Agency, National Security Agency, intelligence organizations of the separate military services, and the State Department Bureau of Intelligence and

Research. These other units are also responsible to their parent departments. The DCI's authority has never matched his responsibility, and attempts to assert his control have frequently been resisted. The Defense Department and its services in particular have complained that CIA analysts have delved too far into the analytical territory of the military. Unless we are to return to a pre–Pearl Harbor system of completely decentralized intelligence, however, the DCI has to have a mandate to coordinate. The limits of that mandate are important, and can be determined by no one but the president. This problem of authority, of course, is only part of the challenge to improving foreign intelligence. The appointment of a political confidant as DCI will probably, in itself, increase the clout of the top manager. If William Casey devotes his attention to covert action rather than to improving the production of estimative intelligence, however, or tries to purge "liberal" analysts and to deliberately skew analysis toward hard-line "realism," blind spots in intelligence will persist, simply in another direction. The most important function of intelligence is to tell decision-makers what they don't want to hear. For that function to be fulfilled, though, decision-makers themselves must not only tolerate analysts who do not share their assumptions; they must encourage them (see Betts 1980).

Finally, there is the question of how free a rein the president wants to give his political appointees as opposed to that given the permanent professionals in their agencies. In the domestic area, Reagan has appeared committed to clipping the wings of the bureaucracy and enforcing major policy changes from the top. On foreign policy, his rhetoric has suggested that strong political leadership will ensure that the career foreign service does not simply carry on business as usual. This interest, however, does not clearly carry over to defense policy, where many conservative Republicans have been advocating a diminution of the power of civilian staffs in the Pentagon and some restoration of programmatic decision-making authority to the professional military.

The Office of Program Analysis and Evaluation (PA&E) has been a particular irritant to the services. If PA&E is cut back, however, the question involves how to deal with the trade-offs between the programs of the different services, since the American military does not have a fully developed general staff on the Prussian model. Given the necessity of providing firepower support for ground force operations, for example, how much should be invested in army artillery or in air force fighter-bombers? Each service would prefer to be self-sufficient. Simply aggregating all their programs, though, would cost far more than even a much-expanded defense budget could supply and would be wastefully duplicative. The president and secretary of defense can force the Joint Chiefs of Staff to resolve the trade-offs by bargaining among themselves under the constraint of a fixed budget ceiling, but this still risks increasing the gaps or overlaps in capabilities that a supraservice analytical staff might help to avoid. There are certainly serious disadvantages in relying on civilian program analysts.[4] Streamlining the input side of the bureaucracy, however, does not necessarily support efficiency in the output: an integrated and complementary set of military capabilities.

The effectiveness of any of these management choices depends on two more general considerations: the president's personal preference for how *he* wishes to function in the policymaking process, and the manner in which he tempers the results of executive branch deliberations with concern for the constraints of public opinion and congressional power.

LEADERSHIP STYLE

The basic management choice for a chief executive is whether to function as a referee and "magistrate," delegating the details of policy formation to his subordinates and their agencies, encouraging bureaucratic consensus, or as an "activist," fostering bureaucratic competition that forces issues to the top, reserving the maximum number of decisions to himself (Destler 1977, pp. 164–65). In recent times Dwight Eisenhower and Gerald Ford have most typified the former type, and Franklin Roosevelt, John Kennedy, Richard Nixon, and Jimmy Carter, the latter. Harry Truman and Lyndon Johnson fell in between, though closer to the activist model. Until recently, political scientists tended to favor the activist model of leadership, perhaps in part because it coincided with their own partisan preferences.[5] Distaste for the results of activism by Nixon and Carter, and a growing nostalgia for the stability of policy in the 1950s, have led many analysts toward greater appreciation for the "magistrate" style.[6]

The problem with executive activism is overload; there are not enough hours in the day for the president to master the intricacies of all complex issues, talk to a sufficient range of contending experts, and resolve second- or third-order policy disputes. The problem with emphasizing delegation is that it fosters conservatism (in the literal sense), harnesses policy to bureaucratic constipation and compromise, and almost guarantees that policy change will be slow and incremental rather than dramatic. Thus the president's choice of administrative practice cannot be divorced from the substance of his goals. If Reagan wishes to play safe in piloting the ship of state in the international arena, there are advantages to letting the foreign affairs agencies bargain among their competing concerns while he reserves his attention for the few insoluble bureaucratic disputes that flag critical issues. If he wishes to change the nation's course sharply, however, it will be difficult to do so without personally grabbing as many reins as possible and dictating what he wants to do, irrespective of the views of some experts who disagree. This requires taking risks, and perhaps limiting debate within the bureaucracy. The extreme example of this was Nixon's secret orchestration of the dramatic rapprochement with China. In reality, of course, the choice normally lies between the extremes. An organizational pattern of communication and authority will emerge, depending on how the evolution of the president's working relationships matches the formal plans he establishes early in the administration.

Controlling his own subordinates will be difficult for the president, as any student of bureaucracy knows. But, at least in the executive branch, officials must obey direct orders if the president gives them and follows them up. Congress, however, is a body that the president must convince and cooperate with. The transfer of power to the Republican party in the Senate will help Reagan by eliminating some of the problems of divided government that hampered Eisenhower, Nixon, and Ford. But much of the tension between the executive and legislative branches is institutional rather than partisan. Carter lacked staunch support on Capitol Hill, despite the Democratic party's control of both branches.

The vaunted growth of legislative activism in the 1970s was in large part a reaction to the Vietnam war and Watergate. Congressional power to ratify treaties is unlikely to hamstring Reagan as it did Carter, because any treaty Reagan negotiates is likely to be more advantageous than the minimum demands of a substantial majority in Congress. Even the most visible example of Congress's reassertion of its foreign policy role—the War Powers Act—is not a severe constraint on the president. In the post-Afghanistan climate it is difficult to envision a situation, given the new conservative complexion of Congress, in which the president would undertake a major use of force (longer than sixty days) that Congress would not endorse.

The principal area in which legislative-executive relations could be critical is the appropriation of funds, and the defense budget is the financial hub of foreign policy. Democratic control of the House of Representatives builds in potential friction, though it is notable that Congress, under

Carter, favored higher military spending than the president. Unless Reagan decides to push for truly massive defense increases—say, over 6 or 7 percent real growth in obligational authority—the legislative branch is unlikely to obstruct him.

The crucial arena of conflict will be the executive branch, as defense planning confronts the fiscal restraint of the Treasury Department and the Office of Management and Budget (OMB). If the president tries to leave decisions on the proper level of military expenditure to negotiations within his cabinet, he needs a secretary of defense who shares the priorities of his principal economic advisors—and Caspar Weinberger headed the OMB under Nixon—or else he needs to be ready, himself, to stipulate the size of the defense budget. Otherwise, given the contradictorily ambitious demands of the economic and defense policies articulated during the campaign, the internal disarray of his government on this issue will make the Carter administration look like a model of coherence.

The final area in which the president's leadership style is vital is in dealing with public opinion. There are a few specific issues on which interest-group pressure will pose distinct limits to his freedom of maneuver: for example, the Arab-Israeli conflict, relations with Greece and Turkey, and Japanese imports. Should he choose policies that challenge the preferences of organized domestic constituencies on these matters, success will depend on his skill in invoking the notion of broader national interest, selling it rhetorically and mobilizing support among constituencies with less intense interests. On most other foreign policy questions, however, public opinion will become a constraint only retrospectively—if policies fail dramatically.

TOWARD PRESIDENTIAL GOVERNANCE
IN FOREIGN POLICY

Many of the problems President Reagan faces in developing, implementing, and nurturing effective policies for national security are constant: how to use and oversee a cumbrous and complex bureaucracy, accommodate with Congress, and carry on a consistent diplomacy in a world where American interests and involvements are so extensive and changeable that it is almost impossible to integrate them completely. These are problems of management, and success depends on the match between the president's general goals and personal administrative habits, on one hand, and the pattern of political appointments he makes, on the other.

The constant problems of process, however, are not the most difficult ones. At worst, they can compound the substantive problems, which have grown more challenging. The U.S. position in the world is not as precarious as Reagan's campaign rhetoric suggested, but there is less room for mistakes than there was earlier in the postwar era when the U.S. economic and military power was relatively greater. Part of the solution does lie in the restoration of American power by unilateral initiatives. But relative power can never be restored to the level of twenty years ago. If the Carter administration erred through too blithe an acceptance of the assertiveness of other nations and a diminished global military role for the United States, the danger for the Reagan administration lies in unrealistic nostalgia for a world order that has changed for many reasons besides American failures of will.

As a successful politician, and as the only official in his own administration who must deal with the entire span of policy considerations, Reagan has more reason than his advisors to be sensitive to constraints and trade-offs. He may have to take the lead himself in recognizing that novel means of *influence* will have to compensate to some degree for the reduction in material *power* that used to be available to U.S. presidents. Such influence requires firmness and confidence, but also nimble political finesse and inventiveness in negotiation. Carter was finally compelled by international realities to move away from the liberal idealism and crude antimilitarism of many of his appointees to the foreign policy bureaucracy and toward more pragmatic balance-of-power policies, but he moved too late. His electoral defeat, however, was due more to domestic economic disarray than to failures abroad.

RECOMMENDATIONS

Leaving aside the question of whether President Reagan agrees with the outline of general preferences implicit in this chapter's presentation of foreign policy problems, I will offer a short list of recommendations he should consider.

Military policy. In the short term, massive across-the-board budget increases should be avoided. This is not just because the competing goal of domestic economic rehabilitation is vital. Huge new defense programs would overload the decayed defense production base, causing logjams, confusion, and inefficiency in procurement. That could rebound against long-term improvement by fueling another cycle of disillusionment with Pentagon "waste." Real growth of 3 or 4 percent a year in the defense budget, if allocated efficiently and especially if sustained for a prolonged period, would be better than a spurt of twice that rate for a few years followed by a decline. Increasing military pay is one useful measure that would not cause such problems, although for the longer term —if the Soviet threat does not diminish and U.S. rhetoric about the need to meet it is to be taken seriously by allies— the possibility of a return to conscription should be left open.

For both the short and long terms, *selected* improvements in readiness should be a high priority. Maximal readiness for *all* components of military forces would be wasteful and would reduce the funds available for increasing force levels. Many elements can be brought to high levels of readiness given the warning from a severe international crisis. Improvements should focus on the forces most vital for countering a surprise attack or a fast-breaking crisis. This suggests enhancing the day-to-day posture of the U.S. Seventh Army in Europe, possibly rebasing inland more of the Strategic Air Command's bombers, and investing heavily in airlift capability for the Rapid Deployment Force. Looking to the future, the administration should force the services and the research and development establishment to subordinate the qualitative "gold plating" orientation in weapon design to considerations of quantity and maintainability, in order to achieve a better high-low mix of capabilities.

In force structure investments, growth is needed in all areas, but the administration should avoid a nuclear fixation. More tanks and ships are as important as new missiles. To restrain growth in the Soviet nuclear advantage while U.S. strategic programs develop, President Reagan would do well to settle for a cosmetically modified SALT II treaty. To address longer-range requirements, the U.S. negotiating position should offer limitations on MX deployment geared to reductions in Soviet heavy ICBMs. Similarly, the Russians should know that the extent of U.S. theater nuclear force modernization will vary directly with their deployment of missiles such as the SS–20.

Economic policy. The most critical U.S. requirement is to reduce vulnerability to an interruption of oil supplies. Filling the scandalously low petroleum reserve is the most immediate response. Saudi objections should be politely rejected; after all, the Saudis should hardly be expected to have confidence in American power and protection if we voluntarily relinquish control of our own security. At the same time, Washington should make it clear that we are committed to the defense of Israel but will not support indefinite Israeli retention of Arab territory. The better solution, of course, is overall reduction of U.S. energy dependence, which is a matter of more slowly evolving domestic policy (conservation as well as expansion and diversification of energy sources) as much as foreign policy.

In dealing with Third World demands, such as the movement for a "new international economic order," there is nothing to be gained by blunt frankness. If the West is going to resist calls for unilateral redistribution of resources, Washington might as well cushion the policy with sugarcoated rhetoric. Avoiding symbolic provocation serves U.S. interests as does discriminating but increased foreign economic aid.

Diplomacy. If there is to be any chance of salvaging a modus vivendi with the USSR during the "window of vulnerability" while the United States rebuilds its military power—and if that rebuilding is not to be completely neutralized by additional Soviet military programs—American firmness must be coupled with restraint in rhetoric. Policy should be *articulated* in terms of regaining *parity* (even if the *real* goal is some degree of net advantage). Whether or not their motives are utterly cynical or paranoid, U.S. "superiority" is a codeword guaranteed to provoke vigorous counteraction by the Russians. Call the U.S. goal a "margin of safety" or whatever, but don't call it "superiority."

Diplomacy toward nations at the other end of the spectrum of international power should not repeat (in the opposite direction) the Carter administration's twin mistakes of overestimating the importance of relations with all Third World countries and assuming the need for an undiscriminating single standard for U.S. support. "Friendly" regimes should not be backed unconditionally, irrespective of their human rights policies. Rather, they should know that the United States will approach them in terms of its own national interests. Thus we should support countries such as South Korea, where it is strategically vital to do so despite unhappiness with the character of the regime, and should not support friendly but objectionable regimes such as South Africa, where it is strategically advisable not to do so. (Gains from better relations with Pretoria would be outweighed by damage to relations with many other countries, such as oil-rich Nigeria.)

Management. Assuming that President Reagan's personal style leans toward the "magistrate" model emphasizing delegation of authority, he should insist on the highlighting of subordinates' disagreements within the option papers that are passed to him, even when he asks for the consensus recommendation of NSC-level officials. This will at least alert him to potential uncertainties behind policy choices, toward which he should keep his antennae tuned as policies unfold. If he required his assistant to the president for national security affairs to monitor and investigate exceptions to interagency consensus without taking a personal position on the disputes, this would promote the coordinating function—as opposed to the more recent policy advocacy role—of that office, thus reinforcing the norm that the foreign policy staff in the White House avoid competing for power with the secretaries of state and defense.

Departmental officials should avoid reorganization except where absolutely necessary. Constant reorganization has proved to be a snipe hunt seeking easy procedural fixes for tough substantive problems. With the exception of *major* changes (as opposed to those that simply shuffle units around on the organization charts) such as the Defense Department reorganization of 1958 or the creation of new functions such as systems analysis, there is scant evidence that structural changes measurably improve policy output. And constant tinkering disrupts bureaucratic productivity.

Reagan's appointments have already revealed the priority he attaches to rebuilding the economy and his recognition of the need to move toward more centrist compromises in foreign policy than were represented in the views of his longest-standing supporters. The test of his effectiveness in the international sphere now depends on how pragmatic he can be while long-term economic policies take precedence over short-term military fixes. This requires skill in differentiating necessary trouble from unnecessary ideological confrontations with nonaligned states, friction with allies, and provocation of the Soviet Union. To do all that without sacrificing some of his ambitious goals will require not only skill, but luck.

V

Coda

14

ARNOLD J. MELTSNER

Politics and Governance

The need for governance. Critical early decisions—a time for caution. The short list of priorities. Popularity and leadership. Choice in a context of change. Interest groups, lobbyists, congressmen, the courts, and the press. The president and his policies. The use of crisis.

If we are not living in an age of discontent, we are certainly living in an age of disappointment. Faced with increasing taxes and inflation and an unstable international situation, Americans are feeling increasingly insecure and are questioning the competence and legitimacy of their governmental institutions. Many citizens ask not whether government is too large, but whether government at any level works at all. If government does not ensure our sense of security in the present and our prospects for the future, then it all too

readily can be seen as a waste of both the energies of the
people involved in it and the taxpayer money which supports
it. With the election of a new president and the installation of
a new administration, disappointment will give way to expectations for improvement. Americans put their faith and hope
in the new president without understanding the constraints
under which he must operate. Thus President Reagan has a
dual problem—to sustain the confidence of the people in him
and in their government while dealing practically with the
realities of the political system.

GOVERNMENT THROUGH POLITICS

Some observers believe that the president cannot govern.
Power is too diffuse and the authority of our political and economic institutions has been dissipated. In their view, a major
overhaul of our constitution is needed to give the president
the formal and informal powers to do the job. Such a view is
not particularly unique. Every period seems to call forth its
reformers who argue for more or less presidential power.
Those who clamor for more agree with how the president
might use it, while those who want less disapprove the way
past presidents have used their office and want to constrain
future ones. Regardless of the particular reform—a six-year
term, responsible party government, congressional
budgeting—it is not likely to affect the current president.
Major reforms, constitutional or otherwise, take time to
design and implement, and in the meantime the president
has to do the job. He cannot wait for some reform to come
about to make things easier. He must take the office as it is,
modify it to fit his style and needs, and govern. *Despite
difficulties and problems, the president can govern*. He has no
other choice but to do so.
    We have written this book for the president and his ad-
visors. Our objective was to enhance their ability to govern

by increasing an understanding of the political framework for action. It may seem strange that such an understanding should need to be increased, given that the new president has just been elected in a difficult campaign. But running for office is not the same thing as governing. Governing involves more than gathering present support; it also requires having a conception of the future. It means setting out in a steady direction and selecting policies.

Governance in the United States means to steer, and steering should not be confused with control. Past presidents all too often have attempted to control other participants in the political process, and have discovered the limits of their powers. In developing policies and setting out directions, the president must take into account the *systemic* nature of politics—the way institutions and political people connect and interact. Railing at one institution or trying to control another will likely only strengthen other participants and possibly precipitate unforeseen problems.

Despite the president's many formal and constitutional powers, personal persuasion and negotiation will be the principal aides in most of what he can accomplish. The president cannot simply order bureaucrats to eliminate waste or independent sovereign nations to behave in a predictable way. There are relatively few areas where he can act unilaterally and expect that his wishes will be accomplished. This puts the president in the uncomfortable position of being the citizens' chief problem-solver, without the resources to ensure effective implementation. While the president can determine his domain of action, he is dependent on others for the success of his actions.

THE VALUE OF CAUTIOUS OPTIMISM

In the aftermath of electoral victory and the inauguration, the president may come into his office with inflated expectations of what he can accomplish. If so, he will be in danger of believing his own campaign rhetoric, believing that he, as an individual, can actually "get the country moving." His staff and trusted confidants will also share in the general euphoria, and will be unwilling at times to present a more restrained picture of political reality. They will call for immediate and dramatic action. Having won the White House, everything seems possible, and Cassandras are likely to be shunned by an overly optimistic president and his staff.

This period at the beginning of an administration is one of great danger. What a president does then can often determine the reception and success of his entire term of office. His initial actions set a tone for future actions. He can easily waste the support of the country's citizens and the good wishes of the world's leaders. It should be a period of reflection, careful planning, and selection of critical policies. Instead, this period is often characterized by much option and wheel-spinning. The president all too often is confronted with reports of numerous task forces, briefing books, and advice from many friends and enemies. Everybody in this period, including me, has something to say to the president about how he should conduct his office and what he should do.

Part of the activity in the early months of an administration is necessary: positions must be filled and certain decisions must be made. There will be those, however, who will urge action because no time can be lost, since the congressional elections are less than two years off and the party must consolidate its position. No doubt a sensible objective for the president to pursue, but which action to take—and its timing—are not as clear. The notion that a great deal of proposed legislation must be sent up to Congress—otherwise the president will lose the initiative to other people—may be wrong. In the rush to get there first, presidents are apt to ignore the problems of congressional scheduling and timing and perhaps lose the support of the leadership and members.

Action in the congressional arena slows down by design. The Congress is supposed to deliberate and take its time to consider diverse views and interests. There are few reasons for a member of Congress to overcome resistance caused by partisanship, personal spite, constituent pressures, and genuine concern. Unfortunately for the president who wants immediate action, many of our problems of public policy have been with us for some time, and chronic problems help those who want to defer action. It takes time to build coalitions to pass legislation, and that is one reason why the president should take his time.

The president should also take his time to avoid mistakes. During this early period, presidents have been known to make the most severe foreign policy mistakes of their administration—recall the Bay of Pigs, for example. This is not to say that the president and his staff should not consult their advisors and listen to what they say. But the key to this period is to take time for reflection and for second thoughts, and particularly to select a clear policy agenda and strategy.

BE SELECTIVE

Being selective is not easy for a president when his transition task force, his advisors, and his close confidants all have incentives to present things for him to do. Part of the reward system for an advisor is acceptance of his advice; each advisor therefore has enormous incentives to push his own ideas for action. It is particularly important that the president know his own priorities and insist on phasing them in throughout the entire period of his administration. He must develop his own *short list* of priorities and objectives.

Suppose the president has five to ten key objectives he wants to accomplish in his administration. He should not try to put all of them in motion—at least, in visible motion—at once. Instead, he should select one or two, and work these out carefully before they are presented to Congress or to international leaders.

For legislation, it would be a serious mistake to send up to Congress ill thought-out bills—bills with holes in them—which can be easily defeated by simple questions and which lack necessary political support. The White House, in other words, must do its homework before wading into political waters. If this sounds like overly simple advice, many presidents in the past have ignored it and thus have wasted political resources. Because of the prevailing unhappiness that citizens feel toward their elected leaders and governmental institutions, it is particularly important at this time that the president start out correctly at the beginning of his administration to ensure its success. Everything should be done to encourage the development of confidence in our leaders and in the competence of our institutions. And it is essential that the president lead the way.

EPHEMERAL POPULARITY

Being selective will not be easy, given the recent history with single-term presidents. The president himself will feel pressed to get many things moving at the same time. As long as this activity is kept within the family, there should be no major problems. But the president may feel the need to present his program to a broader audience while he is still popular with the people, with congressional supporters, and, to a lesser extent, with the wait-and-see press. His judgment in fact may be correct, as past presidential popularity has declined with time in office. It is certainly easier for a president to govern when he is popular. The only hitch is that he is not likely to remain popular, and overloading the visible policy agenda will aggravate his problem. As he publicly presents his policies and programs for approval, they will be criticized; soon he will be, too.

The source of a president's decline in popularity lies in the conflicting expectations of citizens and in the imperatives of leadership. We want our presidents to be consistent, firm, decisive—but we also want them to be flexible. We want our presidents to have high ethical standards, but we are unhappy when they lack political skill and knowledge to get things done. Then how can a president lead without incurring some pain? We want the president to put the country's interests first, at least up to the point that they conflict with our own. A good rule is: don't expect to be loved, though a foreign policy crisis might come along and rescue your popularity. In general, however, one would think it better to be unpopular and not to have to cope with intractable and dangerous problems. There is some solace in the prospect that popularity may return at the end of the president's term or in subsequent history books. In the meantime, the president should be selective in choosing what to do.

CHOICE AND CHANGE

The president obviously has many choices when he comes into office. He must not only make choices about how to organize his office; he must also make choices about when to lead and which strategies to adopt to encourage cooperation. Moreover, he will have to make critical policy choices to manage our economy, to develop our human and natural resources, and to strengthen our national defense.

Choices will be made in a changing context. As a point of departure, it is important to understand the framework for presidential action—the constraints and opportunities which the president will face. For this, the president must understand and assess the major changes which have taken place in our political system in the last five to ten years.

One of these changes, a critical one, involves the enormous growth in size and complexity of the public sector. If we can judge by the number of people employed, most of this growth has occurred at the state and local level. At the federal level, growth has been in budgets and programs and in the use of more professional and skilled personnel. As the federal budget has grown to well over six hundred billion dollars, the financing of governmental services has become more centralized, and there has been increased emphasis on "contracting" for services through states, localities, and the private sector. At the state level, such financial centralization has taken place through vehicles such as Proposition 13; at the national level, centralization has grown through such popular programs as revenue sharing.

As a result, lobbying—particularly by public organizations—has increased at the federal level. Washington, D.C., has become the place to make sure that other levels of government are being cared for. Thus, at present, at least seven umbrella organizations, thirty-one states, and over a hundred cities have lobbying offices in the District of Columbia. Like bees going to honey, lobbyists from government, business, unions, consumer groups, and the like, have settled in Washington, where the money and action are.

With the rise of single-interest groups and effective lobbying activities, we have also witnessed a decline in our political parties. This is not to say that the decline has been permanent, as one could feel life in the party system during the recent election. The party that helped select a president, however, may not help him to govern.

Consider that many members of Congress are elected mainly through their own efforts, with little help from national or local party organizations. When they come to Congress, congressmen find that power is greatly fragmented and that, along with the decline of seniority, their party leaders cannot always deliver votes or control party members. Coupled with the increase of staff resources, each congressman has become a decision-maker in his own right, a fact also reflected in the growth of subcommittees in both houses. The president thus cannot rely on the party to gather political support. Indeed, he will have to build coalitions from members of both parties for each policy initiative.

An interesting change in the political environment has been the increasing use of policy experts and policy professionals at all levels of government. These professionals combine with experts in the bureaucracy, in Congress, and in various interest groups to form what Hugh Heclo calls "issue networks." Instead of the president being faced with a number of small subgovernments—"iron triangles" formed from representatives of the bureaucracy, interest groups, and Congress—the issue networks are much larger, more fluid, and provide a modicum of more maneuvering room for the president. The presidential staff must consult with members of these networks to design policies, incorporating their points of view in the proposed legislation.

The press and the court will go their own way, and in doing so they will sometimes set the policy agenda for the president. The courts do so by enforcing old rights or establishing new ones; the press, by creating or publicizing issues. The president should not expect too much of a honeymoon from the media, as its incentives and inclinations to look for warts on the body politic are too engrained.

The interest in investigative reporting and the post-Watergate media mentality feed voters' usual and healthy suspicion of politics, creating a citizenry that is more than ever distrustful of politicians and government. Despite the electoral landslide, according to the Federal Election Commission only some 54 percent of eligible voters turned out in the 1980 election. This means that the president was elected by a minority of our citizens. Thus we have a large number of citizens who do not vote, who are not identified with parties, and who believe that government does not know what it is doing. To make matters worse, the more complex policies become and the more experts are required to understand them, the more difficult it becomes to build a popular consensus. Indeed, as the slogans and philosophy of the New Deal have worn thin, no new themes or philosophies have taken their place, and citizens at present are simply distrustful and not sufficiently anchored to the political system. As citizens, we look to the president to restore our confidence in government.

DEPENDING ON THE PRESIDENT

The political environment thus leads us as citizens to depend on the president, and much of what happens depends on him—even though he must perform in a conflicting context of great expectations and of prevailing public disagreement about what he should do.

The president must begin by setting, for his administration, a theme, a public philosophy, which will attract the allegiance of citizens and ensure support for his programs. He will have to spend a great deal of time educating the public and leaders alike about what is at stake.

But even if he articulates his theme persuasively, at best he may be able to achieve only half the legislation which he proposes to Congress. He therefore cannot put the prestige of the presidency behind every bill and assert, as in the past, that his administration will be a failure if the bill does not pass, because it is just as likely that it will not pass. Not only must he be selective about what he looks at; he must also be selective about setting the congressional agenda.

Similarly, when it comes to organizing his office, staff, and sources of advice, a great deal depends more on the president and his style of operations and less on structural fixes such as having a special office for long-range policy studies. If he wants to make greater use of his cabinet, this will depend on his own willingness to do so, since there will be many other political tugs on cabinet members. Having them sit in the White House will not reduce these tugs, and only a president's treatment of individual cabinet members will counteract these contrary forces.

One can urge that a president not isolate himself from outside advisors, but this good advice still depends on the president's willingness to listen to people who will tell him things he does not want to hear. A great deal of commentary, for example, has been written about the tendency of certain presidents to isolate themselves from their advisors and to make decisions with a small group of people or by themselves. Pundits usually feel that the president should open himself up to greater consultation. But again, this requires that the president be willing and that he have a personality that is consistent with an open style of operation.

Presidential style also determines whether he will confuse governance with administration. He has many experienced people in his cabinet, in the agencies, and in the staff who can follow through on the operating details of programs and policies, and it is important that he conserve his energies and not be personally involved in everything. That way his subordinates will not only take the credit and blame; more important, they will also do the work. Some presidents, however, cannot resist nuts-and-bolts. Much is made of the tremendous demands that are placed on a president by outside forces, and there is some truth in this. But there is little understanding of how many demands presidents personally place on themselves. If a president insists on getting into the details of particular programs, there will be no way of keeping him out. When he does this, he will manage or attempt to monitor the activities of other people and he will be afraid of the mistakes they will make. What he will not be doing is governing.

A president should not be personally involved in everything, and he does not have the resources to be so. He must be careful about what draws his attention. Given that he must choose how to spend his time, it would be preferable that he continue to provide overall direction for his administration and to give content to its general theme.

THE POLICY AGENDA

All too often presidents adopt slogans such as "re-industrialization" without following through and giving them policy content. While it makes sense to use slogans in a campaign, the president has to go beyond slogans when governing. Governance implies the ability to convert ideas and slogans about the scope of governmental activity into specific policies and programs. In this book we devoted several chapters to policy questions. The citizens' call for a change is also a call for changes in our foreign and domestic policies. In our chapters on the policy agenda we did not address all of the issues which the president will have to confront, only those which seem to be most pressing—those dealing with the economy, energy, and national security. Developing a long-run strategy to deal with our economic problems while incurring short-run economic and political costs is no easy task. Nor is it simple to resolve the perplexing questions about the development of our natural and synthetic fuel resources without penalties to our environment or to disadvantaged Americans. Finally, the question of national security and the need to develop credible and predictable policies is critically important.

In considering specific policy areas, sometimes we overstate the differences in arena and politics between domestic and foreign policy; we do not realize the importance of the effects of our foreign policies on domestic questions and vice versa. All too often the president, lulled into believing that he can be more influential in foreign policy, gives less attention to domestic policy.

Even if this feature of our policy were true most of the time, it still does not tell a president how to act or how to commit his valuable resources. Should the president, for example, try to recreate in Congress the norms of bipartisanship in foreign policy? Since the Vietnam war, Congress has shown renewed interest in foreign policy. With this renewed interest, it will probably bring back domestic and local concerns into the consideration of foreign policy. In this light, one wonders about the feasibility of bipartisanship in the creation of foreign policy. In any event, given the difficulty of maintaining our alliances and our own interests in protecting domestic industries, the president and his staff will have to consider the implications of foreign and domestic policy at the same time. If he does not, congressmen and other political participants surely will.

BEING POLITICAL

Much of what happens in the next few years will depend heavily on the president and his political conception of the presidency. Being political and enjoying being a politician can help ensure the success of his administration. It is true that he will be badly constrained and will not always have the political resources to do what he would like. On the other hand, how he acts can make a difference. If he decides, for instance, to put a lot of personal effort into building his political party—which many presidents have not done—it may not help *him*, even if it does help the party. Increasing the strength of the party will only emphasize differences and develop local antagonists. In addition, if he respects the bureaucracy instead of undermining it, he will find it an important source of expertise and help. It is true that civil servants may pursue their own interests and notions about programs, and it is also true that they will leak and make end runs. Still, on balance, there is a great deal of competence to be used. Similarly, the Congress at this point is somewhat amorphous, and power is fragmented and spread out among many participants. The president therefore should not do anything which would make him the enemy of Congress and thus unify it against him. Consulting with Congress will help facilitate development of his program and certainly will enhance his leadership.

Being political means using tactics. It involves knowing when it pays to send up a trial balloon for a suggested change, and when to implement a policy while keeping it secret and then take credit after it works. I find it difficult to understand why presidents and their staffs telegraph so much of what they intend to do. Obviously there are complex issues which require laying groundwork and preparing the public to support individual policies. But in the case of internal management decisions, for example, there is little reason to announce a new form of collegial or super-cabinet government or to insist publicly that the secretary of state will be the sole voice of foreign policy. Sometimes these announcements are premature and, when things do not work out as planned, they can embarrass the president and undermine the public's perception of his competence. There will be enough times when, without his help, events will force a president to backtrack, to look foolish and inconsistent.

CRISIS MANAGEMENT

The best way to manage a crisis is not to have one. There are advantages for the president to appear stable, calm, in charge, for the government to appear to know what it is doing, and for things to seem stable and under control. The president and his staff, however, can take any set of events and attempt to make them into a crisis. A combat brigade in

Cuba can be construed as an extension of training requirements or as a deliberate, bellicose action. My point is that
there must be some political or policy reason for a president
to insist that the country is facing a crisis.

Most of what we have discussed in this book has been how
to cope with politics as usual. But when there is a crisis, the
political situation becomes more fluid, and what is feasible
often is greatly enlarged. This is one advantage to calling a
situation a crisis. An acknowledged crisis such as World War
II or the depression made it easier to get quick action from
the Congress and cooperation from the bureaucracy. If the
public in the 1970s had waited in gas lines over a long period
and the president then had presented a straightforward,
easily understood, energy program to Congress, there would
have been a fairly rapid legislative response. In such situations the president need not have a delicate sense of
timing—all he need do is to take advantage of the crisis. He
would not have had to make many speeches to get an energy
program.

Despite the image of constant flaps and fire drills in Washington policymaking, the president will usually confront
chronic policy problems, particularly domestic ones. His advisors will be prone to see some of these as having crisis
dimensions. With the best intentions, they will manufacture
a crisis and encourage the president to declare the solution to
be the moral equivalent of war.

The transition effort provides us with a recent example.
The economy is in sad shape; the problems are serious, and it
is going to take time to get out of high inflation, low growth
and productivity, and high unemployment. But is this economic mess a crisis? Is it sensible to call for a national
emergency or to suggest that the nation is on the brink of an
economic Dunkirk? What are the political and policy advantages in resorting to such exaggerated language? President
Reagan does not need it to get citizens and policymakers to
focus on the problem because he was just elected to deal with

the economic situation. He does not need a mandate to act
because most people expect him to act. Moreover, use of a
crisis metaphor will not automatically bring consensus on
the president's solutions. Liberals will not want taxpayers in
upper brackets to get a break, and conservatives will want
additional fiscal cuts to match tax cuts. How does the crisis
contribute to forming a political coalition to pass the president's program?

When policies are formulated under crisis conditions,
serious problems can result. While the policies chosen may
be appropriate, unless the perception of crisis is widely
shared disagreement and obstruction may emerge to thwart
the president's purposes and make him appear ineffectual. If
the policies are inappropriate, the president may have to
change both his mind and the policy and thus may appear inconsistent. Even a correct policy may take too long to show
positive effects; when the situation appears not to have improved, the president can then be accused of being an
alarmist.

Declaring a crisis raises the political stakes, and with them
the political risks. If the chances for success may be improved by declaring a crisis, so too may the prospects and
costs of failure. For a situation to be tagged as a crisis, calling
for drastic and quick action, most citizens and officials have
to see —or can easily be drawn to see—the situation as such.
If only a few advisors and elected officials in and out of the
White House see the crisis, the president should be cautious
in adapting and pursuing a crisis metaphor. When everyone
is pleading with the president to do something, then it makes
sense to talk in crisis terms. But when the president has to
convince others that there is a problem *and that his solutions
will work*, there is no crisis, at least not politically. If every
problem is a crisis, none is.

THE ART OF GOVERNANCE

There are no schools for presidents. No matter how experienced and intelligent a president may be, he will not be prepared entirely for the office. He cannot model his presidency on the basis of a previous president; he is different, and so are the times. He will have to learn on the job, and that is why I have urged a modicum of caution and reflection. He can accomplish a great deal personally by such small gestures as being able to put his colleagues at ease and getting them to do things that they do not want to do. In addition to personal charm and persuasion, he needs to know what he wants to accomplish: he needs a short list of policy objectives and the will to accomplish them. He can govern, and the nation sorely needs someone who can.

NOTES

3. Jack Citrin: "The Changing American Electorate"

1. Throughout this section the words "eligible voters" refer to those old enough to vote, even if they fail to meet other registration requirements. See *U.S. Statistical Abstract 1979*, Table 835.

2. These data are from the University of Michigan's National Election Studies. Evaluations of the presidential candidates were based on how they were rated on "feeling thermometers" from 0 to 97, with 50 as the neutral midpoint. Scores under 50 are considered "alienated" answers. Indifference simply means that the candidates were given the same thermometer rating. See Brody 1978, p. 21.

3. I am greatly indebted to Professor Raymond Wolfinger for providing me with these figures from his forthcoming book on Independents.

4. This section owes much to the illuminating analysis by Lipset and Ladd (1980).

5. To examine the trend, see the differences between the results in Stouffer 1955 and National Opinion Research Center 1973–77. See also *Public Opinion* 3, 5 (Oct./Nov. 1980):27–28.

6. *Public Opinion* 3, 4 (Aug./Sept. 1980):39; NORC 1978.

7. See *Public Opinion* 3, 3 (June/July 1980): 38–39, for data on attitudes toward regulation.

8. Ibid., p. 39.

9. The material on public opinion regarding taxes and spending is drawn from the discussion in Citrin 1979.

10. See *Public Opinion* 3, 5 (Oct./Nov. 1980):24–25.

11. For example, the proportion favoring a government program to provide medical care at low cost rose from 64 percent in 1964 to 85 percent in 1978.

12. See Citrin 1977, Lipset and Ladd 1980, and the debate between Pat Caddell and Warren Miller in *Public Opinion* 2, 5 (Oct./Nov. 1979).

13. This measure was developed by Arthur Miller (see Miller et al. 1973).

14. See Citrin et al. 1975 and Sniderman and Brody 1977 for an extended analysis of the link between personal circumstances and political trust.

15. Kavanaugh 1980 has an excellent analysis of this point.

4. Everett Carll Ladd, Jr.: "Political Parties and Governance in the 1980s"

1. The 1952 Election Study conducted by the Survey Research Center of the University of Michigan.

2. Survey conducted by Market Opinion Research, September 1980. This 1980 survey employed the very same measure of partisan identification that the Michigan SRC had used in 1952.

3. Survey by the Gallup Organization, 16–19 May 1980.

4. Survey by the Institute for Social Inquiry, University of Connecticut, 11–16 September 1980, based on 500 state residents.

5. For further data and discussion of the public's frustration over its perceived lack of control with regard to government and public policy, see Ladd 1978, pp. 40–48.

5. Robert M. Entman: "The Imperial Media"

1. The figures vary from year to year. See Gans 1979, pp. 9–10; see also Kumar and Grossman 1980, pp. 5–7, 10–11; and Balutis 1976, p. 511.

2. See the findings of Kingdon 1973, pp. 169–91, and Clausen 1973, pp. 192–212, who finds presidential impact only on issues of international involvement; cf. Davis 1979, pp. 465–79, Neustadt 1980, pp. 212–16.

3. For evidence of weak correlations between approval ratings and success, see Edwards 1976, pp. 101–13.

7. Francis E. Rourke: "Grappling with the Bureaucracy"

1. The concept of the "iron triangle" has been widely discussed in the literature of modern American politics. It received its most systematic analysis in Freeman 1955.

2. Illustrative of this White House staff point of view is Schlesinger 1965; see especially pp. 406, 412–17.

3. For an analysis of the factors that gave rise to bureaucratic independence, see Rourke 1979.

4. For the full study from which this article was drawn, see Kahn et al. 1975b.

5. Among recent studies of the implementation problem are Pressman and Wildavsky 1973, Bardach 1977, and Edwards 1980.

8. Martin M. Shapiro: "The Presidency and the Federal Courts"

1. *Amalgamated Meat Cutters* v. *Connally*, 337 F. Supp. 737 (D.D.C. 1971).

2. *Mourning* v. *Family Publications Services, Inc.*, 411 U.S. 356 (1973).

3. Idem.

4. This development is traced in detail in Davis 1976.

5. See *Vermont Yankee Nuclear Power Corp.* v. *Natural Resources Defense Council*, 435 U.S. 519 (1978).

9. Hugh Heclo: "The Changing Presidential Office"

1. A brief description is contained in National Academy of Public Administration 1980, Chapter 2.

2. The current advisory mechanisms available to the president are surveyed in Pious 1979, Chapters 7–10.

3. Wayne Coy Paper, "Memorandum of October 26, 1940," in Franklin D. Roosevelt Presidential Library, Hyde Park.

10. Peter Szanton: "Reconstructing the Presidency"

1. It well may be argued, as Lloyd Cutler (1980, pp. 126–43), among others, has done, that our system of government provides fatally little incentive for such relations, and that only a more nearly parliamentary system, created by constitutional change, can so link the fates of legislators and presidents as to induce such collaborative action. However that may be, constitutional amendment of this kind is not yet in prospect. The operational task for this decade will be to see whether the current system can be made once again to function acceptably. It is far from clear that it cannot.

2. The staff numbers include professionals and supporting personnel; in most EOP staffs, professionals alone would comprise roughly two-fifths of these totals.

3. President Carter's more ambitious intentions came to even less. The extensive studies he commissioned of possible super-cabinet departments of Natural Resources, Community and Economic Development, and Trade, Technology, and Industry, were abandoned when the degree of interest group and executive branch opposition became clear, and before any proposals had been submitted to the Congress.

4. Variants of this and some of the following proposals are discussed at greater length in Allison and Szanton 1976, pp. 76–90.

5. These gains would not come free. The main danger is that members of such an inner cabinet will have even more limited influence over their own departments than most secretaries do. Adding the pressures (and satisfactions) of counseling a president to the burden of congressional testimony, public appearances, and ceremonial and political chores means that there will be painfully little time left in which these officials, however able, can lead or manage their own departments. Capable deputy secretaries and strong departmental staffs would have to be chosen to fill in under them.

6. Current arrangements have often proven inadequate to meet even far more modest standards. President Carter attempted to make final decisions on the FY 1980 defense budget while consulting three separate sets of staffing papers—from Defense, OMB, and NSC staff—which characterized the issues in conflicting terms and disagreed as to critical facts. See Odeen 1980, pp. 111–29.

7. The Tokyo Round accomplishment was particularly striking. There (with the assistance of special statutory procedures limiting the number of congressional players and with strong and adroit leadership from Robert Strauss) a complex, sensitive, and potentially controversial set of trade agreements was embodied in a bill that passed the House by 395 to 7 and the Senate by 90 to 4. See Destler and Graham 1980, pp. 53–70.

12. Robert S. Pindyck: "An Agenda for American Energy Policy"

1. It is true that U.S. oil imports fell substantially in 1980 compared to 1978 and 1979 levels. However, it must be remembered that 1980 was a year of economic recession, and most of the drop in oil imports is directly attributable to the reduced growth of economic output.

2. This is discussed in MacAvoy and Pindyck 1975 and in Pindyck 1977.

3. These arguments were examined in considerable detail in a research project conducted by Joskow and Pindyck at the Center for Energy Policy Research of the MIT Energy Laboratory. For a more detailed discussion of those issues, see Joskow and Pindyck 1979.

4. For a discussion of some of the statistical evidence and an analysis of energy demand, see Pindyck 1979.

5. For example, I do not deal here with the future of the Department of Energy. The real issues are whether we will decontrol prices and move away from the large-scale subsidization of synthetic fuels, and *not* the particular organizational framework that will be used to administer energy policy. Also, I do not deal with nuclear power, a complex issue that goes beyond the scope of this chapter.

6. For example, this claim was made in Stobaugh and Yergin 1979.

7. This point is discussed in some detail in Hall and Pindyck 1980.

8. The effect of price shocks is discussed in idem.

13.   Richard K. Betts: "Managing Foreign and Defense Policy"

1. If Japanese and Chinese defense budgets are added to NATO's, as a cautious Soviet defense planner might calculate, Moscow and its allies are outspent by a very large margin. For data on defense budgets, see Central Intelligence Agency 1980 and Arms Control and Disarmament Agency 1979. See also Posen and Evera 1980, pp. 99–106, 109.

2. For an example of arguments that denigrate the danger of numerical imbalance, see Panofsky 1973 and Jervis 1979–80.

3. "Coordination is rarely neutral. . . . Inevitably it advances some interests at the expense of others." Seidman 1970, p. 168.

4. The systems analysis and program budgeting revolution brought to the Pentagon by Robert McNamara may have created as many problems as it solved. See Kanter 1979, pp. 79–94.

5. The classic scholarly brief for this preference is Neustadt 1960.

6. Some also debunk the image of Eisenhower's passivity: Greenstein 1979–80, Quester 1979.

REFERENCES

Aberbach, Joel D., and Rockman, Bert A. 1976. "Clashing Beliefs within the Executive Branch: The Nixon Administration Bureaucracy." *American Political Science Review* 70, 2 (June).

Abraham, Henry. 1974. *Justices and Presidents*. New York: Oxford Press.

Allison, G., and Szanton, P. 1976. *Remaking Foreign Policy: The Organizational Connection*. New York: Basic Books.

American Political Science Association. 1950. *Toward a More Responsible Two-Party System*. A Report of the Committee on Political Parties of the American Political Science Association. New York: Rinehart and Company.

Arms Control and Disarmament Agency. 1979. *World Military Expenditures and Arms Transfers 1968–1977*. Washington, DC: Arms Control and Disarmament Agency (October).

Balutis, Alan P. 1976. "Congress, the President, and the Press." *Journalism Quarterly* 53.

Barber, James David. 1979. "Not the *New York Times*." *Washington Monthly* 11 (September).

Bardach, Eugene. 1977. *The Implementation Game: What Happens after a Bill Becomes a Law*. Cambridge, MA: MIT Press.

Barker, Ernest. 1958 (1942). *Reflections on Government*. New York: Oxford University Press.

Betts, Richard K. 1980. "Intelligence for Policymaking." *Washington Quarterly* 3, 3 (Summer).

Broder, David S. 1970. "Political Reporters in Presidential Politics." In *Inside the System: A Washington Monthly Reader*, ed. Charles Peters and Timothy J. Adams. New York: Praeger.

Brody, Richard. 1978. "The Puzzling Picture of Political Participation in America." In *The New American Political System*, ed. Anthony King. Washington, DC: American Enterprise Institute.

———, and Page, Benjamin I. 1975. "The Impact of Events on Presidential Popularity: The Johnson and Nixon Administrations." In *Perspectives on the Presidency*, ed. Aaron Wildavsky. Boston: Little, Brown.

Burt, Richard. 1980. "Pentagon Reports Serious Difficulties in Trident Program." *New York Times*, 25 November 1980.

Caddell, Patrick. 1979. "Yes, It's Real." *Public Opinion* 2.

Califano, Joseph A., Jr. 1978. Remarks of Joseph A. Califano, Jr., before the Economic Club of Chicago, 20 April. News release: U.S. Department of Health, Education, and Welfare.

Central Intelligence Agency. 1980. *National Basic Intelligence Factbook.* Washington, DC: Central Intelligence Agency.

Choper, Jesse H. 1980. *Judicial Review and the National Political Process.* Chicago: University of Chicago Press.

Citrin, Jack. 1978. "The Alienated Voter." *Taxing & Spending* 1 (Oct./Nov.).

———. 1979. "Do People Want Something for Nothing?" *National Tax Journal* 30 (June).

———. 1977. "Political Alienation as a Social Indicator: Attitudes and Action." *Social Indicators Research* 4.

———; McClesky, H.; Shanks, M.; Sniderman, P. M. 1975. "Personal and Political Sources of Political Alienation." *British Journal of Political Science* 5.

Clausen, Aage R. 1973. *How Congressmen Decide: A Policy Focus.* New York: St. Martin's Press.

Clubb, J.; Flanigan, W.; Zingale, N. 1976. "Partisan Realignment since 1960." Unpublished paper delivered at meeting of American Political Science Association in Chicago, IL, 2–5 September.

Cole, Richard L., and Caputo, David A. 1979. "Presidential Control of the Senior Civil Service: Assessing the Strategies of the Nixon Years." *American Political Science Review* 73, 2 (June).

Converse, P., and Markus, G. 1979. "Plus ca change . . . " *American Political Science Review* 73.

Cooper, Chester. 1970. *The Lost Crusade.* New York: Dodd, Mead.

Cronin, Thomas E. 1980. *The State of the Presidency.* 2d ed. Boston: Little Brown.

Crouse, Timothy. 1973. *The Boys on the Bus.* New York: Random House.

Crozier, M.; Huntington, S.; Wanatuki, J. 1975. *The Crisis of Democracy.* New York: New York University Press.

Cutler, Lloyd N. 1980. "To Form a Government." *Foreign Affairs* 59, 1 (Fall).

Davis, Eric L. 1979. "Legislative Reform and the Decline of Presidential Influence on Capitol Hill." *British Journal of Political Science* 9.

Davis, K. C. 1976. *Administrative Law of the 70s.* Rochester, NY: Lawyers Cooperative.

Destler, I. M. 1977. "National Security Advice to U.S. Presidents: Some Lessons from Thirty Years." *World Politics* 29, 2 (January).

———. 1972. *Presidents, Bureaucrats, and Foreign Policy.* Princeton: Princeton University Press.

———, and Graham, Thomas R. 1980. "United States Congress and the Tokyo Round: Lessons of a Success Story." *The World Economy* 3, 1.

De Vries, W., and Torrance, V. L. 1972. *The Ticket Splitter: A New Force in American Politics.* Grand Rapids, MI: William B. Eerdsmans Publishing Co.

Dry, Murray. 1980. "Legislative Veto—Pro." *Staff: The Congressional Staff Journal.* 96th Congress, Issue 10.

Duignan, Peter, and Babushka, Alvin. 1980. *The United States in the 1980s.* Stanford, CA: Hoover Institution Press.

Easton, D. 1965. *A Systems Analysis of Political Life.* New York: John Wiley & Sons.

Edwards, George C. III. 1980. *Implementing Public Policy.* Washington, DC: Congressional Quarterly Press.

———. 1976. "Presidential Influence in the House: Presidential Prestige as a Source of Presidential Power." *American Political Science Review* 70.

Ely, John Hart. 1980. *Democracy and Distrust: A Theory of Judicial Review.* Cambridge, MA: Harvard University Press.

Fenno, Richard F., Jr. 1973. *Congressmen in Committees.* Boston: Little Brown.

———. 1978. *Homestyle: House Members in Their Districts.* Boston: Little Brown.

Fiorina, Morris P. 1977. *Congress: Keystone of the Washington Establishment.* New Haven, CT: Yale University Press.

Fisher, Louis. 1978. *The Constitution between Friends: Congress, the President, and the Law.* New York: St. Martin's.

Fiss, Owen. 1979. "The Forms of Justice." *Harvard Law Review* 93.

Fortune. 1979. "Candid Reflections of a Businessman in Washington" (29 January).

Freedman, James O. 1978. *Crisis and Legitimacy: The Administrative Process and American Government.* Cambridge: Cambridge University Press.

Freeman, J. Leiper. 1955. *The Political Process: Executive Bureau—Legislative Committee Relations.* New York: Random House.

Gans, Herbert J. 1979. *Deciding What's News.* New York: Pantheon.

Greenstein, Fred I. 1979–80. "Eisenhower as an Activist President." *Political Science Quarterly* 94, 4 (Winter).

Grossman, Michael B., and Rourke, Francis E. 1976. "The Media and the Presidency: An Exchange Analysis." *Political Science Quarterly* 91.

Haight, Timothy R., and Brody, Richard A. 1977. "The Mass Media and Presidential Popularity, Presidential Broadcasting and News in the Nixon Administration." *Communications Research* 4.

Hall, Robert E., and Pindyck, Robert S. 1977. "The Conflicting Goals of National Energy Policy." *The Public Interest* (Spring).

———. 1980. "Energy and the Western Economies." MIT Energy Laboratory Working Paper No. EL80–033WP (September).

Hammond, Paul Y. 1962. "NSC−68: Prologue to Rearmament." In *Strategy, Politics, and Defense Budgets*, ed. Warner R. Schilling, Paul Y. Hammond, and Glenn H. Snyder. New York: Columbia University Press.

Hand, Learned. 1958. *The Bill of Rights*. Cambridge, MA: Harvard University Press.

Heclo, Hugh. 1978. "Issue Networks and the Executive Establishment." In *The New American Political System*, ed. Anthony King. Washington, DC: American Enterprise Institute.

Hess, Stephen. 1976. *Organizing the President*. Washington, DC: The Brookings Institution.

Hibbs, Douglas A., Jr.; Rivers, R. Douglas; Vasilatos, Nicholas. 1980. "On the Demand for Economic Outcomes: Macroeconomic Performance and Mass Political Support in the United States, Great Britain, and Germany." Paper delivered at the annual meeting of the American Political Science Association, Washington, DC, 28−31 August.

Horowitz, Donald. 1977. *Courts and Social Policy*. Washington, DC: The Brookings Institution.

Huntington, Samuel P. 1961. *The Common Defense: Strategic Programs in National Politics*. New York: Columbia University Press.

Jervis, Robert. 1979−80. "Why Nuclear Superiority Doesn't Matter." *Political Science Quarterly* 94, 4 (Winter).

Joskow, Paul L., and Pindyck, Robert S. 1979. "Synthetic Fuels: Should the Government Subsidize Non-Conventional Energy Supplies?" *Regulation* (American Enterprise Institute; September).

Kahn, Robert L.; Gutek, Barbara A.; Barton, Eugenia; and Katz, Daniel. 1975a. "Americans Love Their Bureaucrats." *Psychology Today* 9, 1 (June).

———. 1975b. *Bureaucratic Encounters: A Pilot Study in the Evaluation of Government Services*. Ann Arbor, MI: Survey Research Center, Institute for Social Research, University of Michigan.

Kanter, Arnold. 1979. *Defense Politics: A Budgetary Perspective*. Chicago: University of Chicago Press.

Kavanagh, D. 1980. "Political Leadership: The Labors of Sisyphus." In *Challenge to Governance*, ed. R. Rose. Beverly Hills, CA: Sage Publications.

Kennedy, John F. 1955. *Profiles in Courage*. New York: Harper & Row.

Kernell, Samuel. 1978. "Explaining Presidential Popularity." *American Political Science Review* 72 (June).

King, Anthony, ed. 1978. *The New American Political System*. Washington, DC: American Enterprise Institute.

Kingdon, John W. 1973. *Congressmen's Voting Decisions*. New York: Harper & Row.

Kumar, Martha J., and Grossman, Michael B. (with Leslie Lichter-Mason). 1980. "Images of the White House in the Media." Paper delivered at the annual meeting of the American Political Science Association, Washington, DC, 28−30 August.

Ladd, Everett Carll, Jr. 1980. "Opinion Roundup." *Public Opinion* 3.

————. 1978. "What the Voters Really Want." *Fortune* (18 December).

Lipset, Seymour Martin, ed. 1980. *The Third Century.* Chicago: University of Chicago Press.

————, and Ladd, Everett Carll, Jr. 1980. "Public Opinion and Public Policy." In *The United States in the 1980s,* ed. Peter Duignan and Alvin Babushka. Stanford, CA: Hoover Institution Press.

Lowi, Theodore J. 1969. *The End of Liberalism.* Rev. ed. 1979. New York: W. W. Norton.

MacAvoy, Paul W., and Pindyck, Robert S. 1975. *Price Controls and the Natural Gas Shortage.* Washington, DC: American Enterprise Institute.

Mayhew, David R. 1974. *Congress, the Electoral Connection.* New Haven, CT: Yale University Press.

Mendelson, Wallace. 1961. *Justices Black and Frankfurter: Conflict on the Court.* Chicago: University of Chicago Press.

Michelman, Frank. 1969. "On Protecting the Poor through the Fourteenth Amendment." *Harvard Law Review* 83.

Miller, A. 1974. "Political Issues and Trust in Government: 1964–70." *American Political Science Review* 68.

————; Brown, T.; Raine, A. 1973. "Social Change and Political Estrangement: 1964–72." Unpublished paper delivered at meeting of American Political Science Association in New Orleans, LA, 4–8 September.

————; Goldenberg, E.; Ehbring, L. 1979. "Type-Set Politics: Impact of Newspapers on Public Confidence." *American Political Science Review* 73.

Morris, Roger. 1975. "Carter's Cabinet: The Who's Who Treatment." *Columbia Journalism Review* 14 (Sept./Oct.).

Mueller, John E. 1973. *Wars, Presidents and Public Opinion.* New York: John Wiley.

Nathan, Richard P. 1975. *The Plot That Failed: Nixon and the Administrative Presidency.* New York: John Wiley & Sons.

National Academy of Public Administration. 1980. *A Presidency for the 1980s.* Washington, DC: NAPA.

National Opinion Research Center. 1973–1977, 1978. *Code Book for General Social Survey.* Chicago: NORC, University of Chicago.

Neustadt, Richard E. 1980. *Presidential Power: The Politics of Leadership from FDR to Carter.* New York: John Wiley.

Nisbet, R. 1975. *Twilight of Authority.* New York: Norton.

Nitze, Paul H. 1976. "Assuring Strategic Stability in an Era of Détente." *Foreign Affairs* 54, 2 (January).

————. 1978. *Is America Becoming Number 2? Current Trends in the U.S. Soviet Military Balance.* Washington, DC: Committee on the Present Danger (October).

Odeen, Philip A. 1980. "Organizing for National Security." *International Security* 5, 1 (Summer).

Okamura, T. 1979. "Political Cynicism in Japan." Unpublished paper delivered at meeting of the International Political Science Association in Moscow (August).

Paletz, David L., and Entman, Robert M. 1981. *Media Power Politics*. New York: Free Press.

Panofsky, Wolfgang. 1973. "The Mutual Hostage Relationship between America and Russia." *Foreign Affairs* 52, 1 (October).

Patterson, T. 1980. *The Mass Media Election: How Americans Choose Their President*. New York: Praeger.

Peters, Charles. 1976. "Concerns about Carter." *The Washington Monthly* (December).

——, and Adams,Timothy J., eds. 1970. *Inside the System: A Washington Monthly Reader*. New York: Praeger.

Pindyck, Robert S. 1980. "The American Energy Debate." *The Public Interest* (Spring).

——. 1977. "Prices vs. Shortages: Policy Options for the Natural Gas Industry." In *Options for U.S. Energy Policy*. San Francisco, CA: Institute for Contemporary Studies.

——. 1979. *The Structure of World Energy Demand*. Cambridge, MA: MIT Press.

Pious, Richard. 1979. *The American Presidency*. New York: Basic Books.

Polsby, Nelson W. 1976. *Congress and the Presidency*. 3d ed. Englewood Cliffs, NJ: Prentice-Hall.

Posen, Barry R., and Van Evera, Stephen W. 1980. "Overarming and Underwhelming." *Foreign Policy* No. 40 (Fall).

President's Committee on Administrative Management. 1937. *Report of the Committee with Studies of Administrative Management in the Federal Government*. Commonly known as the Brownlow Report. Washington, DC: Government Printing Office.

Pressman, Jeffrey L., and Wildavsky, Aaron B. 1973. *Implementation: Why It's Amazing that Federal Programs Work at All . . .* Berkeley, Los Angeles, CA: University of California Press.

Purvis, Hoyt, ed. 1976. *The Presidency and the Press*. Austin, TX: Lyndon B. Johnson School of Public Affairs, University of Texas.

Quester, George. 1979. "Was Eisenhower a Genius?" *International Security* 4, 2 (Fall).

Randall, Ronald. 1979. "Presidential Power versus Bureaucratic Intransigence: The Influence of the Nixon Administration on Welfare Policy." *American Political Review* 73, 3 (September).

Robinson, M.; Conover, N.; Sheehan, M. 1980. "The Media at Mid-Year: A Bad Year for McCluhanites." *Public Opinion* 3.

Rose, R., ed. 1980. *Challenge to Governance*. Beverly Hills, CA: Sage Publications.

Rossiter, C. 1960. *The American Presidency.* Rev. ed. New York: Mentor Books.

Rourke, Francis E. 1979. "Bureaucratic Autonomy and the Public Interest." In *Making Bureaucracies Work*, ed. Carol H. Weiss and Allen H. Barton. Beverly Hills, CA: Sage Publications.

Schilling, Warner R.; Hammond, Paul Y.; Snyder, Glenn H. 1962. *Strategy, Politics, and Defense Budgets.* New York: Columbia University Press.

Schlesinger, Arthur M., Jr. 1965. *A Thousand Days: John F. Kennedy in the White House.* Boston: Houghton Mifflin.

Schmidhauser, John. 1958. *Supreme Court as Final Arbiter in Federal State Relations.* Chapel Hill, NC: University of North Carolina Press.

Schuck, Peter. 1979. "The Graying of Civil Rights Law: The Age Discrimination Act of 1975." *Yale Law Journal* 89.

Scigliano, Robert. 1972. *The Supreme Court and the Presidency.* New York: Free Press.

Sears, D.; Citrin, Jack; Tyler, T.; Kinder, D. 1978. "System Support and Public Reactions to the Energy Crisis." *American Journal of Political Science* 22.

Seidman, Harold. 1980. "Legislative Veto—Con." *Staff: The Congressional Staff Journal.* 96th Congress: Issue 10.

———. 1970. *Politics, Position, and Power: The Dynamics of Federal Organization.* New York: Oxford University Press.

Shapiro, Martin. 1980. "Judicial Activism." In *The Third Century*, ed. Seymour Martin Lipset. Chicago: University of Chicago Press.

Sigelman, Lee. 1979. "Rallying to the President's Support: A Reappraisal of the Evidence." *Polity* 11.

Singer, James W. 1980. "Civil Service Reform Means Power for Reagan." *National Journal* 12, 48 (29 November).

Sniderman, P., and Brody, R. 1977. "Coping: The Ethic of Self-Reliance." *American Journal of Political Science* 21.

Sperlich, Peter W. 1975. "Bargaining and Overload: An Essay on Presidential Power." In *Perspectives on the Presidency*, ed. Aaron Wildavsky. Boston: Little Brown.

Stanley, David T.; Mann, Dean E.; and Doig, Jameson W. 1967. *Men Who Govern.* Washington, DC: The Brookings Institution.

Stewart, Richard. 1975. "The Reformation of American Administrative Law." *Harvard Law Review* 88.

Stobaugh, Robert, and Yergin, Daniel, eds. 1979. *Energy Future.* New York: Random House.

Stouffer, S. 1955. *Communism, Conformity and Civil Liberties.* New York: Doubleday.

Sundquist, J. 1980. "The Crisis of Competence in our National Government." *Political Science Quarterly* 95 (Summer).

Tribe, Lawrence. 1980. "Puzzling Persistence of Progress-Based Constitutional Theories." *Yale Law Journal* 89.

Van Cleave, William R., and Thompson, W. Scott. 1979. *Strategic Options for the Early Eighties: What Can Be Done?* New York: National Strategy Information Center.

Wayne, Stephen J. 1980. "Expectations of the President." Paper delivered at the annual meeting of the American Political Science Association, Washington, DC, 28–21 August.

Weiss, Carol H., and Barton, Allen H., eds. 1979. *Making Bureaucracies Work.* Beverly Hills, CA: Sage Publications.

Welborn, David M. 1977. *Governance of Federal Regulatory Agencies.* Knoxville, TN: University of Tennessee Press.

White, William D. 1974. *U.S. Tactical Air Power: Missions, Forces, and Costs.* Washington, DC: The Brookings Institution.

Wildavsky, Aaron. 1975. *Perspectives on the Presidency.* Boston: Little Brown.

Wilkinson, J. Harvie. 1978. *From Brown to Bakke: The Supreme Court and School Integration, 1954–1978.* New York: Oxford Press.

Wilson, Woodrow. 1885. *Congressional Government.* Boston: Houghton Mifflin.

Winograd Commission. 1978. *Openness, Participation and Party Building: Reforms for a Stronger Democratic Party.* Report of the Commission on Presidential Nomination and Party Structure, Morely A. Winograd, Chairman. Washington, DC: Democratic National Committee.

Wolfinger, R., and Rosenstone, S. 1980. *Who Votes?* New Haven, CT: Yale University Press.

ABOUT THE AUTHORS

RICHARD K. BETTS, a Research Associate in Foreign Policy Studies at the Brookings Institution, is a former staff member of the National Security Council and of the Senate Select Committee on Intelligence. A member of the Council on Foreign Relations and of the editorial board of *The Journal of Strategic Studies*, he teaches graduate courses on defense policy at Columbia University and at the Johns Hopkins University School of Advanced International Studies. Betts's first book, *Soldiers, Statesmen, and Cold War Crises*, won the Harold Lasswell Award for the best book on civil/military relations in 1977 and 1978. He coauthored at Brookings *Nonproliferation and U.S. Foreign Policy* (1980) and *The Irony of Vietnam: The System Worked* (1979). The latter won the 1980 Woodrow Wilson Prize for the best book in political science.

JACK CITRIN is Associate Professor of Political Science, University of California—Berkeley. His field is American politics with emphasis on public opinion, elections, alienation, and political protest. He is coauthor with David Elkins of *Political Disaffection among British and American Youth* and of the forthcoming *The California Tax Revolt* with David Sears and Merrill Shanks. His publications also include "The Political Relevance of Trust in Government," *American Political Science Review* (1977), "Do People Want Something for Nothing?" in the *National Tax Journal* (1979), and the forthcoming book, *Political Disaffection in America*.

ERIC L. DAVIS, Assistant Professor of Political Science at Middlebury College, Vermont, spent two years as a Research Fellow and Visiting Scholar at the Brookings Institution. His writings include "Legislative Liaison in the Carter Administration," *Political Science Quarterly* (1979), "Legislative Reform and the Decline of Presidential Influence on Capitol Hill," *British Journal of Political Science* (1979), and "Congressional Liaison: The People and the Institutions" in the forthcoming *Both Ends of the Avenue: The Presidency, the Executive Branch, and Congress in the 1980s*, edited by Anthony King.

ROBERT M. ENTMAN is Assistant Professor of Public Policy Studies at Duke University. His writings include the coauthorship with D. L. Paletz of "Presidents, Power, and the Press," *Presidential Studies Quarterly* (1980), and the forthcoming *Media Power Politics*. He is author of *Legal and Institutional Aspects of Regulating Intermedia Pollution* (1980), and "The Influence of the Mass Media on Political Socialization and Attitude Change" in *Exploring Relationships between Mass Media and Political Culture*, edited by T. J. Volgy (1975).

ROBERT E. HALL, Professor of Economics at Stanford University and Senior Fellow at Hoover Institution, is director of the Economic Fluctuations Program and of the Project on Inflation at the National Bureau of Economic Research. His many writings include "A Theory of the Natural Unemployment Rate and the Duration of Employment," *Journal of Monetary Economics* (1979); "Stabilization Policy and Capital Formation," *American Economic Review* (1980); with Knut A. Mork, "Energy Prices and the U.S. Economy in 1979–1981," *The Energy Journal* (1980); with David Lilien, "Efficient Wage Bargains under Uncertain Supply and Demand," *American Economic Review* (1979); and with Dennis W. Carlton, "The Distribution of Permanent Income" in *Income Distribution and Economic Inequality*, edited by Zvi Griliches et al. (1978).

HUGH HECLO is Professor of Government at Harvard University and former consultant to the German Marshall Fund, the Ford Foundation, and the British Department of Health and Social Security. His writings include *Modern Social Politics in Britain and Sweden: From Relief to Income Maintenance*, which won the 1975 Woodrow Wilson Book Award as "the best book published on government, politics, or international affairs," *A Government of Strangers: Executive Politics in Washington* (1977), *Studying the Presidency* (1977), and, with Arnold Heidenheimer and Carolyn Adams, *Comparative Public Policy: The Politics of Social Choice in Europe and America*, which was chosen by the American Political Science Association for the 1976 Gladys Kammerer Award as "the best political science publication in the field of U.S. national policy."

EVERETT CARLL LADD, JR., is executive director of the Roper Center for Public Opinion Research and director of the Institute for Social Inquiry, University of Connecticut. He is a member of the editorial boards of *Public Opinion, Political Behavior*, and *Politics of Behavior*. His many publications include *Where Have All the Voters Gone? The Fracturing of America's Political Parties* (1978) and, with C. D. Hadley, *Transformations of the American Party System: Political Coalitions from the New Deal to the 1970's* (1975); "A Better Way to Pick Our Presidents," *Fortune* (1980), and "The American Party System Today" in *The Third Century*, edited by Seymour Martin Lipset (1979). He also wrote the chapter on "The Shifting Party Coalitions: 1932–1976" in the institute's book *Emerging Coalitions in American Politics* (1978), edited by Professor Lipset.

ARNOLD J. MELTSNER, Professor of Public Policy in the Graduate School of Public Policy, University of California–Berkeley, is a former analyst with the Rand Corporation and the Research Analysis Corporation. A political scientist, he is the author of *The Politics of City Revenue* (1971), *Urban Outcomes* (1974) written with Aaron Wildavsky and Frank Levy, and *Policy Analysts in the Bureaucracy* (1976). He is editor of *Policy Analysis* and a member of the editorial board of *Public Administration Review*.

CHARLES PETERS is founder and editor-in-chief of *The Washington Monthly*. Winner of the Columbia Journalism Award for 1978, he is the author of *How Washington Really Works* and coauthor of *The Culture of Bureaucracy, Inside the System, Blowing the Whistle: Dissent in the Public Interest*, and *The System*.

ROBERT S. PINDYCK is Professor of Applied Economics at the Sloan School of Management, Massachusetts Institute of Technology. Consultant to the International Bank for Reconstruction and Development, he is associate editor of the *Journal of Economic Dynamics and Control* and of *Energy Economics* and advisory editor of *The Journal of Energy and Development*. The author of many articles on economic policy and the economics of energy and natural resources, his books include *The Structure of World Energy Demand* (1979), *Price Controls and the Natural Gas Shortage* (1975) with P. W. MacAvoy, and *Econometric Models and Economic Forecasts* (1976; 2d ed., 1980), written with D. Rubinfeld.

FRANCIS E. ROURKE, Professor of Political Science at Johns Hopkins University, is a member of the editorial board of *Administration and Society*. Former vice chairman of the Governor's Commission for the Modernization of State Government in Maryland and treasurer of the American Political Science Association, he is the author of *Secrecy and Publicity, Dilemmas of Democracy,*

Bureaucracy, Politics and Public Policy, and *Bureaucracy and Foreign Policy.*

MARTIN M. SHAPIRO is Professor of Law at the University of California—Berkeley. He is the author of "American Federalism" in *Constitutional Government in America* (1980), edited by R. Collins, "Access to Justice and the Welfare State: The American Experience" in *The Prospects for Access to Justice* (in press), edited by Mauro Cappelletti, and, with R. Wolfinger and F. Greenstein, of *Dynamics of American Politics.*

PETER L. SZANTON, vice president of Hamilton, Rabinovitz & Szanton, Inc., policy and management consultants in Washington, DC, is a former associate director for organizational studies in the Office of Management and Budget. A consultant on several phases of operation in the federal government, he is the author of *Reorganizing the Federal Government: What Have We Learned?* (forthcoming), *Remaking Foreign Policy: The Organizational Connection* (1976), and of a number of articles, including "Two Jobs, Not One" in *Foreign Policy* (1980).

INDEX

PUBLICATIONS LIST*

THE INSTITUTE FOR CONTEMPORARY STUDIES

260 California Street, San Francisco, California, 94111

Catalog available upon request

BUREAUCRATS AND BRAINPOWER: GOVERNMENT
REGULATION OF UNIVERSITIES

    $6.95. 171 pages. Publication date: June 1979
    ISBN 0−917616−35− 9
    Library of Congress No. 79−51328

Contributors: Nathan Glazer, Robert S. Hatfield, Richard W. Lyman,
    Paul Seabury, Robert L. Sproull, Miro M. Todorovich, Caspar W.
    Weinberger

THE CALIFORNIA COASTAL PLAN: A CRITIQUE

    $5.95. 199 pages. Publication date: March 1976
    ISBN 0−917616−04−9
    Library of Congress No. 76−7715

Contributors: Eugene Bardach, Daniel K. Benjamin, Thomas E.
    Borcherding, Ross D. Eckert, H. Edward Frech III, M. Bruce Johnson,
    Ronald N. Lafferty, Walter J. Mead, Daniel Orr, Donald M. Pach,
    Michael R. Peevey

THE CRISIS IN SOCIAL SECURITY: PROBLEMS AND PROSPECTS

    $6.95. 214 pages. Publication date: April 1977; 2d ed. rev.,
    1978, 1979
    ISBN 0−917616−16−2/1977; 0−917616−25−1/1978
    Library of Congress No. 77−72542

Contributors: Michael J. Boskin, George F. Break, Rita Ricardo Campbell,
    Edward Cowan, Martin S. Feldstein, Milton Friedman, Douglas R.
    Munro, Donald O. Parsons, Carl V. Patton, Joseph A. Pechman,
    Sherwin Rosen, W. Kip Viscusi, Richard J. Zeckhauser

DEFENDING AMERICA: TOWARD A NEW ROLE IN THE
POST-DETENTE WORLD

    $13.95 (hardbound only). 255 pages. Publication date: April 1977 by
    Basic Books (New York)
    ISBN 0−465−01585−9
    Library of Congress No. 76−43479

*Prices subject to change.

Contributors: Robert Conquest, Theodore Draper, Gregory Grossman, Walter Z. Laqueur, Edward N. Luttwak, Charles Burton Marshall, Paul H. Nitze, Norman Polmar, Eugene V. Rostow, Leonard Schapiro, James R. Schlesinger, Paul Seabury, W. Scott Thompson, Albert Wohlstetter

THE ECONOMY IN THE 1980s: A PROGRAM FOR
GROWTH AND STABILITY
$7.95, (paper). 462 pages. Publication date: June 1980.
ISBN 0−917616−39−1
Library of Congress No. 80−80647
$17.95 (cloth). 462 pages. Publication date: August 1980.
ISBN 0−87855−399−1. Available through Transaction Books, Rutgers−The State University, New Brunswick, NJ 08903
Contributors: Michael J. Boskin, George F. Break, John T. Cuddington, Patricia Drury, Alain Enthoven, Laurence J. Kotlikoff, Ronald I. McKinnon, John Pencavel, Henry S. Rowen, John L. Scadding, John B. Shoven, James L. Sweeney, David Teece

EMERGING COALITIONS IN AMERICAN POLITICS
$6.95. 524 pages. Publication date: June 1978
ISBN 0−917616−22−7
Library of Congress No. 78−53414
Contributors: Jack Bass, David S. Broder, Jerome M. Clubb, Edward H. Crane III, Walter De Vries, Andrew M. Greeley, S. I. Hayakawa, Tom Hayden, Milton Himmelfarb, Richard Jensen, Paul Kleppner, Everett Carll Ladd, Jr., Seymour Martin Lipset, Robert A. Nisbet, Michael Novak, Gary R. Orren, Nelson W. Polsby, Joseph L. Rauh, Jr., Stanley Rothman, William A. Rusher, William Schneider, Jesse M. Unruh, Ben J. Wattenberg

FEDERAL TAX REFORM: MYTHS AND REALITIES
$5.95. 270 pages. Publication date: September 1978
ISBN 0−917616−32−4
Library of Congress No. 78−61661
Contributors: Robert J. Barro, Michael J. Boskin, George F. Break, Jerry R. Green, Laurence J. Kotlikoff, Mordecai Kurz, Peter Mieszkowski, John B. Shoven, Paul J. Taubman, John Whalley

GOVERNMENT CREDIT ALLOCATION: WHERE DO WE GO
FROM HERE?
$4.95. 208 pages. Publication date: November 1975
ISBN 0−917616−02−2
Library of Congress No. 75−32951
Contributors: George J. Benston, Karl Brunner, Dwight M. Jaffe, Omotunde E. G. Johnson, Edward J. Kane, Thomas Mayer, Allen H. Meltzer

NATIONAL SECURITY IN THE 1980s: FROM
WEAKNESS TO STRENGTH
$8.95 (paper). 524 pages. Publication date: May 1980
ISBN 0–917616–38–3
Library of Congress No. 80–80648
$19.95 (cloth). 524 pages. Publication date: August 1980
ISBN 0–87855–412–2. Available through Transaction Books,
Rutgers–The State University, New Brunswick, NJ 08903
Contributors: Kenneth L. Adelman, Richard R. Burt, Miles M. Costick,
Robert F. Ellsworth, Fred Charles Iklé, Geoffrey T. H. Kemp,
Edward N. Luttwak, Charles Burton Marshall, Paul H. Nitze,
Sam Nunn, Henry S. Rowen, Leonard Sullivan, Jr., W. Scott
Thompson, William R. Van Cleave, Francis J. West, Jr.,
Albert Wohlstetter, Elmo R. Zumwalt, Jr.

NEW DIRECTIONS IN PUBLIC HEALTH CARE: AN EVALUATION
OF PROPOSALS FOR NATIONAL HEALTH INSURANCE
$6.95. 277 pages. Publication date: May 1976
ISBN 0–917616–00–6
Library of Congress No. 76–9522
Contributors: Martin S. Feldstein, Thomas D. Hall, Leon R. Kass, Keith
B. Leffler, Cotton M. Lindsay, Mark V. Pauly, Charles E. Phelps,
Thomas C. Schelling, Arthur Seldon

NEW DIRECTIONS IN PUBLIC HEALTH CARE: A PRESCRIPTION
FOR THE 1980s
$6.95 (paper). 290 pages. Publication date: May 1976; 3d ed.
rev., 1980
ISBN 0–917616–37–5
Library of Congress No. 79–92868
$16.95 (cloth). 290 pages. Publication date: April 1980
ISBN 0–87855–394–0. Available through Transaction Books,
Rutgers—The State University, New Brunswick, NJ 08903
Contributors: Alain Enthoven, W. Philip Gramm, Leon R. Kass, Keith B.
Leffler, Cotton M. Lindsay, Jack A. Meyer, Charles E. Phelps,
Thomas C. Schelling, Harry Schwartz, Arthur Seldon, David A.
Stockman, Lewis Thomas

NO LAND IS AN ISLAND: INDIVIDUAL RIGHTS AND
GOVERNMENT CONTROL OF LAND USE
$5.95. 221 pages. Publication date: November 1975
ISBN 0–917616–03–0
Library of Congress No. 75–38415
Contributors: Benjamin F. Bobo, B. Bruce-Briggs, Connie Cheney, A.
Lawrence Chickering, Robert B. Ekelund, Jr., W. Philip Gramm,
Donald G. Hagman, Robert B. Hawkins, Jr., M. Bruce Johnson, Jan
Krasnowiecki, John McClaughry, Donald M. Pach, Bernard H.
Siegan, Ann Louise Strong, Morris K. Udall

NO TIME TO CONFUSE: A CRITIQUE OF THE FORD
FOUNDATION'S ENERGY POLICY PROJECT *A TIME TO
CHOOSE AMERICA'S ENERGY FUTURE*
$4.95. 156 pages. Publication date: February 1975
ISBN 0–917616–01–4
Library of Congress No. 75–10230
Contributors: Morris A. Adelman, Armen A. Alchian, James C. DeHaven,
George W. Hilton, M. Bruce Johnson, Herman Kahn, Walter J. Mead,
Arnold B. Moore, Thomas Gale Moore, William H. Riker

ONCE IS ENOUGH: THE TAXATION OF CORPORATE
EQUITY INCOME
$2.00. 32 pages. Publication date: May 1977
ISBN 0–917616–23–5
Library of Congress No. 77–670132
Author: Charles E. McLure, Jr.

OPTIONS FOR U.S. ENERGY POLICY
$5.95. 309 pages. Publication date: September 1977
ISBN 0–917616–20–0
Library of Congress No. 77–89094
Contributors: Albert Carnesale, Stanley M. Greenfield, Fred S. Hoffman,
Edward J. Mitchell, William R. Moffat, Richard Nehring, Robert
S. Pindyck, Norman C. Rasmussen, David J. Rose, Henry S. Rowen,
James L. Sweeney, Arthur W. Wright

PARENTS, TEACHERS, AND CHILDREN: PROSPECTS FOR CHOICE
IN AMERICAN EDUCATION
$5.95. 336 pages. Publication date: June 1977
ISBN 0–917616–18–9
Library of Congress No. 77–79164
Contributors: James S. Coleman, John E. Coons, William H. Cornog,
Denis P. Doyle, E. Babette Edwards, Nathan Glazer, Andrew
M. Greeley, R. Kent Greenawalt, Marvin Lazerson, William
C. McCready, Michael Novak, John P. O'Dwyer, Robert Singleton,
Thomas Sowell, Stephen D. Sugarman, Richard E. Wagner

POLITICS AND THE OVAL OFFICE: TOWARDS
PRESIDENTIAL GOVERNANCE
$7.95 (paper). 300 pages. Publication date: February 1981
ISBN 0–917616–40–5
Library of Congress No. 80–69617
$18.95 (cloth). 300 pages. Publication date: April 1981
ISBN 0–87855–428–9. Available through Transaction Books,
Rutgers–The State University, New Brunswick, NJ 08903
Contributors: Richard K. Betts, Jack Citrin, Eric L. Davis, Robert M.
Entman, Robert E. Hall, Hugh Heclo, Everett Carll Ladd, Jr.,
Arnold J. Meltsner, Charles Peters, Robert S. Pindyck, Francis E.
Rourke, Martin M. Shapiro, Peter L. Szanton